graphis annual

81|82

graphis annual

The International Annual of Advertising and
Editorial Graphics

Das internationale Jahrbuch der Werbegraphik und der redaktionellen Graphik

Le répertoire international de l'art graphique
publicitaire et rédactionnel

Edited by / Herausgegeben von / Réalisé par:

Walter Herdeg

Graphis Press Corp., Zurich (Switzerland)

graphis annual 81|82

THE INTERNATIONAL ANNUAL OF ADVERTISING AND EDITORIAL GRAPHICS

This is the 29th annual edition of the original cornerstone of the "Graphis trilogy" which, for more than two decades, has richly earned its world-wide reputation as the standard work reflecting the latest international trends in all design fields. This year's collection continues its survey of graphics in advertisements, booklets, editorial design, annual reports, book jackets, trade magazines and magazine covers, calendars, trade marks, letterheads, packaging, record covers. "It is like a garden of international commercial art, and a delight to both professionals and lay browsers. The quality of reproduction is superb." – *Los Angeles Free Press.* "No matter what the creative climate, the *Graphis Annuals* make the best of things." – *Art Direction.* "A splendid art show in print, exciting and provocative." – *Publishers Weekly.* "*Graphis Annual* offers inspiration to everyone in advertising and visual communication and provides a ready reference for ideas." – *Creative Magazine.* "A must for all graphic collections!" – *Umbrella.* "This international survey of advertising and editorial art, in the nearly three decades of its publication, has undoubtedly become the most influential trend setter of all . . . Its superbly printed pages overflow with fresh conceptions and technical solutions for design problems." – *American Artist.*

Other important GRAPHIS Books:

GRAPHIS POSTERS
THE INTERNATIONAL ANNUAL OF POSTER ART

"Simply wonderful." – *Art Direction.* "More than a lavish volume of fascinating designs, the pages of the book are virtually a mirror of the present moment in time, reflecting ideas and the appearance of people, places and things with extraordinary intensity." – *School Arts.* "New ideas, approaches and standards of excellence can be studied and enjoyed." – *Inland Printer/American Lithographer.* Each edition offers visual evidence of the world's best posters arranged in four major categories: Advertising posters, Cultural posters, Social posters, Consumer posters. Published each year in early Spring.

PHOTOGRAPHIS
THE INTERNATIONAL ANNUAL OF ADVERTISING, EDITORIAL AND TELEVISION PHOTOGRAPHY

In this annual are outstanding world-wide achievements in Advertising; Annual Reports; Book Jackets; Editorial Photography; Magazine Covers; Packaging; Calendars; House Organs; Booklets; Television. ". . . eclectic in more than a historical sense, for they present a vast range of artistic styles." – *Publisher's Weekly.* "For anyone working with the photo-image, for any conceivable purpose involving persuasion and communications, this annual is a visual index to the many creative ways, to the changing visual techniques, and to the shifts in emphasis and style apparent in the work of top notch photographers and production people in the Western world." – *Technical Photography.* "This annual becomes more exciting every year." – *American Artist.* Published each year in late Spring.

"Square Books" format (9½" × 9¾")

ARCHIGRAPHIA
ARCHITECTURAL AND ENVIRONMENTAL GRAPHICS

GRAPHIS DIAGRAMS
THE GRAPHIC VISUALIZIATON OF ABSTRACT DATA

Distributed in the United States by

Hastings House

Publishers
10 East 40th Street, New York, N.Y. 10016

[ISBN 0-8038-2715-6]

Contents   Inhalt   Sommaire

Abbreviations	6	Abkürzungen	6	Abréviations	6
Introduction	8	Vorwort	11	Préface	14
Index to Artists and to Designers	14	Verzeichnis der Künstler und Gestalter	14	Index des artistes et maquettistes	14
Index to Art Directors	18	der Künstlerischen Leiter	18	Index directeurs artistiques	18
Index to Agencies	20	der Agenturen und Studios	20	Index des agences	20
Index to Publishers	21	der Verleger	21	Index des éditeurs	21
Index to Advertisers	22	der Auftraggeber	22	Index des clients	22

Advertisements	25	Briefköpfe	234	Annonces	25
Annual Reports	202	Buchumschläge	206	Calendriers	222
Book Covers	206	Fachzeitschriften	182	Couvertures de livres	206
Booklets	60	Firmenpublikationen	200	Couvertures de périodiques	102
Calendars	222	Hauszeitschriften	192	Emballages	244
Corporate Publications	200	Inserate	25	En-têtes	234
House Organs	192	Jahresberichte	202	Illustrations de journaux	160
Letterheads	234	Kalender	222	Illustrations de périodiques	115
Magazine Covers	102	Packungen	244	Journaux d'entreprise	192
Magazine Illustrations	115	Prospekte	60	Marques et emblèmes	230
Newspaper Illustrations	160	Schallplatten-Umschläge	238	Pochettes de disques	238
Packaging	244	Schutzmarken	230	Prospectus	60
Record Covers	238	Zeitschriften-Illustrationen	115	Publications d'entreprise	200
Trade Magazines	182	Zeitschriften-Umschläge	102	Rapports annuels	202
Trade Marks	230	Zeitungs-Illustrationen	160	Revues professionnelles	182

Abbreviations   Abkürzungen   Abréviations

Argentina	ARG	Argentinien	ARG	Allemagne occidentale	GER
Australia	AUS	Australien	AUS	Argentine	ARG
Austria	AUT	Belgien	BEL	Australie	AUS
Belgium	BEL	Brasilien	BRA	Autriche	AUT
Brazil	BRA	Dänemark	DEN	Belgique	BEL
Canada	CAN	Deutschland (BRD)	GER	Brésil	BRA
Czechoslovakia	CSR	Finnland	FIN	Canada	CAN
Denmark	DEN	Frankreich	FRA	Danemark	DEN
Finland	FIN	Grossbritannien	GBR	Espagne	SPA
France	FRA	Hongkong	HKG	Etats-Unis	USA
Germany (West)	GER	Indien	IND	Finlande	FIN
Great Britain	GBR	Italien	ITA	France	FRA
Hong Kong	HKG	Japan	JPN	Grande-Bretagne	GBR
Hungary	HUN	Kanada	CAN	Hongkong	HKG
India	IND	Kuweit	KUW	Hongrie	HUN
Italy	ITA	Mexiko	MEX	Inde	IND
Japan	JPN	Niederlande	NLD	Italie	ITA
Kuweit	KUW	Norwegen	NOR	Japon	JPN
Mexico	MEX	Österreich	AUT	Koweit	KUW
Netherlands	NLD	Polen	POL	Mexique	MEX
Norway	NOR	Portugal	POR	Norvège	NOR
Poland	POL	Schweden	SWE	Pays-Bas	NLD
Portugal	POR	Schweiz	SWI	Pologne	POL
Soviet Union	USR	Sowjetunion	USR	Portugal	POR
Spain	SPA	Spanien	SPA	Suède	SWE
Sweden	SWE	Thailand	THA	Suisse	SWI
Switzerland	SWI	Tschechoslowakei	CSR	Tchécoslovaquie	CSR
Thailand	THA	Ungarn	HUN	Thaïlande	THA
Uruguay	URU	Uruguay	URU	Union Soviétique	USR
USA	USA	USA	USA	Uruguay	URU
Venezuela	VEN	Venezuela	VEN	Venezuela	VEN

In recent years the quality standards in graphic design have improved constantly. Thanks to a more complex education and the many visual and intellectual experiences the graphic designer is exposed to, he has been able to meet with the increasing demands and standards of his public. Those who send us their work regularly, enable us to contribute with our publication a small part to the improvement and preservation of quality, and we are greatful to them for their efforts and cooperation.

Die Interaktion zwischen einem anspruchsvolleren Publikum und dem Graphiker, dessen Horizont sich durch eine breiter gefächerte Ausbildung und eine Vielfalt visueller und intellektueller Eindrücke erweitert hat, führte in den letzten Jahren zu einfallsreichen Arbeiten. Dass wir mit unseren Publikationen auch einen kleinen Teil dazu beitragen konnten, verdanken wir all jenen, die uns regelmässig ihre neuesten Arbeiten einschicken.

L'interaction entre une audience mieux éduquée et plus sophistiquée et des graphistes mieux formés et constamment exposés à une variété d'expériences visuelles et intellectuelles, a produit d'extraordinaires réalisations graphiques contemporaines. Nous sommes heureux d'avoir pu contribuer en quelque sorte à propager ces nouvelles tendances de perspectives agrandies, grâce à nos collaborateurs, qui nous envoient régulièrement leurs réalisations les plus récentes.

SHIGEO FUKUDA, born in 1932, graduated from the Tokyo University of Fine Arts. With his cover illustration for GRAPHIS ANNUAL he has once again given proof of his playfulness, his perceptive, thoughtful and ingenious visual language. The scope of his work includes indoor and outdoor decorations, symbols, posters, editorial and advertising graphics, cartoons and three-dimensional objects. It has been shown in numerous exhibitions and has been awarded many prizes.

SHIGEO FUKUDA, 1932 geboren, studierte an der Kunstakademie Tokio. Seine Umschlagillustration ist ein weiteres Beispiel seines spielerischen Einfallsreichtums, seiner geistreichen, sensiblen, raffinierten visuellen Sprache, die an Intellekt und Fantasie appelliert. Seine Arbeiten reichen von Supergraphiken, Symbolen, Plakaten, redaktioneller und Werbegraphik zu Karikaturen und dreidimensionalen Objekten. Seine Werke wurden an zahlreichen Ausstellungen gezeigt und mit verschiedenen Preisen ausgezeichnet.

SHIGEO FUKUDA, né en 1932, a fait ses études à l'académie des Beaux-Arts de Tokyo. Son illustration de couverture témoigne de son imagination vive, de son langage visuel plein d'esprit, sensible et ingénieux, qui ouvre des univers à la fantaisie et à l'intellect. Il travaille dans tous les domaines de l'art et du design: murs peints, décorations, symboles, affiches, art graphique rédactionnel et publicitaire, caricatures et objets tridimensionnels. Ses œuvres ont été en vue à de nombreuses expositions et plusieurs prix lui ont été décernés.

Karl Fink

Visual Literacy

KARL FINK, a graduate of the Parsons School of Design, has headed his own graphic and industrial design office since 1951. He is a past president of the American Institute of Graphic Arts and of the Package Designers Council, and has been a board member of the Inter-Society Color Council. He has been a consultant/panellist with the United States National Endowment for the Arts for its ongoing Federal Design Improvement Program. He has taught and lectured widely and has published in numerous professional journals; he has written sectional texts or introductory chapters for several GRAPHIS volumes.

Thirty years have passed since the appearance of the first GRAPHIS ANNUAL. While this collection of volumes is not alone in recording the graphic work of those years, it is unique in its value. Rigorously edited over the years by one man, a shelf of GRAPHIS ANNUALS represents continuity in criteria and approach—a search for excellence in all graphic media, a celebration of inventive visual thinking, an impatience with mere trendiness and me-too-ism. From the start, the Annual has pointed the way towards fresh and sound creative approaches.

Leafing through any volume of the Annual can be a stimulating experience for a young designer. And a chronological browse through the Graphis years is something of a revelation for anyone in our profession. The constancy of editorial viewpoint has documented exhilarating growth in all areas of the graphic arts and enrichment of the role and output of graphic artists and designers.

Clearly apparent in recent volumes is the broadening of the graphic artist's view, the un-self-conscious adoption of concepts from the fine arts, the keen awareness of the world beyond the drawing-board, easel or problem to be solved. Also evident is a new respect for the viewer or audience, an assumption that the subtle, the surprising, the unexpected, the visual pun, will be well within its grasp.

The most recent GRAPHIS ANNUALS are, in a sense, the harvest of the widened perspectives of both graphic artists and their audiences. Typically, the education of today's designers and artists encompasses far more than skills training. Many young practitioners are the products of liberal arts colleges and universities whose art curricula have been sufficiently strengthened to attract serious students of design; others are graduates of the many art schools which, recognizing the need to expose students to other disciplines, have incorporated liberal arts and social study courses into their programmes of study.

Whatever their formal education, and regardless of whether they are twenty or sixty years old, today's graphic artists have been exposed to different, more varied visual and intellectual experiences than their counterparts of a generation ago. Travel within their own countries and abroad has been easy and affordable. (Even when money is short, today's casual, back-packing approach to international travel has put young people on the move.) Television and film, despite their shortcomings, have provided the enrapturing visual stimuli of underseas photography, incredible views of our own and other planets, vicarious tours of remote lands and cultures, imaginative journeys into science fiction's worlds of the future. Even a brief documentary on the migration of the hartebeest can be a visual and intellectual adventure.

But a generation of better-educated, better-integrated, more sophisticated designers and artists would be a frustrated generation indeed if the audience for its more intellectually demanding output had not experienced parallel growth. Fortunately, today's graphics are reaching a general public whose horizons have also widened. Better and more highly educated in general and far more accepting of all art forms, these are people who now fill museums and art galleries which once were nearly deserted temples. They crowd the halls for such once-elitist art forms as ballet, modern dance, lieder and chamber music concerts.

Most important, from our point of view, is that today's public—particularly the segment under forty-five—has extraordinarily high visual literacy. It is more receptive to—more demanding of—change and surprise than any previous generation. Accustomed to the constantly switching images of TV and film, trained to adapt speedily to the sequential confusions of live action, stop action, slow motion and instant replay, it is restless of eye and mind's eye, constantly seeking new stimuli. If it is less loyal to the old brands, the old packages, the old trademarks, it is quick to respond to the imaginative new. Far from taking offence at experimental graphics, it embraces them, seizing on such ephemera as posters as exciting, completely appropriate additions to home décor.

The interaction between a more visually experienced audience and humanistically broadened graphic artists has led to the best of contemporary graphics. The audience has both freed and challenged the artist/designer. The public's ability to see more, recognize more, adapt readily to the unexpected, has opened the door to greater latitude in visual arts expression. And the emergence of more complete, more thinking artists has given life to a good deal of highly cerebral graphics—particularly in illustration. The kind of creativity that starts in the head, rather than on the drawing-board, the type of idea-based output once associated primarily with political cartoonists, is rampant today. Graphics is far richer—and often more fun—for it.

This is not to say that all aspects of graphics are progressing at the same pace. Some of the very publications that carry the cream of current illustration are often self-consciously designed, overdesigned, or tritely designed, with layouts, typography and trappings overshadowing the very work they feature.

And progress is less than heartening in such areas of ordered design as trademarks and packaging. Trademark design, particularly, finds itself in a kind of cul de sac after nearly exhausting the possible permutations of abstract and letter forms. It may be that the time has come to explore new visual directions. However, it is not altogether fair to criticize the less innovative design of packaging and trademarks. To some extent, it is attributable to the longer commercial lives these designs are expected to live. To an even greater extent, it is attributable to the fact that, while most illustration is commissioned by art directors or editors, trademark and packaging assignments usually come from non-design-oriented people whose decisions frequently are made with timidity and, too often, in committee.

This brings us to a weak link in our visual chain and to an area which our educational systems still are not serving adequately. Students of business and finance—the young people who will increasingly move into the middle and top management positions of corporations with the greatest need for effective design—seldom receive even minimal preparation for design decision-making. And design students rarely are given insight into the business realities which are valid elements of business decision-making.

Some type of forced educational cross-fertilization is indicated. It might be in the form of required courses in "Graphics for the Non-Graphics Student" and "Business Fundamentals for the Graphics Professional". In universities offering both curricula, there are possibilities for shared seminars, informal meetings, or even role-playing sessions built around graphics projects.

With educators putting their minds to it, our visual world, which is increasingly being shaped by corporate graphics or corporate patronage of art, can become more reflective of our complete society.

Karl Fink

Visuelle Bildung

KARL FINK promovierte an der Parsons School of Design und leitet seit 1951 sein eigenes Studio für Graphik und Produktgestaltung. Er war Präsident des American Institute of Graphic Arts und des Package Designers Council, wie auch Vorstandsmitglied des Inter-Society Color Council. Für die nationale Stiftung zur Förderung von Kunst und Kultur (U.S. National Endowment for the Arts) arbeitet er als Berater und Diskussionsteilnehmer an einem neuen Programm, das auf nationaler Ebene eine Verbesserung der graphischen Gestaltung anstrebt. Er hält regelmässig Vorlesungen und Vorträge, und seine Artikel wurden in zahlreichen Fachzeitschriften publiziert. Für GRAPHIS schrieb er einleitende Texte zu verschiedenen Publikationen.

Dreissig Jahre sind seit dem Erscheinen des ersten GRAPHIS ANNUAL vergangen. Während diese Reihe von Jahrbüchern nicht die einzige Aufzeichnung des graphischen Schaffens dieser Jahre ist, so ist sie doch in ihrer Bedeutung einzigartig, denn kaum eine andere Werkreihe wurde über die Jahre von ein und demselben Mann betreut und zeichnet sich durch diese Kontinuität in Auswahlkriterien und Anschauung aus. Sie spiegelt die Suche nach ausserge- wöhnlichen Leistungen in allen graphischen Bereichen, ein Hervorstreichen einfallsreichen visuellen Denkens, ein Ablehnen reiner Trenderscheinungen und Nachahmungen. Von Anbeginn war GRAPHIS ANNUAL wegweisend im Aufzeigen kreativ neuer Richtungen.

Beim Durchblättern irgendeines Bandes findet der Designer eine Fülle von Anregungen. Eine chronologische Durchsicht der Annual-Jahrgänge ist für jeden in unserem Berufsstand eine Offenbarung. Dank der Konstanz des verlegerischen Standpunktes wird auch eine erfreuliche Öffnung in allen Bereichen der graphischen Künste sichtbar, die der Arbeit von Graphiker und Designer eine Vielfalt neuer Aspekte verleiht.

Die neueren Bände zeigen deutlich, dass sich der Horizont des Graphikers über Reissbrett, Staffelei und Problemstellung hinaus erweitert hat und dass Konzepte aus der Kunst gekonnt übernommen und angewendet werden. Ebenso offensichtlich wird die neue Haltung gegenüber dem Zielpublikum, von dem vorausgesetzt wird, dass es subtile, unerwartete und überraschende visuelle Pointen versteht und entschlüsselt.

Die jüngsten Bände enthalten gewissermassen die Ausbeute dieser Arbeiten. Die Ausbildung von Graphikern und Künstlern umfasst heute mehr als nur das Erlernen handwerklicher und technischer Fertigkeiten. Viele junge Künstler sind Absolventen humanistischer Gymnasien oder Universitäten, deren Lehrveranstaltungen in Kunst so weit gefasst sind, dass sie auch von ernsthaften Designstudenten besucht werden. Auch Kunstakademien und Design- schulen kamen zur Einsicht, dass ihren Studenten Kenntnisse in Human-, Natur- und Sozialwissenschaften vermittelt werden sollten.

Unabhängig von Ausbildung und Alter ist der Graphiker heute einer grösseren Vielfalt visueller und intellektueller Erfahrungen ausgesetzt, als sein Kollege vor dreissig Jahren. Reisen im In- und Ausland sind problemloser und erschwinglicher. (Auch wenn das Geld knapp ist, trampen die jungen Leute in ihrer unkomplizierten Art durch alle Kontinente.) Trotz etlicher Mängel und Oberflächlichkeiten liefern Film und Fernsehen mitreissende visuelle Stimuli mit Unterwasseraufnahmen, unglaublichen Ansichten unseres und anderer Planeten, Reiseberichten über ferne Länder und unbekannte Kulturen, fantastische Expeditionen in die Science-fiction- Welt der Zukunft. Sogar ein Dokumentarfilm über die periodischen Wanderungen der Kuhantilope kann zu einem visuellen und intellektuellen Abenteuer werden.

Diese Generation von gebildeteren, integrierteren und anspruchsvolleren Künstlern und Designern wäre jedoch total frustriert, wenn sich das Publikum nicht parallel zu den intellektuell anspruchsvolleren Arbeiten entwickelt hätte. Glücklicherweise richtet sich die Graphik heute an ein Publikum, dessen Horizont sich ebenfalls beträchtlich erweitert hat. Dank der allgemein breiter gefächerten Ausbildung, dem grösseren Interesse und der Offenheit gegenüber allen Kunstformen, beleben diese Leute heute Museen und Galerien, die ehemals verlassenen Kultur- tempel. Heute strömen sie in einst elitäre Kultur-Veranstaltungen, wie Ballett- und moderne Tanzdarbietungen, Liederabende und Kammermusik-Konzerte.

Weit wichtiger aus unserer Sicht ist, dass das heutige Publikum – vor allem unter 45 – einen aussergewöhnlich hohen visuellen Bildungsstand hat. Es ist offener – viel empfänglicher – für neue Kunstrichtungen und Überraschungseffekte als frühere Generationen. An die schnell wechselnde Bildfolge in Film und Fernsehen gewohnt, geübt, sich in der verwirrenden Abfolge von Direktübertragung, Standbild, Zeitlupe und Rückblende augenblicklich zurechtzufinden, sucht das Publikum mit rastlosem Auge und Geist stets neue Anreize. Ist es alten Marken, Packungen und Warenzeichen gegenüber auch weniger treu, so stürzt es sich sichtlich auf einfallsreiche Novitäten. Experimentelle Graphik wird völlig in seine Umwelt einbezogen und so ephemere Dinge wie Plakate beleben die häusliche Atmosphäre.

Das Zusammenspiel eines visuell erfahreneren Publikums und eines humanistisch gebildeteren Graphikers hat zu Bestleistungen in zeitgenössischer Graphik geführt. Das Publikum gesteht Künstlern und Designern mehr Freiheit zu, fordert sie gleichzeitig aber stärker heraus. Die Fähigkeit des Publikums, mehr zu sehen, mehr zu erkennen, Unerwartetes bereitwillig anzunehmen, lässt dem Künstler freien Spielraum für neue visuelle Ausdrucksmöglichkeiten. Diese gründlicher geschulten, die Probleme überdenkenden Künstler, haben – besonders im Bereich der Illustration – eine Menge ungemein intellektueller Arbeiten geschaffen. Die im Kopf und nicht auf dem Reissbrett geborene Kreativität, die bis anhin mit ideen- und ereignisgebundenen politischen Karikaturen verglichen wurde, ist heute gang und gäbe. Dies ist mit ein Grund, weshalb die Graphik heute vielgestaltiger und oft auch unterhaltsamer ist.

Das heisst natürlich nicht, dass die Graphik in jeder Hinsicht mit der allgemeinen Entwicklung Schritt hielt. Einige einschlägige Publikationen, welche nur trendgebundene Bestleistungen zeigen, sind im Design oft zu befangen, zu übertrieben oder zu trivial, wobei Layout, Typographie und Aufmachung die gezeigten Arbeiten förmlich erdrücken.

Der Fortschritt auf dem Gebiet von produktmässig vorgegebenen Markenzeichen oder Packungen ist nicht sonderlich ermutigend. Besonders die Gestaltung von Markenzeichen befindet sich in einer Sackgasse, nachdem alle Möglichkeiten der abstrakten und herkömmlichen Wiedergabe bis zur Erschöpfung abgewandelt wurden. Mag sein, dass die Zeit gekommen ist, neue visuelle Bereiche zu erforschen. Jedenfalls ist es nicht angebracht, weniger einfallsreiche Konzepte für Packungen und Markenzeichen hier zu kritisieren. In gewisser Hinsicht hängt dies damit zusammen, dass eine langfristige, marktgerechte Marken- oder Produkt-Identifizierung im Vordergrund steht. Wichtiger ist in diesem Zusammenhang aber, dass Markenzeichen und Packungen meistens von Leuten in Auftrag gegeben werden, die von Design keine Ahnung haben und deren Entscheidungen häufig in Absprache mit irgendeinem Geschäftsausschuss getroffen werden, während die meisten übrigen Illustrationen von Art Direktoren oder Verlegern bestellt und ausgewählt werden.

Dies bringt uns zu einem schwachen Glied in der visuellen Gestaltung und in unserem Bildungssystem. Studierende an betriebswirtschaftlichen und handelswissenschaftlichen Instituten – junge Leute also, die in die Kaderpositionen der Grossbetriebe nachrücken, wo wirkungsvolles Design eminent wichtig ist – haben in den seltensten Fällen die Voraussetzungen, die ihnen Entscheidungen in Fragen des Designs erleichtern würden. Umgekehrt erhalten Design-Studenten kaum Einblick in die Geschäftsrealität, die Entscheidungsprozesse massgeblich beeinflusst.

Ein gegenseitiges Aufarbeiten wäre hier vonnöten. Dies könnte in Form von Pflichtfächern wie «Graphik für Nicht-Graphiker» oder «Betriebswirtschaftliche Grundkenntnisse für Graphiker» geschehen. Universitäten mit beiden Fachrichtungen könnten interdisziplinäre Seminare, informelle Diskussionen oder Arbeitsgruppen, in welchen graphische Projekte im Rollenspiel abgehandelt werden, organisieren.

Wenn diesem Problem in der Ausbildung vermehrt Beachtung geschenkt würde, könnte unsere visuelle Umwelt, die von globalen Erscheinungsbildern und Firmenmäzenatentum geprägt ist, ein genaueres Bild unserer Umwelt geben.

Karl Fink

L'alphabétisation visuelle

KARL FINK a fait ses études à la Parsons School of
Design et depuis 1951 il a son propre studio d'art
graphique et d'esthétique industrielle. Il a été président de
L'American Institute of Graphic Arts et du Package
Designers Council et appartenait au comité directeur de
l'Inter-Society Color Council. En sa qualité de conseiller
de la fondation nationale pour la promotion des arts (U.S.
National Endowment for the Arts) en rapport avec le
nouveau programme visant à améliorer le design
graphique sur le plan national, il a pris part dans nombre
de discussions. Il donne régulièrement des conférences et
ses articles ont été publiés dans de nombreux périodiques
professionnels. Pour GRAPHIS, il a écrit plusieurs textes
d'introduction pour diverses publications.

Trente ans ont passé depuis la parution du premier volume de GRAPHIS ANNUAL. Si la
collection de ces annuels n'a pas le monopole de l'enregistrement de la production graphique
de ces trois dernières décennies, elle reste néanmoins unique en ce qu'elle incarne une rare
continuité des critères appliqués et de l'approche choisie. Réalisée en effet par le même
éditeur responsable au fil des années, la série des GRAPHIS ANNUALS se situe imperturbable-
ment à un niveau optimal que garantissent la recherche assidue du meilleur à travers tous
les secteurs des médias graphiques, la priorité accordée au langage visuel créatif, le dédain teinté
d'impatience face à toute mode passagère et au vedettariat abusif. Depuis qu'il existe, GRAPHIS
ANNUAL a frayé sans défaillir la voie à tout ce qui perdure dans sa fraîcheur et sa nouveauté.

C'est ainsi que le jeune designer se trouve grandement stimulé par l'étude de n'importe quel
volume de cette collection. Pour qui entreprend la lecture chronologique des GRAPHIS
ANNUALS, cette mine de trésors réserve des surprises de taille – une véritable révélation pour
le professionnel. L'orientation conséquente maintenue à travers tous ces volumes ne fait
ressortir que davantage la prolifération étonnante et combien gratifiante des arts graphiques
et l'importance croissante du rôle et de la production des graphistes et des designers.

Les derniers volumes en particulier attestent l'élargissement des vues de l'artiste graphique,
l'adoption sans problème de mainte conception dérivée des beaux-arts, la prise de conscience
aiguë du monde existant par-delà la planche à dessin, le chevalet ou le problème hic et nunc à
résoudre. Ce qui est également manifeste, c'est le respect accru de l'audience, du public et le
souci de mettre à sa portée tout élément de subtilité, de surprise, d'inattendu, de jeu de mots
visuel, pour qu'il puisse rester pleinement réceptif.

Quant aux tout derniers GRAPHIS ANNUALS, ils engrangent en quelque sorte la moisson des
perspectives agrandies des artistes créateurs et de leur public. C'est que la formation du designer
et de l'artiste graphique porte de nos jours sur bien autre chose que la simple acquisition de
techniques. Un grand nombre de jeunes professionnels sortent de collèges et universités
des beaux-arts aux programmes rénovés de manière à attirer les étudiants du design; les
autres ont reçu leur formation dans les nombreuses écoles d'art conscientes de la nécessité
d'ouvrir l'esprit de leurs élèves à des disciplines nouvelles, des beaux-arts aux sciences
sociales.

Quel que soit leur degré d'éducation formelle, quel que soit leur âge, vingt ou soixante ans, les
graphistes d'aujourd'hui ont été exposés à une variété d'expériences visuelles et intellectuelles
bien plus grande que leurs aînés de la génération précédente. Ils ont pu se déplacer à travers
leur propre pays et à l'étranger, même si c'était le sac au dos. La télévision et le cinéma, tout
défaillants soient-ils, les ont assaillis de stimuli visuels époustouflants, de vues sous-marines et
astronautiques, d'explorations ethnologiques insolites, de voyages où l'imaginaire s'empare
en triomphe des visions du futur à travers la science-fiction. Sans compter les
documentaires scientifiques qui ouvrent des univers fantastiques à la vision et à l'intellect.

Pourtant, une génération de designers et d'artistes mieux formés, mieux intégrés, plus sophisti-
qués serait vouée à une frustration intolérable si l'évolution du public devant réceptionner
leurs visions enrichies n'avait pas suivi un cours parallèle. Il est heureux de constater que les
productions graphiques d'aujourd'hui atteignent un public dont l'horizon a sensiblement
reculé. Mieux éduqué et accédant à un niveau de formation supérieur, ouvert à toutes les
formes imaginables de l'art, ce public parcourt volontiers les musées et les galeries d'art encore
naguère quasi déserts. Et on le retrouve nombreux à ces spectacles réputés d'élite que sont le
ballet, la danse moderne, les récitals de lieder, les concerts de musique de chambre.

Le point que nous apparaît capital, c'est que le public d'aujourd'hui, surtout la tranche des
moins de 45 ans, jouit d'une alphabétisation visuelle extraordinairement rapide. Plus qu'aucune
génération précédente, il est avide de changement, de surprise. Entraîné au défilement
rapide des séquences télévisées et des images cinématographiques, à faire prestement la part
des confusions inhérentes au vécu en direct, au ralenti, à l'arrêt, au retour en arrière, il a l'œil

constamment en alerte, l'esprit qui traite les informations visuelles également, constamment à l'affût d'informations visuelles nouvelles. Moins fidèle aux marques confirmées, aux emballages éprouvés, aux produits traditionnels, il répond d'autant plus facilement aux nouveautés qui stimulent son imagination. L'expérimentation graphique ne le choque plus, elle lui paraît au contraire nécessaire, et il s'empare avidement de productions éphémères telles que les affiches et les posters pour rehausser son cadre de vie privé et faire vivre les murs de son foyer.

L'interaction constante entre une audience plus expérimentée sur le plan visuel et des graphistes bénéficiant d'une ouverture plus grande sur le fait humain a produit d'extraordinaires réalisations graphiques contemporaines. L'audience a libéré l'artiste et le designer tout en lui lançant de nouveaux défis. L'aptitude du public à voir davantage, à reconnaître davantage, à mieux s'adapter à l'insolite a ouvert toute grande la porte donnant sur la multiplicité des expressions artistiques visuelles. Et l'apparition d'artistes plus complets, plus réfléchis s'est traduite par une masse importante de créations très cérébrales, notamment dans le domaine illustratif. Le genre de créativité née du cerveau et non pas de la planche à dessin, jadis cantonnée dans la satire politique, fait tache d'huile de nos jours, enrichissant sensiblement la matière graphique et l'investissant souvent d'un humour bienvenu.

Il ne faut pas en déduire que tous les aspects de l'art graphique progressent au même rythme. Certaines publications illustratives importantes sont trop souvent graphiquement outrancières ou banalisées, le layout, la typo et tout un fatras inutile noyant l'essence même du travail.

Sans compter que le progrès s'avère plus que modeste dans des secteurs ordonnés du design tels que la conception de marques déposées et d'emballages. Les marques déposées notamment sont dans une impasse après avoir épuisé la presque totalité des permutations possibles de formes pures et de caractères. Il se pourrait bien que le moment soit venu d'explorer des voies nouvelles. A y réfléchir, on se gardera pourtant de critiquer le moindre degré de renouvellement de créations destinées à une certaine longévité et qui ne sont pas commandées à l'artiste par un directeur artistique ou un rédacteur en chef, mais généralement par des personnes sans contact avec le design, peu sûres d'elles en cette matière artistique et se fiant aux décisions en comité.

Ceci nous amène à parler d'un maillon bien faible dans notre chaîne visuelle et d'un domaine où nos systèmes éducatifs ne rendent pas encore les services que l'on est en droit d'attendre. Les étudiants en sciences économiques et financières qui feront un jour le gros du peloton des cadres moyens et supérieurs d'entreprises dont la survie est liée à un design efficace reçoivent rarement une formation même sommaire qui leur permettrait de prendre des décisions adéquates en matière de design. De leur côté, les designers en herbe sont rarement confrontés aux réalités de la vie de l'entreprise qui conditionnent ces processus de décision préalables à toute création publicitaire au service du commerce et de l'industrie.

Il serait grand temps d'imposer sous quelque forme que ce soit un transfert d'information fécond de la formation de cadres à celle des designers et vice-versa, quelque chose dans le genre de cours d'art graphique pour non-graphistes et de notions fondamentales de la vie des affaires pour professionnels des arts graphiques. Au sein des universités offrant une formation économique et une formation artistique appliquée, des séminaires interfacultés, des réunions interdisciplinaires, voire des séances de sociodrame avec échange des rôles professionnels respectifs seraient les bienvenus, avec pour axe central un projet de réalisation graphique commun.

A condition que les éducateurs s'en préoccupent, notre univers visuel, qui porte toujours davantage l'empreinte des programmes d'identité globale de marque ou du patronage des arts exercé par les grandes entreprises, pourra devenir une surface réfléchissante plus fidèle pour l'image totale de la société qui s'y incarne.

Index to Artists and Designers
Verzeichnis der Künstler und Gestalter
Index des artistes et maquettistes

ABDALLA, SANDRA; BRA. 434
ACKER, FRED; USA. 213, 214
ADDUCI, SALVATORE; SPA. 42, 43
AKIZUKI, SHIGERU; JPN. 723, 724
ALCORN, STEPHEN; USA. 511
ALDRICH, CATHERINE; USA. 388, 389, 391, 392, 396, 397
ALLEN, TERRY; USA. 391
ALTEN, JERRY; USA. 245–247
ALTSCHULER, FRANZ; USA. 155–158
AMSEL, RICHARD; USA. 247
ANDERSON, CAL; USA. 7
ANDERSON, KJELL IVAN; SWE. 549, 550, 609
ANDRESEN, MARK; USA. 254
ANGELI, PRIMO; USA. 730
ANTHONY, PAUL; GBR. 676, 676a
AOKI, KAZUO; JPN. 630
ARGENZIANO, JOSEPH; USA. 148, 174
ARIOLA-EURODISC/STUDIOS; GER. 689, 696
ARISMANN, MARSHALL; USA. 261, 364, 365
ARNOLD, HANS; SWE. 424, 425
AXON, C.W.; GBR. 241

BALZI, JUAN JOSÉ; SPA. 486
BANUCHI, CHARLES; USA. 75–78
BARILE, CARL; USA. 406
BARL, V.; GER. 205
BARNES, JEFF; USA. 172
BARRAYA; FRA. 118, 120
BARRETO, ANÉLIO; BRA. 434
BARTH; FRA. 270, 272, 273, 275
BARTON, KENT; USA. 435, 436, 438
BASS, IRIS; USA. 588
BATTLE, DAVID; USA. 316, 591, 592
BECK, IAN; GBR. 631
BELIN, GILDA; GER. 291
BELSER, BURKEY; USA. 505
BENDELL, NORM; USA. 678
BENEDICT, FRANK; USA. 679
BERG, JOHN; USA. 695, 700, 706, 709
BERNARD, WALTER; USA. 257, 258, 261
BILEY, MARK; GBR. 149
BILLOUT, GUY; USA. 406
BISSELL, ALICE; USA. 686
BLACKWELL, PATRICK; USA. 264, 395, 445, 449, 452
BLASUTTA, MARY LYNN; USA. 253
BLATCH, BERNARD; NOR. 558, 612
BLONDEAU, DOMINIQUE. 347
BONNELL, BILL; USA. 108
BOYD HARTE, GLYNN; GBR. 632
BOYKIN, EVERETT; USA. 12, 13
BRALDS, BRALDT; USA. 168, 354, 694
BRESLIN, LYNN DREESE; USA. 703, 710
BRIMMER, HENRY; USA. 143
BROCK, MICHAEL; USA. 336, 337
BROD, STAN; USA. 516, 517
BRÖMSE, BEATE; GER. 276, 277, 292
BROSI, ANNE; GER. 359
BROUTIN, CHRISTIAN; FRA. 48–50
BROWN, LANCE; USA. 41
BROWN, MICHAEL DAVID; USA. 127, 128, 130, 443
BROWNFIELD, MICK; GBR. 529
BROWNING, PAUL; CAN. 102
BRÜSCH, BÉAT; SWI. 194, 203, 283, 299, 300, 390
BÜCHELMAIER, GISELA; GER. 224
BURGER, DIETMAR; GER. 670
BURGERT, HANS-JOACHIM; GER. 512
BURNS, JENNIE; GBR. 685

CAMES, NORBERT; GER. 633
CAMPISI, RONN; USA. 263–265, 393–395
CÁNOVAS, EDUARDO A.; ARG. 641

CAPPELLATO, S. & F.; ITA. 652
CARNASE, TOM; USA. 513, 616
CARPENTER, ROGER; USA. 340
CARRUTHERS, ROY; USA. 212
CARUGATI, ERALDO; USA. 155–158, 260, 278, 279
CARVER, STEVE; USA. 343, 702, 704
CATO, KEN; AUS. 243, 500
CHALLINOR, MARY; USA. 485
CHARMATZ, WILLIAM; USA. 213, 214
CHERMAYEFF, IVAN; USA. 202, 663, 686
CHO, SHINTA; JPN. 628
CHWAST, SEYMOUR; USA. 31, 89, 334, 450, 538, 540, 542, 543, 587, 615, 674, 674a, 727
CIESLEWICZ, ROMAN; FRA. 496, 611
CISS, JULIUS; CAN. 38–40
COBER, ALAN; USA. 506, 510
COLLIER, TERRY; CAN. 44
CONDAK, HENRIETTA; USA. 692
COOPER, HEATHER; CAN. 102, 588
CORRIGAN, DENNIS; USA. 34, 35
COSTELLO, STEPHEN; CAN. 491
CRAFT, KINUKO; USA. 368, 369, 381, 386
CRAINE, JON; USA. 103, 104, 144
CRAWFORD, ELAINE; USA. 248
CROCKETT, PETER; USA. 115
CUMMINS, JEFF; USA. 340

DADDS, JERRY; USA. 197–200
DALEY, JOANN; USA. 378
DALY, GERRY; USA. 507
DANIELS, GAIL; USA. 97, 100
DANION, PATRICK; FRA. 36
DÁNOS, JUDITH; HUN. 669
DE CESARE, JOHN; USA. 507, 509
DEFRIN, BOB; USA. 694
DEGEN, PAUL; USA. 534
DE HARAK, RUDOLPH; USA. 667, 679
DELESSERT, ETIENNE; SWI. 323–325, 693
DENYER, BRIAN; GBR. 142
DEVITO, FRED; USA. 79
DE VRIES, SJOERD; NLD. 554
DI-MACCIO; USA. 370, 371
DISPIGNA, TONY; USA. 638, 655, 660
DOLBY, JOHN; USA. 37
DOMINGO, RAY; USA. 251, 252
DOSIL, ROBERTO; CAN. 134, 135
DRAPER, DAVE; GBR. 45–47
DRATE, SPENCER M.; USA. 707
DUBOIS, ANY; FRA. 518, 519
DUFOUR, JL; FRA. 119, 121
DURIN, BERNARD; FRA. 33

EBEL, ALEX; USA. 97, 100
EBERT, DIETRICH; GER. 57–60, 93
EBERT, IRMGARD; GER. 716
EDELMANN, HEINZ; NLD. 572–580
EICHENBERG, FRITZ; USA. 594
EICHINGER, INC.; USA. 503
EKSELL, OLLE; SWE. 147
ELLIS, BRAD; USA. 707
ENDICOTT, JAMES; USA. 408, 409
ENDRIKAT AG; GER. 164, 230
ENGSTRÖM, OLLE; SWE. 549, 550
ENOS, RANDALL; USA. 478–480, 493, 494, 497
ESCHNER, UDO; SWI. 131
EVANS, TOM; USA. 110, 111, 526
EVENHUIS, FRANS; NLD. 355

FARLEY, BILL; GBR. 241
FENECH, SERGE; FRA. 312
FERRÁNDIZ; SPA. 161
FERRARA, LIDIA; USA. 605

FILANCIA, CAMILLA; USA. 586
FISHAUF, LOUIS; CAN. 215, 216
FISHER, DOUG; USA. 32
FISHER, MARK; USA. 454
FLETCHER, ALAN; GBR. 685
FLETT HENDERSON & ARNOLD PTY LTD; AUS. 498
FLORVILLE, PATRICK; USA. 687
FLOURY, CHANTAL; FRA. 519
FOLON, JEAN MICHEL; FRA. 51, 52, 248
FOREMAN, MICHAEL; GBR. 349, 350
FORT, ESTEVE; SPA. 42, 43
FOUNTAIN, MICHAEL; USA. 24
FRAMPTON, DAVID; USA. 388, 389
FRANCEKEVICH, AL; USA. 63, 64
FRANÇOIS, ANDRÉ; FRA. 6, 10
FRATERNALE, OTELLO; ITA. 53, 54
FRICK, URS; GER. 1
FRIEDMAN, CAROL; USA. 705
FRINTA, DAGMAR; USA. 333
FRIZ, R.G.; GER. 14
FUCHS, ERNST. 372, 373
FUKUDA, SHIGEO; JPN. 286, 287

GALE, ROBERT A.; USA. 665, 666
GALLONI, ADELCHI; ITA. 415
GASS, WILLIAM; USA. 544, 545
GASSNER, CHRISTOF; GER. 22, 223, 225, 226
GAUTHIER, ALAIN; FRA. 597
GEIBEL, STUDIO; GER. 1
GEISMAR, THOMAS; USA. 640
GEISSBUHLER, STEFF; USA. 683
GERICKE, MICHEL; USA. 680
GERLACH, CAMERON; USA. 197–200
GIBBS, STEVE; USA. 187, 188
GIBSON, KURT; USA. 217
GIBSON, WAYNE; USA. 18–20
GIUSTI, GEORGE; USA. 629
GIUSTI, ROBERT; USA. 61, 62, 246, 701, 703, 710
GLASER, BYRON; USA. 80–82, 714
GLASER, MILTON; USA. 30, 123, 266, 341
GLOOR; SWI. 271
GNIDZIEJKO, ALEX; USA. 21
GOEDICKE, HANS; NLD. 90, 688
GOFFIN, JOSSE; BEL. 621–624
GOMEZ, IGNACIO; USA. 155–158, 338
GOOSSENS, CARLA; NLD. 357
GOSLIN, CHARLES; USA. 167, 527
GÖTTLICHER, ERHARD; GER. 356, 360, 379, 604
GOTTSCHALK, FRITZ; SWI. 145, 146
GRAELLS, FRANCISCO (PANCHO); VEN. 487–489
GRAHAM, STEVE; AUS. 67–69, 728
GRANDJEAN, JEAN-PIERRE; SWI. 36
GRASSO, MARIO; SWI. 422
GREEN, NORMAN; USA. 162, 163
GREENE, DIANE; USA. 497
GREIF, GENE; USA. 699
GRIEDER, WALTER; SWI. 416, 421
GRIESBACH, CHERYL; USA. 211
GRIGG, BOB; USA. 181
GRILO, RUBEM CAMPOS; BRA. 473, 474, 476
GROSSMAN, ROBERT; USA. 15, 267, 706
GROVE, DAVID; USA. 7
GUTHER, GEORGE; GER. 386, 387

HABERFIELD, BOB; AUS. 243
HAGIO, KUNIO; USA. 402, 403
HAGIWARA, SAKUMI; JPN. 101
HAMBLIN, GEORGE; USA. 37
HANDS, JENE; GBR. 554
HANSEN, BRUCE; USA. 377
HARDER, ROLF; CAN. 154
HARRIS, ROBIN; GBR. 504

HARROD, BRIAN; CAN. 38–40
HEINER, JOE; USA. 250
HELNWEIN, GOTTFRIED; AUT. 140, 141, 387
HENRICH, ANDREAS; GER. 136, 137
HERMAN, SIDNEY; USA. 657
HERRERO, LOWELL; USA. 598
HESS, MARK; USA. 281, 282, 698, 700
HESS, RICHARD; USA. 595
HILL, LEE; USA. 413, 414
HILLMAN, DAVID; GBR. 105–107, 159, 160
HILLMER, KEITH; CAN. 44
HIVELY, CHARLES; USA. 89
HOBBS, DAN; USA. 98
HOCKNEY, DAVID; USA. 217
HODEL, MARCUS; SWI. 552
HOEFIG, NANCY; USA. 84, 86, 87, 94–96
HOFRICHTER, FRITZ; GER. 30, 31
HOGLUND, RUDOLPH; USA. 255, 256, 260, 262
HOKANSON, LARS; GBR. 720
HOLLAND, BRAD; USA. 382, 444, 465, 477
HOLLYN, LYNN; USA. 588, 598
HORNE, JIM; USA. 569
HORNER, SUE; GBR. 124
HUBERT, GUY; CAN. 134, 135
HUERTA, GERARD; USA. 695
HUGHES, ED; USA. 129
HULL, CATHY; USA. 410, 456
HUTCHCROFT, JOSEPH; USA. 635
HUYSSEN, ROGER; USA. 155–158
HYATT, JOHN; USA. 521

IGARASHI, TAKENOBU; JPN. 717, 718
INGHAM, THOMAS; USA. 384
INNAMI, NORIO; JPN. 204
INSHAW, DAVID; GBR. 585

JARREAU, JULIEN; USA. 150–152
JAY, JOHN C.; USA. 75–78
JEANMARD, JERRY; USA. 525
JEMERSON; USA. 173
JENKINS, STEVE; USA. 171
JETTER, FRANCES; USA. 328, 466, 470–472, 492
JOHNSON, V. COURTLANDT; USA. 155–158
JOHNSON, LONNIE SUE; USA. 509
JOHNSTON, SKIP; USA. 278–282
JONES, MARK; USA. 730
JONSSON, DAN; SWE. 318
JOST, HEINZ; SWI. 193
JÜSP; SWI. 274

KAISER, URSULA; CAN. 419
KANISE, YUKIO; JPN. 524
KATSUI, MITSUO; JPN. 553, 627–630
KEEBLER, WES; USA. 182, 183
KELLER, BERND; GER. 566
KENNEDY, SHARON; CAN. 66
KENSINGER, EDWARD C.; USA. 551
KIDD, IAN; AUS. 67–69
KIEHLE, JAMES; USA. 338
KING, GREG; USA. 559
KISELËV, V. P.; ITA. 219–222
KLEIN, RENEE; USA. 263, 447, 448
KNIGHT, JACOB; USA. 348
KOPPEL, TERRY; USA. 447–455
KORBET, STEVE; USA. 654
KOVAR, CONSTANCE; USA. 677
KRISTENSON, STELLAN; SWE. 593
KUNISADA, GORO; JPN. 708
KURAHASHI, TADASHI; JPN. 72
KURELEK, WILLIAM; CAN. 625, 626
KURI, YOJI; JPN. 268, 269, 293, 294, 523
KURLANSKY, MERVYN; GBR. 124, 673

KYSAR, ED; USA. 561

LAKES, FRANKLIN; USA. 551
LAMB, JIM; USA. 564, 565
LANE, TONY; USA. 702, 704
LANG, CHRISTIAN; SWI. 209
LANGE, DIETRICH; GER. 314, 610
LARGIADER, PHILIPP; SWI. 734
LARRIÈRE, JEAN-JACQUES; FRA. 25, 26
LAURENT, ALAIN; FRA. 16, 17
LEES, W. JOHN; USA. 664
LEHR, PAUL; USA. 13
LENGREN, ZBIGNIEW; POL. 329
LERNER, ROBERT; USA. 242
LESNIEWICZ, TERRY; USA. 713
LESSER, GILBERT; USA. 231–240
LEU, OLAF; GER. 30, 31
LEUNG, HANNAH; USA. 719
LEUPIN, HERBERT; SWI. 191, 192
LEVINE, DAVID; USA. 262
LEWIS, CHRIS; NLD. 90
LIEBOLD, ROBERT; USA. 736
LINDGREN, LISBETH; SWE. 185
LLEWELLYN, SUE; USA. 288
LLOYD, JOHN; CAN. 44
LLOYD, PETER; USA. 336, 337
LOESCH, UWE; GER. 636, 637
LOHRER, UWE; GER. 670
LOPEZ, ANTIONIO; USA. 75–78
LUBALIN, HERB; USA. 506, 510–517
LUBY, JODI; USA. 684
LUTZ, ALFRED; GER. 562, 563
LYKES, JOHN; USA. 155–158, 327
LYNCH, DAN; USA. 87

MABRY, MIKE; USA. 109
MACHADO, JOÃO; POR. 195
MADER, GERLINDE; GER. 244, 556, 557
MADER'S DESIGN; GER. 244
MAFIA, DANIEL; USA. 351
MAILE, BOB; USA. 719
MALERBA, CARLO; ITA. 643
MALISH, MIRO; CAN. 215, 216, 419
MALLIE, DALE; USA. 63, 64
MANTEL, RICHARD; USA. 182, 183, 535–545, 581, 614
MARCELLINO, FRED; USA. 589
MARSALA, JAMES J.; USA. 736
MARSH, JAMES; GBR. 255, 256, 385, 608
MARSHALL, ROBERT; AUS. 712
MARTIN, JOHN; CAN. 126, 313, 342, 362, 546, 547
MARTUCCI, STANLEY; USA. 211
MATSUNAGA, SHIN; JPN. 321
MATTELSON, MARVIN; USA. 257, 258
MATTHEWS, JOHN; USA. 79
MATTHIJSEN, BOB; BEL. 169, 170
MATUSIK, JIM; USA. 172
MAU, BRUCE; CAN. 125, 126, 166, 311
MAUMARY, F.; SWI. 726
MCCONNELL, JOHN; GBR. 149, 725
MCFARLAND, JIM; USA. 150–152, 212
MCLEAN, WILSON; USA. 375
MCPHERSON, CAROL; USA. 705
MEDIAVILLA, FRA. 117
MEDNICK, SCOTT A.; USA. 661
MEEK, BRUCE. 690
MEHLMAN, ELWYN; USA. 181
MEISNER, JÁN; CSR. 711
MELANDER, LARS; SWE. 83
MENDELL, PIERRE; GER. 14
MENEAR, DAVID; CAN. 184
MICHAELSON, JAMES L.; USA. 80–82

MIGNON, I.; FRA. 116
MIHAESCO, EUGENE; SWI. 297, 442, 458, 459, 461, 463, 464
MIHO, JAMES; USA. 122, 123
MILLER, RON; USA. 485
MILLER, STEPHEN; USA. 559
MINOR, WENDELL; USA. 363, 605, 613
MIRAN (OSWALDO MIRANDA); BRA. 55, 467–469
MITCHELL, DICK; USA. 85, 88, 672
MIYAUCHI, HARUO; USA. 567
MONGUZZI, BRUNO; SWI. 219–222
MONTONE, KEN; USA. 8, 9
MORGAN, CLINT; USA. 92
MORGAN, JACQUI; USA. 71, 376
MORIKAMI, SATCH; JPN. 204
MORROW, BRIAN; GBR. 11
MORTENSEN, CHRISTINE; USA. 155–158
MORTENSEN, GORDON; USA. 155–158, 326, 327
MOSS, GEOFFREY; USA. 153, 208, 296, 298, 483, 501, 606, 607

NAGAI, KAZUMASA; JPN. 27–29, 646, 651
NAGEL, PAT; USA. 377
NAKAGAWA, KENZO; JPN. 204
NAPRSTEK, JOEL F.; USA. 21
NAVARRE, AL; USA. 713
NENZI, DANDA; ITA. 114
NESSIM, BARBARA; USA. 308, 627
NEUBECKER, ROBERT; USA. 433
NEUMEIER, MARTY; USA. 80–82, 675, 714
NEWMAN, BOB; USA. 412
NEWMAN, CODY; USA. 658
NOBLE, DENNIS; CAN. 125
NORD-SÜD VERLAG; SWI. 620, 620a
NORRINGTON, BOB; GBR. 590
NOWLAND, JOHN; AUS. 132, 715
NUBIOLI, DANILO; ITA. 647
NUMAN, MARIET; NLD. 361

OCHAGAVIA, CARLOS; USA. 12
ODOM, MEL; USA. 398–401, 404
OHANIAN, NANCY; USA. 441
OHASHI, TADASHI; JPN. 2, 3, 531, 532
OHNISHI, YOSUKE; JPN. 481
OKA, DON; USA. 560
OLBINSKI, RAFAL; POL. 617, 618
O'LEARY, DAN; CAN. 625, 626
OPIT S.R.L.; ITA. 5
OSTERWALDER, UTE; GER. 319, 320, 322

PAGANUCCI, BOB; USA. 210, 570, 571
PALIX, MICHEL; FRA. 518
PARDUE, JACK; USA. 508
PARONI, EMILIO; SWI. 201
PARRISH, GEORGE I.; USA. 280
PAUL, GREG; USA. 251–254, 345–347
PAVEY, JERRY; USA. 555
PAXTON, MAUREEN. 310
PEASE, ROBERT; USA. 648, 649, 659
PECKOLICK, ALAN; USA. 138, 139, 616, 650, 662
PENNEY, DAVID; GBR. 105–107, 159, 160
PERICOLI, TULLIO; ITA. 315, 317, 601, 602
PETEET, REX; USA. 94–96
PFANZELT, HARRY; GER. 671
PINTO, ZÉLIO ALVES; BRA. 91
PLAZZOGNA, G. VITTORIO; ITA. 114
PLOURDE, DAVID; USA. 150–152
POISSON, GINNY; CAN. 65, 66
POPE, KERIG; USA. 382, 398–401, 404
POST, BOB; USA. 368, 369, 378
PRATO, RODICA; USA. 186
PRECHTL, MICHAEL MATHIAS; GER. 600

PRÜSSEN, EDUARD; GER. 411, 437, 530, 533
PRYOR, ROBERT; USA. 446
PUSH PIN STUDIOS, INC.; USA. 182, 183

RACHETER, YVES; SWI. 548
RAMPAZZO, GIUSEPPE; ITA. 599
RAU, HANS-JÜRGEN; GER. 175, 176
RAUCH, HANS-GEORG; GER. 420
RAZZI, GUIDO; ITA. 405
REDMOND, PATRICK; USA. 418
REESER, COURTNEY; USA. 561
REIL, DONETTE; USA. 182, 183
RICCA, PIETRO; ITA. 227–229
RIEDIGER, MANFRED; GER. 168
RIEFLER, JULIE; USA. 719
RIGHETTO, MARIO; SWI. 639
ROBERTS, CHERYL; USA. 307
ROGERS, RICHARD; USA. 242
ROGNER, FRED-JÜRGEN; GER. 289, 290, 380, 383, 407
ROSOCHA, WIESLAW; POL. 330
ROTHMAN, FRANK; USA. 490
ROVILLO, CHRIS; USA. 88
RUDNAK, THEO: USA. 345

SALINA, JOE; CAN. 184
SALISBURY, MIKE; USA. 250
SALPETER, BOB; USA. 180
SANDLER, BARBARA; USA. 536, 537
SAWKA, JAN; USA. 331, 392, 396, 397, 451, 455,
    457, 460
SAWYER, ARNIE; USA. 453
SCARISBRICK, ED; USA. 250
SCHER, PAULA; USA. 698, 699, 701
SCHLEINKOFER, DAVID; USA. 352
SCHMID, HELMUT; JPN. 729, 731
SCHMIDT, SAM; USA. 682
SCHMITTSIEGEL, HELMUT M.; GER. 224
SCHONGUT, EMANUEL; USA. 539, 541
SCHROEDER, BINETTE; GER. 620, 620a
SCHULTHEIS, K.; GBR. 720
SCHUMACHER, FRANZ; GER. 633, 634
SCHWARTZ, RENATE. 520
SCHWORTZ, BARRIE; USA. 155–158
SEARLE, RONALD; FRA. 596
SEPPELT-DEAKIN, LYNNE; AUS. 715
SESSIONS, STEVEN; USA. 51, 52, 525
SHAKESPEAR, GEORGE; USA. 668
SHIELDS, CHARLES; USA. 155–158
SHINODA, SHOZO; JPN. 99
SHOFFNER, TERRY. 309
SHORTEN, CHRIS; USA. 83
SHOSTAK, MITCH; USA. 482
SHRAMENKO, JOHN; HKG. 249
SIDJAKOV & BERMAN ASSOC.; USA. 56, 109, 521
SIDJAKOV, NICOLAS; USA. 56, 109

SILVIA, KEN; USA. 306, 307
SLANSKY, W.; GER. 205
SMITH, JAMES PENDLEY; USA. 8, 9
SMITH, MAIRE; AUS. 619
SOMMESE, LANNY; USA. 218
SOO HOO, PATRICK; USA. 735
SOREL, EDWARD; USA. 259, 692
SOYKA, ED; USA. 155–158, 326, 482, 503
SPANNFELLER, JIM; USA. 514
SPINA, BARBARA; USA. 493, 494
SPRINGMAN, STUDIO; GER. 556, 557
SREBNIK, CRAIG; USA. 656
STAEBELL, JOSEPH; USA. 522
STAHL, NANCY; USA. 23, 568
STAMATY, MARK ALAN; USA. 462
STEINER, HENRY; HKG. 249
STIEDEL, HELMUT; AUT. 374
STIRES, LARRY; USA. 153
STUART, DAVID; GBR. 725
SUARÈS, JEAN-CLAUDE; USA. 335, 344, 427–432
SULLIVAN, RON; USA. 644
SUMICHRAST, JOZEF; USA. 24, 155–158
SUSSMAN, ABIE; USA. 21
SUSUKI, BOB; CAN. 491
SWANWICK, BETTY. 697, 697a
SWIERZY, WALDEMAR; POL. 500

TAKEI, KOJI; USA. 560
TANI, GORDON; USA. 661, 737
TAYLOR, SCOTT; CAN. 102
TEICHBERG, IRA; USA. 186
TEL DESIGN; NLD. 177–179
TELLEZ, FRANCISCO; MEX. 645
TERRY, MIKE; GBR. 528
THOEN, PETTER; USA. 181
THOM, JOHN; GBR. 112
TIM; FRA. 475
TINA; USA. 71
TINKELMAN, MURRAY; USA. 515
TOGUCHI, TSUTOMU; JPN. 284, 285
TOOKER, GEORGE; USA. 366, 367
TORRÉ, MODESTO; USA. 363
TRICKETT & WEBB LTD; GBR. 631, 632
TUCKER, BARRIE; AUS. 67–69, 619, 728

ULRICH, MARK; USA. 189, 190, 346
UNO, YASUYUKI; JPN. 99, 101
UNRUH, JACK; USA. 41
URBANSKI, NANCY; USA. 197–200

VAN DEN BOGAARD, THEO; NLD. 90
VANDERBYL, MICHAEL; USA. 653
VAN DER JAGT, MARTIJN; NLD. 353, 357
VICKERS, PAUL; GBR. 673
VISKUPIC, GARY; USA. 413, 414

VITALE, ETTORE; ITA. 642
VON KORNATZKI, PETER; GER. 196
VORMSTEIN, MOUCHE; GER. 696
VORMSTEIN, TOM; GER. 689

WALD, CAROL; USA. 490
WALDRON, SARAH; USA. 730
WALKER, NORMAN; USA. 569
WALLER, CHARLES; USA. 265, 417, 439, 440
WALSH, JAMES T.; USA. 495
WALUKANIS, RICHARD; USA. 148, 174
WALDREP, RICHARD; USA. 197–200
WASILEWSKI, MIECYSLAW; POL. 502
WASSMER, STEFAN; SWI. 145, 146
WATSON, KAREN; USA. 306
WATTS, STAN; USA. 339
WEIDNER, BEA; USA. 484
WEISBECKER, PHILLIPE; USA. 499
WEISS, OSKAR; SWI. 131
WELKIS, ALLEN; USA. 495
WELLER, DON; USA. 245, 555
WESTERMAN, YOKE; NLD. 353
WESTMAN, CHRISTIAN; FRA. 681
WHITE, CHARLES; USA. 165
WHITE, ED; GBR. 11
WHITE, KEN; USA. 564, 565
WIDENER, TERRY; USA. 84, 187, 188
WIDMER, JEAN; FRA. 206, 207
WIELGUS, STEFAN; POL. 332
WIESMÜLLER, DIETER; GER. 295
WILCOX, DAVID; USA. 129, 699
WILKING, JOAN; USA. 1–113
WILKINSON, CHUCK; USA. 32
WILLIAMS, NANCY; GBR. 105–107, 159, 160
WILLIAMS, RODNEY; USA. 485
WILLIGES, MEL; USA. 393, 394
WILLIS, LEN; USA. 381, 384, 402, 403
WILSON, GAHAN; USA. 18–20
WINDS, HEIDE; GER. 359
WITZIG, FRED; USA. 112
WOLF, J.; USA. 586
WOLIN-SEMPLE, RICK; USA. 737
WORTMANN, WILLI; GER. 634
WYSS, HANSPETER; SWI. 423, 426

YAMADA, TADAMI; JPN. 358, 603
YANG, LARRY; USA. 217
YEALDHALL, GARY; USA. 197–200
YELDHAM, ADAM; GBR. 585
YOKOO, TADANORI; JPN. 70, 72–74, 301–305,
    582–584
YOSHIOKA, ATSUSHI; JPN. 708

ZELAYA, MARIO; USA. 659
ZIEGENFEUTER, DIETER; GER. 691

Index to Art Directors
Verzeichnis der künstlerischen Leiter
Index des directeurs artistiques

ACKER, FRED; USA. 213, 214
ADAMEK, TINA; USA. 507, 509
ADDUCI, SALVATORE; SPA. 42, 43
ADLER, PETER; USA. 112
AKIZUKI, SHIGERU; JPN. 723, 724
ALTEN, JERRY; USA. 245–247, 348–352
ANDERSON, BETTY; USA. 586
ANDERSON, CAL; USA. 7
ANDERSON, MARITA; SWE. 185
ANGELI, PRIMO; USA. 730
ANSEL, RUTH; USA. 266, 267
AUSTOPCHUK, CHRIS; USA. 331, 333, 334
AXON, C.W.; GBR. 241

BALZI, JUAN JOSÉ; SPA. 486
BARL, V.; GER. 205
BARNES, JEFF; USA. 172
BARRET, RON; USA. 534
BARTON, KENT; USA. 435, 436, 438
BATTLE, DAVID; USA. 316, 591, 592
BENDELL, NORM; USA. 678
BERG, JOH; USA. 695, 700, 706, 709
BERGER, GERHARD; GER. 291
BERMAN, JERRY; USA. 109
BERNARD, WALTER; USA. 257–259, 261
BIERMAN, KERRY; USA. 129
BLACKER, ROGER; USA. 250
BONNELL, BILL; USA. 108
BOSS, DAVID; USA. 343
BOWDEN, SIMON; USA. 15
BOYD, DOUGLAS; USA. 661, 737
BOYKIN, EVERETT; USA. 12, 13
BRACE, MICHELLE; USA. 505
BRESLIN, LYNN DREESE; USA. 703, 710
BRIGHT, KEITH; USA. 719
BROCK, MICHAEL; USA. 336–340
BROOKS, JOE; USA. 407–409
BROWN, LANCE; USA. 41
BURNS, ROBERT; CAN. 102

CADE, PAUL; CAN. 44
CAMPISI, RONN; USA. 263–265, 388, 389,
  391–397, 449
CÁNOVAS, EDUARDO A.; ARG. 641
CAPPELLATO, S. & F.; ITA. 652
CATO, KEN; AUS. 243, 500
CAYEA, JOHN; USA. 440
CHERMAYEFF, IVAN; USA. 202, 663, 668, 686
CHWAST, SEYMOUR; USA. 535–545, 587, 674,
  674a, 727
CLIVE, BOB; USA. 410
CONDAK, HENRIETTA; USA. 692
CONOLLY, JOSEPH; USA. 480
CORRIGAN, DENNIS; USA. 34, 35
COSTELLO, STEPHEN; CAN. 311, 491
CRAINE, JON; USA. 103, 104, 108, 144
CRAWFORD, ELAINE; USA. 248
CROCKETT, PETER; USA. 115
CURL, TED; AUS. 61, 62
CUTLER, MAY; CAN. 625, 626

DADDS, JERRY; USA. 197–200
DÁNOS, JUDIT; HUN. 669
DATTEL, MICHEL; USA. 143
DAVIDSON, BARRIE; USA. 483
DAVIS, JIM; USA. 606, 607, 616
DEFRIN, BOB; USA. 694
DELESSERT, ETIENNE; SWI. 693
DELMERICO, GEORGE; USA. 428
DE MOEI, DICK; NLD. 353–357, 360, 361
DENYER, BRIAN; GBR. 142
DERLING, ROBERT; USA. 211

DERSCHKA, PETER; GER. 504
DESGRIPPES, JOEL; FRA. 732, 733
DEVINO, FRANK; USA. 289, 290, 364–367, 370–373, 375
DEVITO, FRED; USA. 79
DEVRIES, SJOERD; NLD. 554
DOLBY, JOHN; USA. 37
DORFSMAN, LOU; USA. 186
DOSIL, ROBERTO; CAN. 134, 135
DOSS, LAURA; USA. 296
DRAPER, DAVE; GBR. 45–47
DRATE, SPENCER M.; USA. 707
DUBACHER, OSWALD; SWI. 131

EBERT, D. & I.; GER. 93
EBERT, IRMGARD; GER. 716
EDELMANN, HEINZ; NLD. 572–580
EICHINGER, BOB; USA. 503
EISENBERG, ARTHUR; USA. 658
EISMONT, ROSTISLAV; USA. 499
EKSELL, OLLE; SWE. 147
ENDRIKAT, K.; GER. 164, 230
ENGSTRÖM, OLLE; SWE. 549, 550

FALL, DOROTHY; USA. 477
FEITLER, BEA; USA. 308
FENDELMAN, JUDY; USA. 479
FERRARA, LIDIA; USA. 589, 595, 605
FILLER, WITOLD; POL. 329, 330, 332
FISHAUF, LOUIS; CAN. 215, 216
FISHER, DOUG; USA. 32
FISZMAN, GILLES; BEL. 621–624
FLETT HENDERSON & ARNOLD PTY LTD.; AUS. 498
FLORVILLE, PATRICK; USA. 687
FOUNTAIN, MICHAEL; USA. 24
FOY, RICHARD; USA. 680
FRANCFORT, J.H.; SWI. 194
FRICK, URS; GER. 1
FRIEDMAN, CAROL; USA. 705
FUKUDA, SHIGEO; JPN. 286, 287

GALE, ROBERT A.; USA. 665, 666
GALLONI, ADELCHI; ITA. 415
GARLAN, JUDY; USA. 298
GEISMAR, THOMAS H.; USA. 640
GEISSBUHLER, STEFF; USA. 683
GIBBS, STEVE; USA. 187, 188
GIBSON, WAYNE; USA. 18–20
GILLESPIE, JOHN; USA. 707
GOEDICKE, HANS; NLD. 90, 688
GOFFIN, JOSSE; BEL. 621–624
GOODMAN, LENNY; USA. 63, 64
GOSLIN, CHARLES; USA. 167
GOTTA, HANS-JÜRGEN; GER. 295
GRANDJEAN, JEAN-PIERRE; SWI. 36
GREEN, NORMAN; USA. 162, 163
GREIF, PAULA; USA. 308
GROFF, JAMES; USA. 526
GROSSMAN, AL; USA. 363
GROSSMAN, EUGENE J.; USA. 684
GROSVENOR, DAVID; USA. 88
GUIDONE, SILVANO; ITA. 53, 54
GUILDER, MICHEL; FRA. 25, 26

HALDEN, GÜNTER; SWI. 299, 300
HARDER, ROLF; CAN. 154
HARDY, PAUL; USA. 335
HAROUTIUN, GEORGE; CAN. 419
HARROD, BRIAN; CAN. 38–40
HAUSER, JACQUES; SWI. 552, 734
HELLER, STEVEN; USA. 458
HERMAN, SIDNEY; USA. 657
HILLMER, KEITH; CAN. 44

HIVELY, CHARLES; USA. 89
HOBBS, DAN; USA. 98
HOEFIG, NANCY; USA. 84, 86
HOGLUND, RUDOLPH; USA. 255–258, 260, 262
HOLLYN, LYNN; USA. 588, 598
HORNE, JIM; USA. 569
HOSAKA, MITSUTOSHI; JPN. 627–630
HUDSON, RON; USA. 658
HUTCHCROFT, JOSEPH; USA. 635

JARREAU, JULIEN; USA. 150–152
JAY, JOHN C.; USA. 75–79
JEMERSON; USA. 173
JENKINS, STEVE; USA. 171
JOHNSTON, SKIP; USA. 278–282

KAELIN, ALBERT; SWI. 390
KALISH, NICKI; USA. 459
KANISE, YUKIO; JPN. 524
KATSUI, MITSUO; JPN. 553
KEEBLER, WES; USA. 182, 183
KELLER, BERND; GER. 566
KELLER, MARK; USA. 97, 100
KEMPTON, JOHN; USA. 564, 565
KENSINGER, EDWARD C.; USA. 551
KENT, NANCY; USA. 456
KIDD, IAN; AUS. 67–69
KLAWANS, ALAN J.; USA. 567, 568
KOHN, BOB; FRA. 48–50
KOPPEL, TERRY; USA. 445, 447–455
KOVAR, CONSTANCE; USA. 677
KRAUS, JERELLE; USA. 427, 429–432, 442, 444, 461,
  463, 465, 466, 470, 472
KRISTENSON, STELLAN; SWE. 593
KUNISADA, GORO; JPN. 708
KURI, YOJI; JPN. 268, 269, 293, 294

LACKIE, KATE; GBR. 528, 529
LAKES, FRANKLIN; USA. 551
LANE, TONY; USA. 702, 704
LANG, CHRISTIAN; SWI. 209
LAPPAN, CHAR; USA. 613
LARSEN, GUNNAR; FRA. 276, 277, 292
LAWRENCE, JAMES M.; CAN. 309, 310
LAZCYNSKA, LIZ; GBR. 590
LEES, JOHN; USA. 654, 664
LENNON, TOM; USA. 493–495, 497
LEONHART, JERRY; USA. 56
LESNIEWICZ, TERRY; USA. 713
LESSER, GILBERT; USA. 231–240
LEU, OLAF; GER. 30, 31
LEWINE, HARRIS; USA. 581, 614, 615
LIBARDI, ANTHONY; USA. 328
LOESCH, UWE; GER. 636, 637
LOHRER, UWE; GER. 670
LORENZ, LEE; USA. 297
LUBALIN, HERB; USA. 478, 506, 510–517
LUTZ, ALFRED; GER. 562, 563
LYNCH, DAN; USA. 87

MABRY, MIKE; USA. 109, 521
MACHADO, JOÃO; POR. 195
MÄCHLER, FRANZ; SWI. 270–275
MACLEOD, JOHN; USA. 433, 471
MADER, NORFRIED & GERLINDE; GER. 556, 557
MALERBA, CARLO; ITA. 643
MANKE, MANFRED; GER. 691
MARCY, JACQUES; FRA. 312
MARSALA, JAMES J.; USA. 736
MARSON, CHARLOTTE; USA. 127, 128, 130
MASPERO, FRANÇOIS; FRA. 611
MATTHIJSEN, BOB; BEL. 169, 170

MAU, BRUCE; CAN. 166
MCCRAY, STAN; USA. 288
MCFARLAND, JIM; USA. 150–152, 212
MEDNICK, SCOTT A.; USA. 737
MELBOURNE, ROB; CAN. 313
MENDELL, PIERRE; GER. 14
MENEAR, DAVID; CAN. 184
MIHO, JAMES; USA. 122, 123
MILLER, STEPHEN; USA. 559
MIRANDA, OSWALDO; BRA. 55, 467–469
MITCHELL, DICK; USA. 85, 672
MONGUZZI, BRUNO; SWI. 219–222
MONTONE, KEN; USA. 8, 9
MORGAN, JACQUI; USA. 71
MORROW, BRIAN; GBR. 11
MORTENSEN, GORDON; USA. 155–158, 326, 327

NAGAI, KAZUMASA; JPN. 27–29, 646, 651
NAKAGAWA, KENZO; JPN. 204
NAKAHARA, YASUHARA; JPN. 627–630
NAVARRE, AL; USA. 713
NÉRET, GILLES; FRA. 496
NEUMEIER, MARTY; USA. 80–82, 714
NICHOLS, JESSE R.; USA. 508
NOWLAND, JOHN; AUS. 132, 715
NUBIOLI, DANILO; ITA. 647
NUTI, JEAN-CLAUDE; FRA. 16, 17

OHASHI, TADASHI; JPN. 2, 3, 531 532
OHMER, TOM; USA. 560, 561
OHNISHI, YOSUKE; JPN. 481
OPIT S.R.L.; ITA. 5
OSTERWALDER, MARCUS; GER. 319, 320, 322

PAGANUCCI, BOB; USA. 210, 570, 571
PARMENTIER, JEAN; FRA. 283, 323–325
PAUL, ARTHUR; USA. 381, 402, 403
PAUL, GREG; USA. 251–254, 345–347
PAVEY, JERRY; USA. 555
PEASE, ROBERT; USA. 648, 649, 659
PECKOLICK, ALAN; USA. 138, 139, 638
PELHAM, DAVID; GBR. 608
PETEET, REX; USA. 94–96
PETERS, JÜRGEN; GER. 314
PETERS, MICHAEL; GBR. 720
PFANZELT, HARRY; GER. 671
PLATZ, HANS-PETER; SWI. 416, 420–426
PLAZZOGNA, GIAN VITTORIO; ITA. 114
POKROSS, NANCY C.; USA. 501

PÜTZ, ROBERT; GER. 6, 10, 168

RADUCKI, MACIEJ; POL. 617, 618
RAMPAZZO, GIUSEPPE; ITA. 599
RAU, HANS JÜRGEN; GER. 175, 176
REDMOND, PATRICK; USA. 418
REICH, JACK; USA. 242
REIL, DONETTE; USA. 182, 183
REINHARDT, SUSAN; USA. 341
ROBERTS, ELLEN; USA. 406
ROHRER, MELANIE; USA. 208
ROTHMAN, FRANK; USA. 490
RUTTEN, TIM; USA. 441

SALPETER, BOB; USA. 180
SAMBONET, ROBERTO; ITA. 219–222
SANDS, COLIN; GBR. 631, 632
SANTROCH, HARRIET GOLFOS; CAN. 65, 66
SCHENK, ROLAND; GBR. 504
SCHER, PAULA; USA. 698–701
SCHMID, HELMUT; JPN. 729, 731
SCHMITTSIEGEL, HELMUT M.; GER. 224
SCHUMACHER, FRANZ; GER. 633, 634
SENNEFELDER, MARIA-CHRISTINA; GER. 4
SESSIONS, STEVEN; USA. 51, 52, 525
SHISHIDO, YOSHIO; JPN. 603
SHORTEN, CHRIS; USA. 83
SHOSTAK, MITCH; USA. 482
SIDJAKOV, NICOLAS; USA. 109, 521
SILVIA, KEN; USA. 306, 307
SLANSKY, W.; GER. 205
SMITH, ANDREW; CAN. 546, 547
SMITH, JAKE; USA. 484
SMITH, MIRIAM; USA. 412–414
SOMMESE, LANNY; USA. 218
SOO HOO, PATRICK; USA. 735
SPRANG, WOLFGANG; GER. 136, 137
SREBNIK, CRAIG; USA. 656
STAEBLER, TOM; USA. 368, 369, 377, 378, 382, 384,
    398–404
STAHEL, RAINER; SWI. 191, 192
STANFORD, TONY; GBR. 528, 529
STEINER, HENRY; HKG. 249
STEINER, KURT F.; GER. 244
STIEDL, HELMUT; AUT. 374
STIRES, LARRY; USA. 153
SUARÈS, JEAN-CLAUDE; USA. 344
SUGIYAMA, YOSHIMI; JPN. 603
SULLIVAN, RON; USA. 644

SUSSMAN, ABIE; USA. 21
SUTER, BRUNO; FRA. 33

TANABE, FRANCIS; USA. 443
TEICHBERG, IRA; USA. 186
THOEN, PETER; USA. 181
THOMAS, DICK; USA. 23
TORA, SHINICHIRO; USA. 627–630
TRIBONDEAU, JACQUES; FRA. 518, 519
TRICKETT, LYNN; GBR. 631, 632
TUCKER, BARRIE; AUS. 67–69, 619, 712, 728

ULRICH, MARK; USA. 189, 190
UNO, YASUYUKI; JPN. 99, 101

VANDERBYL, MICHAEL; USA. 653
VASSIL, PAMELA; USA. 460
VERA, JOE; MEX. 645
VIDAL, FRANÇOIS RUY; FRA. 597
VITALE, ETTORE; ITA. 642
VORMSTEIN, MANFRED; GER. 689, 696

WALLER, CHARLES; USA. 417, 439
WALLER, MANFRED; GER. 610
WALUKANIS, RICHARD; USA. 148, 174
WASILEWSKI, MIECZYSLAW; POL. 502
WATERS, JOHN; USA. 92
WATT, ROGER; GBR. 385
WEBB, BRIAN; GBR. 631, 632
WEBER, ULI; GER. 57–60
WESTMAN, CHRISTIAN; FRA. 681
WHITE, KEN; USA. 564, 565
WHITE, TOM; USA. 110, 111
WIDMANN, JOACHIM; GER. 295
WIJSENBEEK, S.; NLD. 177–179
WILKING, JOAN; USA. 113
WINDS, HEIDE; GER. 359
WIRTZ, GERARD; SWI. 416, 420–426
WOLF, SHEILA; USA. 492
WOLGENSINGER, JACQUES; FRA. 520
WÖRTMANN, RAINER; GER. 376, 379, 380,
    383, 386, 387

YAMADA, TADAMI; JPN. 358
YELDHAM, ADAM; GBR. 585
YOKOO, TADANORI; JPN. 70, 72–74, 301–305, 582–584
YOUNG, JACKIE; CAN. 342, 362

ZEBROWSKI, ANDREAS; GER. 600

Index to Agencies and Studios
Verzeichnis der Agenturen und Studios
Index des agences et studios

ACKER DESIGN; USA. 213, 214
ACKERMAN & MCQUEEN ADVERTISING, INC.; USA. 97, 100
ADLER, SCHWARTZ, INC.; USA. 112
ADVERTISING DESIGNERS, INC.; USA. 560, 561
ALLAN, KENT, DESIGN GROUP; CAN. 134, 135
AMERICAN HOSPITAL SUPPLY CORP./DESIGN DEPARTEMENT; USA. 129
ANGELI, PRIMO, GRAPHICS; USA. 730
ANISDAHL/CHRISTENSEN AS; NOR. 558
ANSPACH, GROSSMANN, PORTUGAL, INC.; USA. 684
ANTON, JERRY, ASSOCIATES; USA. 162, 163
ARBEITSGEMEINSCHAFT FÜR VISUELLE KOMMUNI-KATION; GER. 636, 637
ART-AGENCY; POL. 617, 618
AXON GARSIDE & CO. LTD.; GBR. 241

BALZI, ESTUDIO; SPA. 486
BAXTER & KORGE, INC.; USA. 51, 52, 525
BBDM ADVERTISING; USA. 37
BELSER, BURKEY; USA. 505
BLOOMINGDALE'S; USA. 75–79
BM GRAPHIC DESIGN; BEL. 169, 170
BONNELL & CROSBY, INC.; USA. 108
BOYD, DOUGLAS, DESIGN & MARKETING; USA. 661, 737
BRIGHT & ASSOCIATES; USA. 719
BRIMMER DESIGN; USA. 143
BROWN, MICHAEL DAVID, INC.; USA. 127, 128, 130, 443
BRÜSCH, BÉAT; SWI. 194, 203, 283, 299, 300, 390
BURNS, COOPER, HYNES LTD.; CAN. 102
BURSON MARSTELLER; USA. 115

CANOVAS, ESTUDIO; ARG. 641
CARABOSSE SA; SWI. 693
CATO HIBBERD DESIGN PTY LTD.; AUS. 243, 500
CBS/BROADCAST GROUP; USA. 186
CBS RECORDS; USA. 692, 695, 698–702, 704, 706, 709
CEVEY KELLER; GER. 566
CHERMAYEFF & GEISMAR ASSOC.; USA. 202, 640, 663, 668, 686
CIBA-GEIGY/ZENTRALE WERBUNG; SWI. 209
CIBA-GEIGY DESIGN; USA. 153
CLASSIC PROPAGANDA; BRA. 91
COMMUNICATION ARTS, INC.; USA. 680
COMPUGRAPHIC CORP.; USA. 113
CONTAINER CORPORATION OF AMERICA/COMMUNICATION DEPT.; USA. 172, 635
CORRIGAN ADVERTISING; USA. 34, 35
CREATIVE SERVICES, INC.; USA. 98
CUNNINGHAM & WALSH, INC.; USA. 7
CURRENT CONCEPTS, INC.; USA. 569

DAILEY & ASSOC.; USA. 56
DANCER FITZGERALD SAMPLE; USA. 181
D'ARCY, MACMANUS & MASIUS; USA. 83
DE HARAK, RUDOLPH, & ASSOCIATES, INC.; USA. 667, 679
DENYER DESIGN ASSOCIATES; GBR. 142
DESGRIPPES, BEAUCHANT, GOBÉ; FRA. 732, 733
DRUID, J. R., ASSOC.; USA. 211

EATON, T., & CO. LTD.; CAN. 65, 66
EICHINGER, INC.; USA. 503
EISENBERG, INC.; USA. 658
ELDORADO; FRA. 33
ENDRIKAT, K., AG; GER. 164, 230

EUCALYPTUS TREE STUDIO; USA. 197–200
EUROTEAM; SPA. 42, 43
EXIGENCE; FRA. 25, 26

FARM CREDIT ADMINISTRATION; USA. 555
FIFTY FINGERS, INC.; CAN. 125, 126, 166, 311, 313, 342, 362, 546, 547
FION, ALAIN; GER. 93, 716
FLETT HENDERSON & ARNOLD PTY LTD.; AUS. 498
FLORVILLE, PATRICK, GRAPHIC DESIGN; USA. 687

GALE, ROBERT A., INC.; USA. 665
GALLERY ART KURI JIKKEN KOBO; JPN. 268, 269, 293, 294
GLASER, MILTON, INC.; USA. 266, 341
GOTTSCHALK + ASH LTD.; CAN. 721, 722
GOTTSCHALK + ASH INTL.; SWI. 145, 146
GRAPHIC COMMUNICATION LTD.; HKG. 249
GRATAMA & DE VRIES; NLD. 554

HAMILL TOMS LTD.; GBR. 45–47
HARDER, ROLF, & ASSOC.; CAN. 154
HERMAN & LEES ASSOC.; USA. 654, 657, 664
HOFFMAN YORK, INC.; USA. 63, 64
HOWARD, MERRELL & BOYKIN; USA. 12, 13

IBM CORP.; USA. 144, 217, 551
IGARASHI, TAKENOBU, DESIGN; JPN. 717, 718
INSTITUT FÜR COMMUNICATION; GER. 224
INX, INC.; USA. 433, 471

JENKINS, STEVE; USA. 171
JONSON, PEDERSEN, HINRICHS & SHAKERY; USA. 567, 568

KOPPEL, T., GRAPHICS; USA. 445, 447–455
KOVAR, CONSTANCE, LTD.; USA. 677
KVH/GGK INT. BV; NLD. 90, 688

LEONHARDT & KERN; GER. 57–60
LESNIEWICZ/NAVARRE; USA. 713
LEU, OLAF, DESIGN & PARTNER; GER. 30, 31
LINIE-GRAFIK; GER. 359
LOHRER, ATELIER; GER. 670
LORD, GELLER, FEDERICO, EINSTEIN; USA. 23
LORD, SULLIVAN & YODER, INC.; USA. 32
LUBALIN PECKOLICK ASSOC., INC.; 138, 139, 506, 510–517, 616, 638, 650, 655, 660, 662

MAGNUS NANKERVIS & CURL; AUS. 61, 62
MALERBA, CARLO; ITA. 643
MARTIN AGENCY; USA. 18–20
MCCANN-ERICKSON; CAN. 38–40, 44
MCCANN-ERICKSON, INC.; USA. 8, 9
MENDELL & OBERER; GER. 14
METZDORF ADVERTISING AGENCY, INC.; USA. 89
MIHO, INC.; USA. 122, 123
MINOR, WENDELL, DESIGN; USA. 363, 605, 613
MIRAN ESTUDIO; BRA. 467–469
MIT DESIGN SERVICES; USA. 501
MOMENTUM DESIGN; CAN. 184
MORGAN, JACQUI, STUDIO; USA. 71
MORTENSEN DESIGN; USA. 155–158, 326, 327

NEEDHAM, HARPER & STEERS, INC.; USA. 15
NESTLÉ/ATELIER GRAPHIQUE; SWI. 548
NEUMEIER DESIGN TEAM; USA. 80–82, 675, 714
NIPPON DESIGN CENTER; JPN. 27–29, 204, 646, 651
NIPPON INTERNATIONAL AGENCY; JPN. 729, 731

NUBIOLI STUDIO; ITA. 647
NUTI & ASSOC.; FRA. 16, 17
NOWLAND, JOHN, GRAPHIC DESIGN; AUS. 132, 715

OPIT S. R. L.; ITA. 5

PAGANUCCI, BOB; USA. 210, 570, 571
PARTENAIRE; FRA. 48–50
PAUL, GREG, & ASSOCIATES; USA. 251–254, 345–347
PEASE, ROBERT, & CO.; USA. 648, 649, 659
PENTAGRAM; GBR. 105–107, 124, 149, 159, 160, 673, 676, 676a, 685, 725
PETERS, MICHAEL, & PARTNERS; GBR. 720
PFANZELT, HARRY; GER. 671
PIHLGREN, MARIANNE; SWE. 147
PLAZZOGNA, G. VITTORIO, GRAPHIC DESIGN; ITA. 114
PS-MARKETING GMBH; GER. 244
PUBLICIS; FRA. 116–121
PUSH PIN STUDIOS, INC.; USA. 535–545, 581, 587, 614, 615, 674, 674a, 727
PÜTZ, ROBERT, GMBH & CO.; GER. 6, 10, 168

RAU, STUDIO; GER. 175, 176
REDMOND, BARBARA & PATRICK, DESIGN, INC.; USA. 418
REKLAMTEAM AB; SWE. 185
RICHARDS GROUP/RICHARDS, SULLIVAN, BROCK & ASSOC.; USA. 41, 84–88, 94–96, 187, 188, 559, 644, 672
RIGHETTO GRAFIK & WERBUNG; SWI. 639
ROGERS, RICHARD, INC.; USA. 242
ROHER, MELANIE, DESIGN; USA. 208
RUMRILL HOYT, INC.; USA. 24

SALPETER, BOB, INC.; USA. 180
SALVATO & COE; USA. 189, 190
SAMBONET, STUDIO; ITA. 219–222
SANDERS, LUBINSKI & POWELL, INC.; USA. 110, 111
SCHUHMACHER, FRANZ; GER. 633, 634
SERVICEPLAN; GER. 556, 557
SIDJAKOW & BERMAN ASSOCIATES; USA. 109, 521
SIEGEL & GALE; USA. 666
SOMMESE, LANNY, DESIGN; USA. 218
SOO HOO, PATRICK, DESIGNERS, INC.; USA. 735
SREBNIK DESIGN; USA. 656
STONE, JENNI, PARTNERSHIP; GBR. 631, 632
SUDLER & HENNESSEY, INC.; USA. 150–152, 212

TBWA LTD.; GBR. 11
TESTA, ARMANDO, S. P. A.; ITA. 53, 54
TOGUCHI ART STUDIO; JPN. 284, 285
TUCKER & KIDD; AUS. 67–69, 619, 712, 728

UMUARAMA; BRA. 55
UNILEVER LTD./INFORMATION WORKSHOP; GBR. 528, 529
UNIVERSITY OF TSUKUBA/INSTITUTE OF ART AND DESIGN; JPN. 553

VANDERBYL DESIGN; USA. 653
VERA, JOE, & ASOCIADES; MEX. 645
VITALE, STUDIO, ITA. 642

WATERS, JOHN, ASSOCIATES; USA. 92
WEBB SILBERG COMPANIES; USA. 182, 183
WESTMAN, CHRISTIAN; FRA. 681
WHITE, KEN, DESIGN OFFICE, INC.; USA. 564, 565
WILLARDSON & WHITE, INC.; USA. 165

YOUNG & RUBICAM GMBH; GER. 1, 4

Index to Advertisers
Verzeichnis der Auftraggeber
Index des clients

ACADEMY OF ART COLLEGE; USA. 143
ACHILLES, GEBR.; GER. 164
ADELAIDE COLLEGE OF THE ARTS AND EDUCATION;
    AUS. 132
ADG FAD; SPA. 161
AIDOS – ASSOCIAZIONE ITALIANA DIRETTORI
    ORGANIZZAZIONE E SISTEMI; ITA. 652
ALITALIA S. P. A.; ITA. 53, 54
ALLEGHENY GROUP; USA. 656
AMERICAN ASSOC. FOR HIGHER EDUCATION; USA.
    127, 128, 130
AMERICAN HOSPITAL SUPPLY CORP.; USA. 129
AMOCO CHEMICALS CORP.; USA. 37
ANALYTIC RECRUITING INC.; USA. 684
ANCHORAGE, THE; USA. 659
ANDERSON, ARTHUR, LTD.; GBR. 685
ANDERSON; HARRY W.; USA. 682
ANTON, JERRY, ASSOCIATES; USA. 162, 163
ARGENTINA FEDERAL BANK; ARG. 641
ASIAN WALL STREET JOURNAL; USA. 92
ASSOCIATED FILM DISTRIBUTORS; USA. 737
ATLAS COPCO LTD; GBR. 45–47
AT VERLAG; SWI. 140, 141

BALTIMORE AQUARIUM; USA. 640
BAMERINDUS; BRA. 55
BANK OF AMERICA; USA. 83
BANK MEES & HOPE NV; NLD. 554
BAUWENS, THEO, N.V.; BEL. 169, 170
BENSON & HEDGES; USA. 655
BERMAN, MONTY & MYRTLE; GBR. 673
BLOOMINGDALE'S; USA. 75–79
BOBST S.A.; SWI. 194
BOISE CASCADE; USA. 109
BRANCA, F.LLI, DISTILLERIE SPA; ITA. 5
BROADHEAD, PAUL, & ASSOCIATES; USA. 87,
    94–96
BROWN, EDWARD; USA. 665
BUNDESMINISTER FÜR FORSCHUNG UND TECHNO-
    LOGIE; GER. 105–107
BURDA VERLAG; GER. 168

CADEL INDUSTRIA MOBILI S. P. A.; ITA. 114
CAMPBELL, K. M., PTY LTD; AUS. 243
CAMP RAFA-EL; USA. 649
CANADIAN OPERA CO.; CAN. 215, 216
CANADIAN REHABILITATION COUNCIL FOR THE
    DISABLED; CAN. 38–40
CAPSUGEL AG; SWI. 14
CBS TELEVISION STATIONS; USA. 186
CENTRAL PENNSYLVANIA FESTIVAL OF THE ARTS;
    USA. 218
CENTRE CULTUREL RÉGIONAL DELÉMONT; SWI. 203
CENTRO DE ARTE CONTEMPORÂNEA; POR. 195
CENTURY PARTNERS; USA. 653
CHAMPION PAPERS; USA. 122, 123
CHASE MANHATTAN BANK; USA. 138, 139
CHITOSE CONFECTIONERY CO; JPN. 724
CIBA-GEIGY AG; SWI. 209
CIBA-GEIGY; USA. 153, 210
CITY OF SAN ANTONIO; USA. 660
CKARAT ADVERTISING, INC.; USA. 677
COLUMBUS SOCIETY OF COMMUNICATING ARTS;
    USA. 189, 190
COMMERCIAL BANK OF KUWAIT; KUW. 676, 676a
COMMUNICATION WORKERS OF AMERICA; USA.
    663
COMPUGRAPHIC CORP.; USA. 113
CONFIDENCE GOLF CO.; USA. 735
CONTAINER CORPORATION OF AMERICA; USA. 172,
    635
CORPUS CHRISTI NATIONAL BANK; USA. 88
CUIR CENTRE; FRA. 33

DALLAS SERVICES FOR THE VISUALLY IMPAIRED;
    USA. 644
DANOS, JUDIT; HUN. 669
DANVILLE RESOURCES, INC.; USA. 638
DAON SOUTHWEST; USA. 41
DEUTZ, DRUCKHAUS; GER. 633, 634
DEUX MONDES, LES; USA. 679
DIBLO; MEX. 645
DOT BAKER; USA. 672

EATON, T., CO. LTD.; CAN. 65, 66
ELECTA EDITRICE; ITA. 219–222
ELLIS CONTAINER; USA. 661
ESCHER WYSS AG; SWI. 191, 192
ESSELTE; GBR. 124
EVANGELISCHE PUBLIZISTIK E. V.; GER. 196
EVEREST & JENNINGS INTERNATIONAL; USA. 560
EX LIBRIS VERLAG AG; SWI. 131
EZIHEAT; AUS. 715

FACE PHOTOSETTING LTD.; GBR. 149
FACHHOCHSCHULE NIEDERRHEIN; GER. 205
FARM CREDIT BANKS; USA. 555
FERRANTI INSTRUMENTATION LTD.; GBR. 241
FIFTY FINGERS, INC.; CAN. 166
FINANCIAL FEDERATION, INC.; USA. 561
FOUR-LEAF TOWERS; USA. 51, 52

GAST; USA. 115
GEORGIA-PACIFIC CORP.; USA. 8, 9
GERLAND; FRA. 48–50
GOSLIN, CHARLES; USA. 167
GRACE, W. R., & CO.; USA. 12, 13

HASEGAWA, K. K.; JPN. 646
HERCULES PACKAGING GROUP; AUS. 712
HOCHSCHULE FÜR GESTALTUNG OFFENBACH/M;
    GER. 136, 137
HOFFMANN-LA ROCHE LTD.; CAN. 154
HOFFMANN-LA ROCHE & CO. AG; SWI. 734
HORIZON LIGHTING CO.; USA. 667
HOTEL BARMEN'S ASSOCIATION; JPN.
    627, 628, 629, 630
HUIS BV; NLD. 688

IBM CORP.; 23, 103, 104, 108, 144, 180, 217, 242
INDIANA CREDIT UNION LEAGUE; USA. 173
INK TANK; USA. 674, 674a
ISETAN DEPT. STORE; JPN. 204
ISMALIA CENTRAL HOUSING BOARD OF INDIA;
    IND. 664

JAM FACTORY; AUS. 67–69, 728
JCB FRANCE; FRA. 16, 17
JENKINS, STEVE; USA. 171
JOCKEY; GER. 57–60
JOST, HEINZ; SWI. 193

KCBQ RADIO; USA. 658
KIKKOMAN SHOYU CO., LTD.; JPN. 2, 3, 531, 532
KIMBERLY-CLARK CORP.; USA. 736
KUNSTGEWERBESCHULE DER STADT ZÜRICH;
    SWI. 201

LEE/MALMÖ YRKESKLÄDER; SWE. 185
LETRASET; GER. 22
LIFE MAGAZINE; USA. 231–235, 237–240

MARCONA SHIPPING & MINING CO.; USA. 648
MARSHALL FIELD'S; USA. 89
MARTIN, AUGUSTUS, LTD.; GBR. 631, 632
MD PAPIERFABRIKEN; GER. 556, 557
MECANORMA; FRA. 116–121

MEDICAL COURIERS, INC.; USA. 680
MENTAL HEALTH ASSOCIATION; USA. 187, 188
MEXICANA AIRLINES; USA. 56
MITCHEL PRESS; AUS. 619
MOBIL INDUSTRIAL CHEMICALS; USA. 18–20
MOBIL CORP.; USA. 202, 668, 686
MOLINARI, P.G., & SONS; USA. 730
MORRIS, PHILIP, INC.; USA. 208
MORSE SHOE CO.; USA. 657
MORTENSEN DESIGN; USA. 155–158

NACONA BOOT COMPANY; USA. 97, 100
NEDERLANDSE SPOORWEGEN; NLD. 177–179
NEUE GALERIE – SAMMLUNG LUDWIG, AACHEN;
    GER. 230
NEVAMAR CORP.; USA. 32
NICHII CO. LTD.; JPN. 651
NISHIHONGANJI; JPN. 72–74
NORD-SÜD VERLAG; SWI. 620, 620a
NORDWESTLOTTO; GER. 175, 176

OLYMPIA BREWING CO.; USA. 719
OMNI INTERNATIONAL HOTELS, INC.; USA. 98
OPEN DESIGN S. R. L.; ITA. 643
OTSUKA PHARMACEUTICALS; JPN. 729, 731
OWENS-CORNING FIBERGLAS CORP.; USA. 713

PARKE-DAVIS CO.; USA. 150–152, 212
PARTICIPATION; CAN. 125, 126
PENDLETON WOOLEN MILLS; USA. 7
PENTAGRAM; GBR. 159, 160
PFANZELT, HARRY; GER. 671
PHILIPS; CAN. 44
PINAUD, PARFUMS; FRA. 732, 733
PITNEY BOWES; USA. 666
POLYDOR, INC.; USA. 21
POST OFFICE TELECOMMUNICATIONS; GBR. 142
PRÄSIDIALABTEILUNG DER STADT ZÜRICH; SWI.
    191, 192
PREISIG, F., INGENIEURBÜRO; SWI. 145, 146
PREMIERE; USA. 181
PRESSEAMT DER LANDESHAUPTSTADT KIEL; GER.
    206, 207
PRINCESS TORAYA CO., LTD.; JPN. 99, 101
PROFESSIONAL TYPOGRAPHIC SERVICES; USA. 678
PROVINCE OF BRITISH COLUMBIA/MINISTRY OF
    TRANSPORTATION AND HIGHWAYS; CAN. 134, 135
P. T. TOTALIZATOR SPORTOWY; POL. 617, 618
PUSH PIN PRODUCTIONS; USA. 727

QUADRANT FILMS LTD.; CAN. 184
QUAKER STOVE CO.; INC.; USA. 34, 35
QUINOLÉINE, LA, SA; FRA. 25, 26

RAI RADIO TELEVISIONE ITALIANA; ITA. 642
REGGIANA RIMORCHI; ITA. 647
REIKA CO.; JPN. 723
REINSURANCE FACILITIES CORP.; USA. 182, 183
REMINGTON; USA. 24
REPUBLIC AIRLINES; USA. 63, 64
RITZ; USA. 71
RIVELLA INTERNATIONAL SA; SWI. 726
ROHNER, EDUARD; SWI. 145, 146
ROUSE COMPANY; USA. 84–86

SANTA BARBARA BANK & TRUST; USA. 80–82
SCHMIDT, GEBR., GMBH; GER. 30, 31
SCHNEIDER-IMPORT GMBH; GER. 1
SCHWÄBISCH GMÜNDER ERSATZKASSE; GER.
    562, 563
SCHWORTZ, BARRIE M., PHOTOGRAPHY; USA. 675
SEIBU DEPARTMENT STORE; JPN. 70
SEV. DAHL GROUP; NOR. 558

SIEGWERK FARBENFABRIK; GER. 6, 10
SLIDES PLUS; USA. 686
SOCIÉTÉ GÉNÉRALE; FRA. 662
SONY; NLD. 90
STONE, JENNI, PARTNERSHIP; GBR. 631, 632
SUCHARD GMBH; GER. 4
SUGARCO EDIZIONI S. R. L.; ITA. 227–229
SURGIKOS, INC.; USA. 211
SVERIGES PERSONALADMINISTRATIVA; SWE. 147

TAKEO PAPER CO.; JPN. 27–29
TECHNISCHE UNIVERSITÄT MÜNCHEN/LEHRSTUHL
   FÜR LANDSCHAFTSARCHITEKTUR UND ENTWER-
   FEN; GER. 670
THAI AIRLINES; THA. 61, 62
TIME, INC.; USA. 148, 174
TIME EQUITIES; USA. 650
TOLID DARU COMPANY; USA. 213, 214
TRICKETT & WEBB LTD.; GBR. 631, 632

TRITON OIL & GAS CORP.; USA. 559
TUNDRA BOOKS; CAN. 625, 626
TYPE SHOP GMBH; GER. 636, 637

ULTRAVUE; BRA. 91
UNDERGROUND, THE; USA. 236
UNION CARBIDE CORP.; USA. 15
UNIVERSITY OF MARYLAND; USA. 197–200
US DEPARTMENT OF HOUSING AND URBAN
   DEVELOPMENT; USA. 654

VERBAND VON LIEFERANTEN VERSILBERTER
   BESTECKE; SWI. 639
VICKERS, CAMILLE, PHOTOGRAPHY; USA. 683
VOLKSWAGEN OF AMERICA, INC.; USA. 112

WALKER, JOHNNIE; GBR. 11
WATNEY MANN BREWERS LTD.; GBR. 725
WESTERN MEDICAL; USA. 714

WESTMAN, CHRISTIAN; FRA. 681
WHITBREAD & CO., LTD.; GBR. 720
WHITE, CHARLES; USA. 165
WILHELM-LEHMBRUCK-MUSEUM; GER. 224
WOOD WILKINGS LTD.; CAN. 102
WYETH, LABORATOIRES; BEL. 621–624

XEROX CORP.; USA. 110, 111

YELLO SPORT; GER. 93, 716
YER LABORATORIOS; SPA. 42, 43

ZDF ZWEITES DEUTSCHES FERNSEHEN; GER. 223,
   225, 226
ZELL-SCHÖNAU AG; GER. 244
ZEN ENVIRONMENTAL DESIGN; JPN. 717, 718
ZYMA SA; SWI. 36

Index to Publishers
Verzeichnis der Verleger
Index des éditeurs

A.A.A.S.; USA. 485
ANTIOCH REVIEW; USA. 316, 591, 592
ARGOS VERGARA S.A.; SPA. 486
ARIOLA-EURODISC GMBH; GER. 689, 696
ARMSTRONG, JOE GRAVITT; USA. 250
ARTISTS HOUSE; USA. 705
ASIAWEEK LTD.; HKG. 249
ASSOCIATION OF JUNIOR LEAGUES, INC.; USA. 248
ATLANTIC-LITTLE, BROWN; USA. 613
ATLANTIC RECORDING CORP.; USA. 694, 703, 710
A.T. AND T.-LONG LINES; USA. 503
ATTENZIONE MAGAZINE; USA. 335
AUDIOVISUAL INSTRUCTION; USA. 505
AVANT-GARDE MEDIA, INC.; USA. 478

BASLER ZEITUNG; SWI. 416, 420–426
BAUER, HEINRICH, VERLAG; GER. 376, 379, 380, 383, 386, 387
BAYARD PRESSE; FRA. 283, 323–325
BEDSIDE NURSE; USA. 527
BOSTON GLOBE; USA. 263–265, 388, 389, 391–397, 417, 439, 445, 447–455
BÜCHERGILDE GUTENBERG; GER. 604
BURROUGHS AND MAN; JPN. 524

CAMDEN HOUSE PUBLISHING LTD.; CAN. 309, 310
CBS RECORDS; USA. 692, 695, 698–702, 704, 706, 709
CHIEF EXECUTIVE MAGAZINE, INC.; USA. 499
CHIKUMA SHOBO LTD.; JPN. 582–584
CITROËN S.A.; FRA. 520
CITY MAGAZINE; CAN. 313
CITY NEWS; URU. 467–469
COMAC COMMUNICATIONS LTD.; CAN. 311, 419, 491
CONNAISSANCE DES ARTS; FRA. 496
CROWN PUBLISHERS; USA. 606, 607, 616
CROWN ZELLERBACH; USA. 521
CUE MAGAZINE; USA. 298

DALLAS MORNING NEWS; USA. 288
DE GEILLUSTREERDE PERS N.V.; NLD. 353–357, 360, 361
DIAL, THE; USA. 341
DONKEY-PRESS; GER. 533
DYNAMIC YEARS MAGAZINE; USA. 296

EDITIONS DE L'AMITIÉ; FRA. 597
ELECTRIC CO.; USA. 534
ESPRESSO, L'; ITA. 315, 317, 601, 602
ESSO FRANCE; FRA. 518, 519
EUROPÄISCHE BILDUNGSGEMEINSCHAFT; GER. 600

FINANCIAL POST MAGAZINE; CAN. 342, 362
FISCHER-MEDICAL PUBLICATIONS; USA. 493–495, 497
FOLHA DE SÃO PAULO; BRA. 473, 474, 476

GENERALSTABENS LITOGRAFISKA ANSTALT; SWE. 593
GENKOSHA PUBLISHING CO.; JPN. 481
GRADUATE MAGAZINE; CAN. 546, 547
GRUNER & JAHR AG & CO.; GER. 359
GYLDENDAL; NOR. 612

HARBOR PUBLISHERS; USA. 598
HARCOURT, BRACE, JOVANOVICH, INC.; USA. 581, 614, 615
HARPER'S MAGAZINE, INC.; USA. 492

HAWTHORN BOOKS, INC.; USA. 587
HAYAKAWA PUBLISHING, INC.; JPN. 358
HEARST CORP.; USA. 490
HNG CORP.; USA. 525
HOFFMAN-LA ROCHE, F.; SWI. 552

IBM CORPORATION; USA. 551, 570, 571
INC. MAGAZINE; USA. 306, 307
INTERMED COMMUNICATIONS, INC.; USA. 484
INTERNATIONAL TYPEFACE CORPORATION; USA. 506, 510–517
INX, INC.; USA. 433, 471
IRI ISTITUTO PER LA RICOSTRUZIONE INDUSTRIALE; ITA. 405
ITOKI CO., LTD.; JPN. 286, 287

JAPEC; JPN. 284, 285
JORNAL DE TARDE; BRA. 434

KARMA MUSIKPRODUKTION GMBH; GER. 691
KIKKOMAN CORP.; JPN. 531, 532
KING RECORD CO., LTD.; JPN. 708
KLETT-COTTA; GER. 572–580
KNOPF, ALFRED A., INC.; USA. 586, 589, 595, 605
KODANSHA LTD.; JPN. 603
KÖLNISCHE RUNDSCHAU; GER. 437
KRAJOWE WYDAWNICTWO CZASOPISM; POL. 502

LARSEN, GUNNAR; FRA. 275, 277
LAWRENCE PUBLISHING CO.; AUS. 500
LINEA, LA, EDITRICE; ITA. 599
LOS ANGELES TIMES; USA. 441, 446

MANAGEMENT TODAY; GBR. 504
MANAGER MAGAZIN; GER. 504
MAREK, RICHARD, PUBLISHERS; USA. 588
MARY-JOSÉE; FRA. 693
MASPERO, FRANÇOIS; FRA. 611
MASSACHUSETTS INSTITUTE OF TECHNOLOGY; USA. 501
MCCALL PUBLISHING CO.; USA. 363
MCGRAW-HILL, PUBLICATIONS CO.; USA. 507, 509
MEDI-MEDIA; FRA. 312
METHUEN & CO. LTD.; GBR. 585
MIAMI HERALD; USA. 435, 436, 438
MINNEAPOLIS STAR; USA. 418
MODE INTERNATIONAL; GER/FRA. 291, 292
MONDADORI, ARNOLDO; ITA. 415

NACIONAL, EL; VEN. 487–489
NASA; USA. 564, 565
NATION, THE; USA. 344
NATIONAL FOOTBALL LEAGUE; USA. 343
NATIONAL LAMPOON; USA. 278–282
NEBELSPALTER-VERLAG; SWI. 270–275
NESTLÉ S.A.; SWI. 548
NEUER VORWÄRTS VERLAG NAU & CO.; GER. 295
NEW REALITIES MAGAZINE; USA. 326, 327
NEWS, THE; USA. 410
NEWSDAY, INC.; USA. 412–414
NEW YORKER MAGAZINE, INC.; USA. 297
NEW YORK TIMES; USA. 266, 267, 427, 429–432, 440, 442, 444, 456–466, 470, 472
NIPPON UPJOHN LTD.; JPN. 523

OMNI PUBLICATIONS INTERNATIONAL LTD.; USA. 289, 290, 364–367, 370–373, 375
OPUS; CSR. 711
ORAG-VERLAG; AUT. 374

PENGUIN BOOKS LTD.; GBR. 608
PENTHOUSE INTERNATIONAL LTD.; USA. 407–409
PHONOGRAM GMBH; GER. 690, 697, 697a
PIGEON CORP.; JPN. 268, 269
PLAIN DEALER PUBLISHING CO.; USA. 251–254, 345–347
PLAYBOY ENTERPRISES, INC.; USA. 336–340, 368, 369, 377, 378, 381, 382, 384, 398–404
PRENTICE-HALL; USA. 406
PRIME TIME COMMUNICATIONS; USA. 479
PROFESSIONAL PHOTOGRAPHY MAGAZINE; AUS. 498
PUSH PIN GRAPHIC, INC.; USA. 535–545

RAGEOT, G.T.; FRA. 597
RAYMOND, PAUL, PUBLICATIONS LTD.; GBR. 385
RELATIONSKONSULT; SWE. 549, 550
RINGIER VERLAG; SWI. 299, 300
ROLLING STONE; USA. 331, 333, 334
ROWOHLT VERLAG; GER. 596, 610

SANDOZ, INC.; USA. 569
SANRIO CO.; JPN. 293, 294
SCOUTING MAGAZINE; USA. 480
SELF MAGAZINE; USA. 308
SESA-DEUTSCHLAND GMBH; GER. 566
SHELL OIL CO.; USA. 526
SHOGAKUKAN LTD.; JPN. 301–305
SIRE RECORDS COMPANY; USA. 707
SMITH, KLINE & FRENCH LABS.; USA. 567, 568
SOUTHWESTERN BELL; USA. 522
SPHERE BOOKS; GBR. 590
STEMMER HOUSE; USA. 594
SZPILKI; POL. 329, 330, 332

TAGES-ANZEIGER AG; SWI. 390
TIDNINGEN VI; SWE. 318
TIME, INC.; USA. 255–262, 328
TRIANGLE PUBLICATIONS, INC.; USA. 245–247, 348–352

UNILEVER LTD.; GBR. 528, 529
UNIVERSITY OF TSUKUBA; JPN. 553
US DEPARTMENT OF HEALTH, EDUCATION & WEL-FARE; USA. 508
US INTERNATIONAL COMMUNICATION AGENCY; USA. 477

VENTURE MAGAZINE; USA. 483
VILLAGE VOICE; USA. 428
VISEL, CURT; GER. 411, 530

WASHINGTON POST; USA. 443
WELTWOCHE-VERLAG AG; SWI. 475
WESTERMANNS MONATSHEFTE; GER. 314
WHARTON MAGAZINE; USA. 482

ZEITVERLAG GERD BUCERIUS KG; GER. 319, 320, 322
ZINDERMANS; SWE. 609

ERRATUM – GRAPHIS ANNUAL 79/80

■ On page 233 of the last but one volume of GRAPHIS ANNUAL we reproduced in Fig. 688 a row of bottles for various types of table wines marketed by the Mexican Vinicola Vergel SA. We regret that there was an error in the credits given for this item. The design studio was not Burns, Cooper, Hynes Ltd., as indicated; all the bottles and labels were designed by Gianninoto Associates, Inc.

■ In der vorletzten Ausgabe von GRAPHIS ANNUAL zeigten wir auf Seite 233 unter Abb. 688 eine Reihe von Flaschen für drei Kategorien von Tischweinen der mexikanischen Weinhandlung Vinicola Vergel SA. Irrtümlicherweise wurde als Designfirma Burns, Cooper, Hynes Ltd. aufgeführt. Die Flaschengestaltung wie auch die Etikettgestaltung wurde jedoch von Gianninoto Associates, Inc. ausgeführt.

■ Dans l'avant dernière édition de GRAPHIS ANNUAL nous avions montré en page 233, fig. 688 une série de bouteilles pour trois catégories de vins de table du viticulteur mexicain Vinicola Vergel SA. Malheureusement une erreur s'est glissée dans les listes des personnes ayant contribué à la réalisation de ce travail. La conception des bouteilles et des étiquettes n'a pas été assumée par Burns, Cooper, Hynes Ltd., mais par l'agence américaine Gianninoto Associates, Inc.

■ Entry instructions may be requested by anyone interested in submitting samples of exceptional graphics or photography for possible inclusion in our annuals. No fees involved. Closing dates for entries:
GRAPHIS ANNUAL (advertising and editorial art and design): 31 January
PHOTOGRAPHIS (advertising and editorial photography): 30 June
GRAPHIS POSTERS (an annual of poster art): 30 June
Write to: Graphis Press Corp., Dufourstrasse 107, 8008 Zurich, Switzerland

■ Einsendebedingungen können von jedermann angefordert werden, der uns Beispiele hervorragender Photographie oder Graphik zur Auswahl für unsere Jahrbücher unterbreiten möchte. Es werden keine Gebühren erhoben.
Einsendetermine:
GRAPHIS ANNUAL (Werbe- und redaktionelle Graphik): 31. Januar
PHOTOGRAPHIS (Werbe- und redaktionelle Photographie): 30. Juni
GRAPHIS POSTERS (ein Jahrbuch der Plakatkunst): 30. Juni
Adresse: Graphis Verlag AG, Dufourstrasse 107, 8008 Zürich, Schweiz

■ Tout intéressé à la soumission de travaux photographiques et graphiques recevra les informations nécessaires sur demande. Sans charge de participation.
Dates limites:
GRAPHIS ANNUAL (art graphique publicitaire et rédactionnel): 31 janvier
PHOTOGRAPHIS (photographie publicitaire et rédactionnelle): 30 juin
GRAPHIS POSTERS (annuaire sur l'art de l'affiche): 30 juin
S'adresser à: Editions Graphis SA, Dufourstrasse 107, 8008 Zurich, Suisse

Editor and Art Director: Walter Herdeg
Assistant Editors: Stanley Mason, Vreni Monnier
Project Manager: Vreni Monnier
Designers: Martin Byland, Ulrich Kemmner
Art Assistants: Marino Bianchera, Willy Müller, Peter Wittwer

1

Magazine Advertisements

Newspaper Advertisements

Zeitschriften-Inserate

Zeitungs-Inserate

Annonces de revues

Annonces de presse

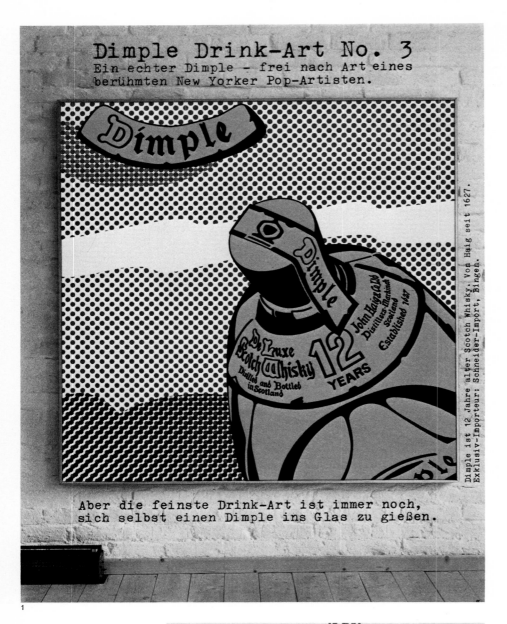

Dimple Drink-Art No. 3
Ein echter Dimple - frei nach Art eines
berühmten New Yorker Pop-Artisten.

Aber die feinste Drink-Art ist immer noch,
sich selbst einen Dimple ins Glas zu gießen.

(Dimple ist 12 Jahre alter Scotch Whisky. Von Haig seit 1627.
Exklusiv-Importeur: Schneider-Import, Bingen.)

1

1 Example from a series of full-page magazine advertisements for *Dimple*. The "Dimple Drink-Art" is a play on words of the German "Art" (way or manner) and the English word, which is why a picture evoking a Roy Lichtenstein painting is shown here. Yellow and black bottle, red and blue dots on white. (GER)
2, 3 From a long-standing series of magazine advertisements for soya sauce by the Kikkoman Corp. published under the title "The Tastes of Japan". Fig. 2 is in dull shades, Fig. 3 is straw coloured. (JPN)
4 Double-spread magazine advertisement for *Milka* milk chocolate by *Suchard*. The illustrations have been taken from a painting competition. (GER)
5 Example from a series of magazine advertisements for *Fernet-Branca*, a drink that aids digestion. Brown mushrooms. (ITA)

1 Beispiel aus einer Serie von ganzseitigen Zeitschriftenanzeigen für *Dimple*. Die Reihe «Dimple Drink-Art» spielt mit den Worten Art und dem englischen Wort (art) für Kunst, weshalb auch ein Roy Lichtenstein nachempfundenes Bild präsentiert wird. Flasche gelb und schwarz, rote und blaue Punkte auf Weiss. (GER)
2, 3 Aus einer langjährigen Serie von Zeitschriftenanzeigen für Soja-Sauce. Abb. 2 in matten Farben, Abb. 3 strohfarben. (JPN)
4 Doppelseitige Zeitschriftenanzeige für *Milka*-Milchschokolade von *Suchard*. Die Illustrationen stammen aus einem Malwettbewerb. (GER)
5 Beispiel aus einer Serie von Zeitschriftenanzeigen für *Fernet-Branca,* der verdauen hilft. Braune Steinpilze. (ITA)

1 Exemple d'une série d'annonces pleines pages pour le whisky *Dimple*. La série intitulée «Dimple Drink-Art» joue avec les deux mots «Art» signifiant en allemand «manière» et en français «art»; pour cette raison on montre une bouteille de *Dimple* devant un tableau évoquant Roy Lichtenstein, le fameux représentant du pop-art. Bouteille en jaune et noir, points rouges et bleus sur blanc. (GER)
2, 3 D'une longue série d'annonces de magazine pour une sauce soja; série intitulée «les saveurs du Japon». Fig. 2 en tons mats, fig. 3 en paille. (JPN)
4 Annonce de magazine double page pour le chocolat au lait *Milka* de *Suchard*. Les illustrations sont des lauréats d'un concours d'illustration. (GER)
5 Exemple d'une série d'annonces de magazine pleine page pour *Fernet-Branca,* un digestif. Bolets bruns. (ITA)

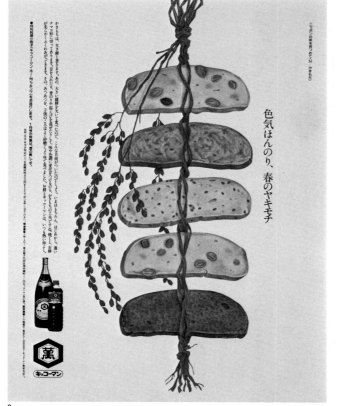

色気ほんのり、春のヤキモチ

2

糸をひく、味ひとすじ

3

Was in einer MILKA-Kuh so alles vorgeht, stellte sich Joachim Müller-Lance aus Umkirch vor.

Na, das war vielleicht eine Überraschung. Fast 80 000 (in Worten: achtzigtausend) lila Kühe trafen zum großen MILKA-Malwettbewerb bei uns ein. Eine schöner als die andere. Und die Schönsten der Schönen zeigen sich auf dieser Doppelseite von ihrer Schokoladenseite.

Das ist keine alte Höhlenmalerei, sondern eine MILKA-Kuh neueren Datums aus einem Skizzenbuch von Klaus Brauer aus Usingen.

Der MILKA-Kuh ein Denkmal gesetzt hat Klaus Wegmann aus Bochum.

Ein Gruppenbild mit lila Kühen hielt Nicolaz Halstenbach aus Wuppertal im Bild fest.

Hendrik Müller aus Rechtmehring malte die MILKA-Kuh zum Anbeißen.

Die Milchkanne im MILKA-Look schickte uns Horst Kraatz aus Bremen.

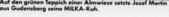

Auf den grünen Teppich einer Almwiese setzte Josef Mertin aus Gudensberg seine MILKA-Kuh.

MILKA im lila Papier. Die zarteste Versuchung, seit es Schokolade gibt.
Nach Schweizer Original-Rezept.

4

ARTIST / KÜNSTLER / ARTISTE:

1 Urs Frick
2, 3 Tadashi Ohashi
5 Opit S. r. l.

DESIGNER / GESTALTER / MAQUETTISTE:

1 Urs Frick/Studio Geibel
2, 3 Tadashi Ohashi
5 Opit S. r. l.

ART DIRECTOR / DIRECTEUR ARTISTIQUE:

1 Urs Frick
2, 3 Tadashi Ohashi
4 Maria-Christina Sennefelder
5 Opit S. r. l.

AGENCY / AGENTUR / AGENCE – STUDIO:

1, 4 Young & Rubicam GmbH
5 Opit S. r. l.

5

6

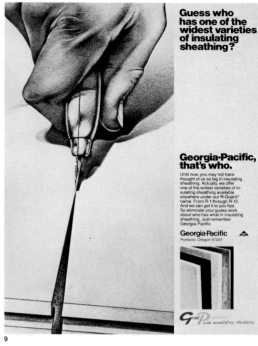

7   8   9

ARTIST / KÜNSTLER / ARTISTE:

6, 10 André François
7 David Grove
8, 9 James Pendley Smith
11 Brian Morrow/Ed White (Photo)

Advertisements
Anzeigen
Annonces

6, 10 Illustration in actual size and double-spread advertisement from the rainbow series for the *Siegwerk* printing inks that has been running for almost fifteen years. (GER)
7 Advertisement for Pendleton Woolen Mills, mainly in shades of blue and brown. (USA)
8, 9 Examples from a uniform advertising series for *Georgia-Pacific* building materials. (USA)
11 Advertisement for a whisky. Bottle and glass in various type sizes. (GBR)

6, 10 Illustration in Originalgrösse und doppelseitige Anzeige aus der nahezu 15 Jahre laufenden Regenbogen-Serie für die *Siegwerk*-Farbenfabrik. (GER)
7 Vorwiegend in Braun- und Blautönen gehaltene Anzeige für eine Wollspinnerei. (USA)
8, 9 Beispiele aus einer einheitlich gestalteten Anzeigenserie für eine Vertriebsorganisation für Baumaterialien, hier für Wandbekleidungen und Isolierplatten. (USA)
11 Flasche und Glas aus Schrifttypen in verschiedenen Graden. Anzeige für einen Whisky. (GBR)

6, 10 Illustration en grandeur originale et annonce double page extraite de la série «arc-en-ciel», devenue depuis une quinzaine d'années le symbole d'une fabrique d'encres d'imprimerie. (GER)
7 Annonce pour une filature de laine. Prédominance de tons bruns et bleus. (USA)
8, 9 Exemple d'une série d'annonces de conception uniforme d'un centre de distribution de matériaux de construction, ici pour des revêtements et des planches isolantes. (USA)
11 Pour un whisky: contours de la bouteille et du verre dessinés en typo de corps variable. (GBR)

DESIGNER / GESTALTER / MAQUETTISTE:

7 Cal Anderson
8, 9 Ken Montone

ART DIRECTOR / DIRECTEUR ARTISTIQUE:

6, 10 Robert Pütz
7 Cal Anderson
8, 9 Ken Montone
11 Brian Morrow

AGENCY / AGENTUR / AGENCE – STUDIO:

6, 10 Robert Pütz GmbH & Co.
7 Cunningham & Walsh, Inc.
8, 9 McCann-Erickson, Inc.
11 TBWA Ltd.

10

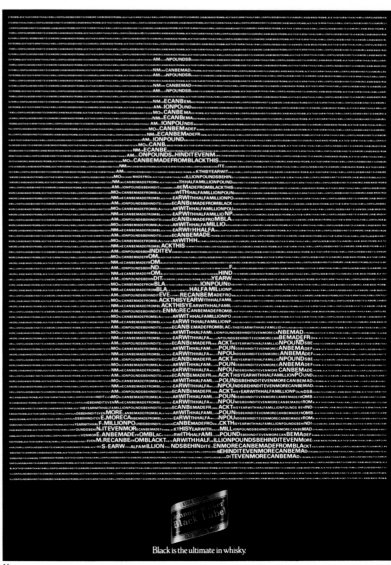

Black is the ultimate in whisky.

11

29

vchugaviu

Young rice needs strong roots to meet what lies ahead.
Before rice seedlings are ready for flooding, they need plenty of special attention. You need to know when to feed your crops as well as what. So when those kinds of questions arise, remember a fellow nearby who's willing to pay special attention to you. He's prepared to offer many helpful suggestions as well as the fertilizers to make all those suggestions work. **There's a Grace dealer down the road.**

GRACE

12

W.R. Grace & Co. Agricultural Products

Will last year's soil be good enough for this year's cotton?
You can't tell much about your land's fertility just by looking at it. You need a soil test. And sometimes some help in deciding what to do about the results. That help may be close by – from someone who'd be glad to do more than just sell you the fertilizer you need. **There's a Grace dealer down the road.**

GRACE

13

Advertisements
Anzeigen
Annonces

12, 13 Examples from an advertising campaign for *Grace* fertilizers. Fig. 12: green rice plants; kettle, water and sky in light blue; Fig. 13: brown stubble-field, pink-violet hand. (USA)
14 From a series of trade advertisements for *Coni-Snap* hard gelatine capsules for the pharmaceutical industry. Capsules in green and yellow-orange or brown and dark pink. (GER)
15 Double-spread trade magazine advertisement for urethane intermediates manufactured by *Union Carbide,* synthetic materials that enable the automobile industry to reduce unnecessary bulky bodywork in the manufacturing of cars. The car is in orange-red. (USA)
16, 17 "Double effort"... of the machine as well as of its concessionaire. From a series of advertisements with full-colour illustrations for machines used in the road-building industry. (FRA)
18–20 Examples from a series of advertisements for *Mobil Chemicals* that appeared in trade magazines. The illustrations are in full colour. (USA)

12, 13 Beispiele aus einer Anzeigenkampagne für ein Düngemittel. Abb. 12: grüne Reispflanzen, Kessel, Wasser und Himmel hellblau; Abb. 13: braunes Stoppelfeld, rosa-violette Hand. (USA)
14 Aus einer Serie von Fachzeitschriftenanzeigen für *Coni-Snap*-Hartgelatinekapseln für die pharmazeutische Industrie. Kapsel grün und gelb-orange, resp. braun und dunkelrosa. (GER)
15 Doppelseitige Fachzeitschriftenanzeige eines Chemiekonzerns, der es der Autoindustrie ermöglichte, dank verschiedenen Kunststoffmaterialien die Wagen einer Schlankheitskur zu unterziehen und unnötige «Fettpolster» abzubauen. Wagen in orange-rot. (USA)
16, 17 «Doppelter Einsatz»... der Maschine wie auch des Konzessionärs. Aus einer Anzeigenserie mit mehrfarbigen Illustrationen für Strassenbau-Maschinen. (FRA)
18–20 Beispiele aus einer in Fachzeitschriften erschienenen Anzeigenserie für chemische Produkte von *Mobil.* Mehrfarbige Illustrationen. (USA)

12, 13 Exemples figurant dans une série d'annonces en faveur d'un engrais. Fig. 12: rizière verte, seau, eau et ciel en bleu clair; fig. 13: chaumes bruns, main rose violette. (USA)
14 D'une série d'annonces de magazine professionnel pour une marque de capsules en gélatine dure utilisées dans l'industrie pharmaceutique. Vert et jaune orange, resp. brun et rose. (GER)
15 Annonce de magazine professionnel sur page double pour une fabrique de produits chimiques: grâce à ces produits l'industrie automobile a pu soumettre les voitures à une cure d'amaigrissement, réduisant ainsi les «bourrelets» superflus. Voiture en orange rougeâtre. (USA)
16, 17 La double efficacité dont on parle dans ces annonces se rapporte d'une part au rendement des pelles et chargeuses JCB, d'autre part au savoir-faire des concessionnaires. (FRA)
18–20 Annonces extraites d'une campagne publicitaire dans des magazines professionnels en faveur des produits chimiques de *Mobil.* Illustration en polychromie. (USA)

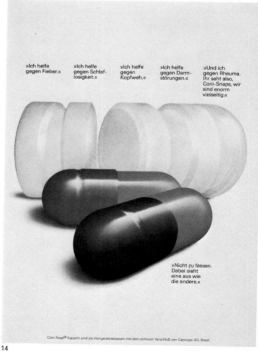

»Ich helfe gegen Fieber.« »Ich helfe gegen Schlaflosigkeit.« »Ich helfe gegen Kopfweh.« »Ich helfe gegen Darmstörungen.« »Und ich gegen Rheuma. Ihr seht also, Coni-Snaps, wir sind enorm vielseitig.«

»Nicht zu fassen. Dabei sieht eine aus wie die andere.«

Coni-Snap® Kapseln sind die Hartgelatinekapseln mit dem sicheren Verschluß von Capsugel AG, Basel.

14

UNION CARBIDE HAS BEEN HELPING THE AUTO INDUSTRY LOSE ITS SPARE TIRE SINCE 1957.

On our diet your automobile loses weight without giving up strength or style.

We began our work back in 1957, when we supplied the polyols for flexible urethane foam topper pads. Then we went on to develop the polymer polyols that eventually created high resilience (HR) foam for auto seating.

In the mid-1960's, we started work on urethane elastomers for RIM. As early as 1973 we had installed the first of our production-scale RIM machines for molding full-sized auto fascia. Because we knew we'd never be satisfied with laboratory experience alone.

Thus, when urethane fascia began to replace steel bumpers in 1975, both our technology and our urethane intermediates were available to the industry. Helping to slim some models by as much as 100 pounds.

Today we are the leading supplier of polyols to the RIM urethane market. In fact, more auto fascia

are based on our NIAX polyols than those of any other supplier.

And, of course, we haven't stopped looking and learning. Our reinforced RIM technology is second to none and we can offer a broad range of intermediates for microcellular and solid urethane elastomer parts.

But the best way to lose weight is with a program tailored to your individual needs. And that is just what your local Union Carbide sales representative would like to talk to you about. Or write to us at Union Carbide Corporation, Dept. JSW, 270 Park Avenue, New York, N.Y. 10017 for more information.

You'll find we're very good at taking worries off your mind, as well as pounds off your automobile.

PEOPLE PLANNING THE FUTURE.

[UNION CARBIDE]
Urethane Intermediates

15

ARTIST / KÜNSTLER / ARTISTE:

12 Carlos Ochagavia
13 Paul Lehr
14 R. G. Friz
15 Robert Grossman
16, 17 Alain Laurent
18–20 Gahan Wilson

DESIGNER / GESTALTER / MAQUETTISTE:

12, 13 Everett Boykin
14 Pierre Mendell
18–20 Wayne Gibson

ART DIRECTOR / DIRECTEUR ARTISTIQUE:

12, 13 Everett Boykin
15 Simon Bowden
16, 17 Jean-Claude Nuti

AGENCY / AGENTUR / AGENCE – STUDIO:

12, 13 Howard, Merrell & Boykin
14 Mendell & Oberer
15 Needham, Harper & Steers
16, 17 Nuti & Assoc.
18–20 The Martin Agency

UNE DOUBLE EFFICACITE [JCB]

DES MACHINES INVENTEES POUR DURER.

16

UNE DOUBLE EFFICACITE [JCB]

DES MACHINES INVENTEES POUR DURER.

17

If your phosphoric acid produces some surprising results, Mobil thinks you should know why.

When you use phosphoric acid, the last thing you can afford is surprises. And should any occur, you need to know why, fast. At Mobil we eliminate guesswork by giving you the right product for your needs and the technical service support to make sure you get the most out of it. Take our DAB 80 as an example. In the bright dip market, its reputation for dependability is second to none. Special brightening and fume suppressant additives assure its superior effectiveness to meet your toughest standards. Yet should questions arise during any phase of your application, Mobil has the complete technology to find the answers. Before they turn into real problems. Technical service back-up is available for all our phosphoric acid products, from our wide range of food grade acids to our mono aluminum and mono magnesium phosphates.

And we'll also promise to deliver your order right when you need it and where you need it, thanks to Mobil's own tank truck equipment.

Technology, service and a broad line of chemical products to meet your requirements. That's the key to Mobil Chemical.

And that's what you can expect from a company that has more experience in phosphorus chemicals than just about anyone else.

From commodity to specialty chemicals, Mobil wants to work with you, to help you get the most out of the products you use.

Because we want you to be as confident about our chemical products as we are.

And that should not come as any big surprise.

For more information on our complete chemical line, write Mobil Chemical Company, Phosphorus Division, P.O. Box 26683, Richmond, Virginia 23261. Or phone (804) 798-4291.

Mobil Chemical

18

Mobil dialkyl alkylphosphonates can offer some surprising solutions you never even dreamed of.

If you've never used our dialkyl alkylphosphonates, you may be missing solutions to problems you thought couldn't be solved. Or improving formulations you didn't believe possible.

You see, our dialkyl alkylphosphonates offer so many opportunities, even we haven't been able to explore them all. But thanks to Mobil technology, we are able to offer findings that may apply to your specific chemical requirements.

For example, compared to trialkyl phosphate esters, our phosphonates offer you higher phosphorus content and greater thermal stability.

In the area of rigid polyurethanes, unsaturated polyesters, and urea formaldehyde foams, our dimethyl methylphosphonate is an effective flame retardant. This phosphonate also exhibits extreme high solvency for hydrophilic substances and contains the highest phosphorus content of all commercially available phosphates or phosphonates.

Mobil also suggests that you evaluate our dibutyl butylphosphonate in combination with di (2-ethylhexyl) phosphoric acid as an extractant for uranium, vanadium and other rare earth elements.

No matter which of our many products you buy, Mobil technology and service support are available to you every step of the way. Working directly with you in developing the best ways for our products to meet your needs. And that's a promise you can count on from the one chemical company that has more experience in phosphorus than just about anyone.

From organic to inorganic chemicals, Mobil has all the specialty and commodity chemicals you've been dreaming about. And a lot you haven't.

For more information, write Mobil Chemical Company, Phosphorus Division, P.O. Box 26683, Richmond, Virginia 23261. Or phone (804) 798-4291.

Mobil Chemical

19

If getting the organic acid phosphates you need is turning into a monster, it's time you saw Mobil.

Take DEHPA, di(2-ethyl hexyl) phosphoric acid, for example.

You already know it's one of the most highly efficient extractants available for uranium and other rare earth elements.

But do you know a source that can guarantee the volume you need, when you need it? Or even more important, that there will be a continuing availability of commodity chemicals you can depend on Mobil.

At Mobil, we're continually expanding our production capabilities for DEHPA, to give you the supply you need today and in the future.

But supply availability is not a promise we make just for DEHPA.

As a specialty chemical company of phosphorus-based products, we offer you organic acid phosphates to meet every need, from metal extractants to acid catalysts. With a line that includes such products as butyl isooctyl 2 ethylhexyl, phenyl and octyl phenyl acid phosphates.

Add to these our extensive range of alkyl phosphites and dialkyl alkylphosphonates, and you have the most reliable source available to meet your phosphorus chemical requirements.

Our organic chemicals, like our full range of inorganic chemicals, are backed by the technology and service capabilities you'd expect from a company that has more experience in phosphorus chemicals than just about anyone else.

Experience that gives us a flexibility to work with you in creating the products you'll need to meet your present and future requirements.

Whenever you need phosphorus-based chemicals, even if it's a monstrous supply, you can depend on Mobil.

For more information on our complete chemical line, write Mobil Chemical Company, P.O. Box 26683, Richmond, Virginia 23261. Or phone (804) 798-4291.

Mobil Chemical

20

GLORIA GAYNOR ON POLYDOR RECORDS & TAPES.

Joel F. Naprstek © 1979

"Never Can Say Goodbye" rocketed Gloria Gaynor to the top of the charts. Gloria was crowned "Queen of the Discos" and credited with launching the disco phenomenon. In Japan, Europe, England, Latin America, Australia—everyplace she toured—entire countries turned into Gloria Gaynor fanatics.
Some people thought that Gloria could never top the huge success of "Never Can Say Goodbye."

YOU CAN TELL A COMPANY BY THE ARTISTS IT KEEPS

But our enthusiasm, belief and commitment run deep, and we don't give up. We sparked the collaboration between Gloria and ace writer/producer Freddie Perren's Grand Slam Productions. Freddie and Dino Fekaris created a slew of hit songs, just for Gloria, and they came through with a perfectly produced gem, "Love Tracks."
Now, "I Will Survive" has brought Gloria the

next step, reaching out across all musical boundaries to a huge new audience.
Gloria Gaynor is just one example of how we've come so far, so fast.
Gloria will continue to grow as an artist, a singer, and as one of the most influential stars on the music scene. We like success. And, we intend to keep it going.

POLYDOR INCORPORATED

ARTIST / KÜNSTLER / ARTISTE:

21 Joel F. Naprstek/Alex Gnidziejko
23 Nancy Stahl
24 Jozef Sumichrast
25, 26 Jean-Jacques Larrière

DESIGNER / GESTALTER / MAQUETTISTE:

21 Abie Sussman
22 Christof Gassner
24 Michael Fountain

ART DIRECTOR / DIRECTEUR ARTISTIQUE:

21 Abie Sussman
23 Dick Thomas
24 Michael Fountain
25, 26 Michel Guilder

WORKING SMARTER VS. WORKING HARDER

Japan's productivity keeps improving.
Germany's too.
"So America's going to have to work harder," people say.
But that's not enough anymore.
We also have to work *smarter*.
America's productivity problem isn't caused by lazy workers. It's partly caused by lazy factories, lazy tools, and lazy methods which dilute the efforts of hard working people.
Working smarter can help change that.
Today, thousands of IBM customers are working smarter by using computers. Insurance companies, retailers, banks, farmers, aerospace companies have all become more productive by making *information* work harder.
In world trade, productivity is a key to success. And America has long been the most productive country on earth.
We got that way by working harder. We can stay that way by working smarter.

IBM

When you're up against one tough number after another, you need the "Grit-Edge" blade.

Remington

21 Magazine advertisement of the *Polydor* record company for the singer Gloria Gaynor. (USA)
22 Trade magazine advertisement with some of the caracters done by *Letraset Deutschland*. (GER)
23 To remain competitive in world markets, IBM calls on the Americans to work more cleverly. (USA)
24 Full-colour trade magazine advertisement for *Remington* "Grit-Edge" blades. (USA)
25, 26 Illustration and complete advertisement for a weedkiller. (FRA)

21 Zeitschriftenanzeige einer Plattenfirma für die Disco-Sängerin Gloria Gaynor. (USA)
22 Fachzeitschriftenanzeige mit einigen von *Letraset Deutschland* geführten Schriften. (GER)
23 Um auf dem Weltmarkt konkurrenzfähig zu bleiben, ruft IBM die Amerikaner auf, raffinierter, nicht nur härter zu arbeiten, z. B. indem sie auf elektronische Datenverarbeitung umstellen. (USA)
24 Mehrfarbige Fachzeitschriftenanzeige für besonders gehärtete Sägeblätter. (USA)
25, 26 Illustration und vollständige Anzeige für ein Unkrautvertilgungsmittel. (FRA)

21 Annonce de magazine de *Polydor* pour lancer Gloria Gaynor, chanteuse de musique disco. (USA)
22 Annonce de magazine professionel présentant divers caractères de *Letraset*. (GER)
23 «Travail raffiné vs travail dur.» Pour mieux supporter la concurrence sur le marché mondial, IBM fait appel aux Américains de travailler avec plus de raffinement, voire avec des ordinateurs. (USA)
24 Annonce de magazine professionnel pour des lames de scie spécialement trempé. (USA)
25, 26 Illustration et annonce complète pour *Eradicane*, un désherbant efficace. (FRA)

Advertisements
Anzeigen
Annonces

AGENCY / AGENTUR / AGENCE – STUDIO:

23 Lord, Geller, Federico, Einstein
24 Rumrill-Hoyt Inc.
25, 26 Exigence

26

25

33

ARTIST / KÜNSTLER / ARTISTE:
27–29 Kazumasa Nagai

DESIGNER / GESTALTER / MAQUETTISTE:
27–29 Kazumasa Nagai

ART DIRECTOR / DIRECTEUR ARTISTIQUE:
27–29 Kazumasa Nagai

AGENCY / AGENTUR / AGENCE – STUDIO:
27–29 Nippon Design Center

27–29 Examples from a long-standing series of trade magazine advertisements in uniform design for the Takeo Paper Co. Fig. 29 is in actual size. (JPN)

27–29 Beispiele aus einer langjährigen, einheitlich gestalteten Serie von Fachzeitschriften-anzeigen für eine Papierfabrik. Abb. 29 in Originalgrösse. (JPN)

27–29 Exemples figurant dans une longue série d'annonces de conception uniforme, parues dans des magazines professionnels: élément de publicité pour une papeterie. Fig. 29 en grandeur originale. (JPN)

DESIGN：KAZUMASA NAGAI

NTラシャ

株式会社 竹尾

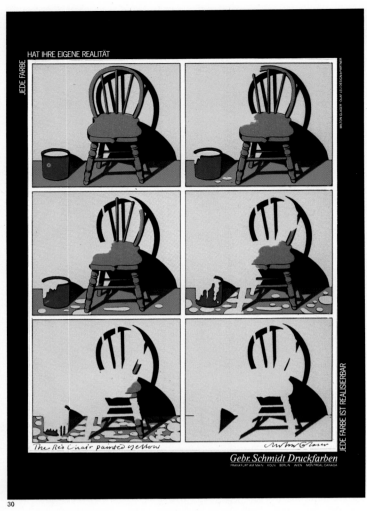

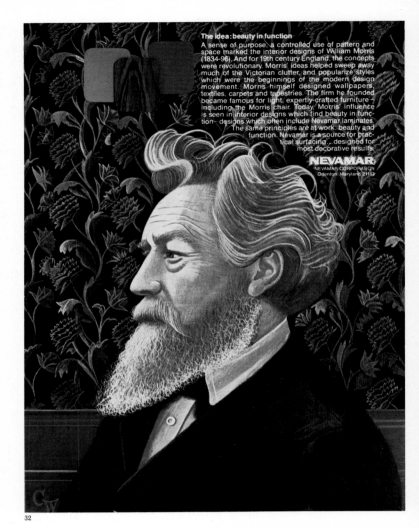

ART DIRECTOR / DIRECTEUR ARTISTIQUE:

30, 31 Olaf Leu
32 Doug Fisher
33 Bruno Suter
34, 35 Dennis Corrigan
36 Jean-Pierre Grandjean

AGENCY / AGENTUR / AGENCE – STUDIO:

30, 31 Olaf Leu Design & Partner
32 Lord, Sullivan & Yoder, Inc.
33 Eldorado
34, 35 Corrigan Advertising

Advertisements
Anzeigen
Annonces

30, 31 "Each colour has its own reality." – "Colours are the most human dictators." Examples from a series of uniform trade magazine advertisements for printing inks made by *Schmidt.* Fig. 30: "The red chair that is being painted in yellow." (GER)
32 The illustration shows William Morris (1834–96), the English poet and skilled craftsman who, amongst other things, designed the Morris Chair and who was a pioneer in modern furnishings – which is why *Nevamar* panelling has incorporated some of his designs. (USA)
33 Magazine advertisement for a French leather centre. Yellow ground. (FRA)
34, 35 Advertisements for *Quaker* stoves, showing Frank Krell and Thomas Incline who both did research work in the field of alternative energy. (USA)
36 "With your head somewhere else." Illustration from an advertisement for a *Zyma* pharmaceutical for fatigue and absent-mindedness. (SWI)

30, 31 Beispiele aus einer Serie von einheitlich gestalteten Fachzeitschriftenanzeigen für die Druckfarbenfabrik Gebr. Schmidt. Abb. 30: «Der rote Stuhl, der gelb gestrichen wird.» (GER)
32 Die Illustration zeigt William Morris (1834–96), englischer Dichter und Kunsthandwerker, der u. a. den Morris-Stuhl entwarf und in der modernen Raumgestaltung bahnbrechend war – deshalb wurden für *Nevamar*-Wandbekleidungen teilweise auch seine Entwürfe übernommen. (USA)
33 Zeitschriftenanzeige für ein französisches Leder-Zentrum. Gelber Grund. (FRA)
34, 35 «Berühmte Fehlschläge in der Energie-Geschichte.» Die Anzeigen einer Ofenbaufirma zeigen F. Krell und T. Incline, die beide auf dem Gebiet der Alternativ-Energie forschten. (USA)
36 «Den Kopf woanders.» Illustration einer Anzeige der Arzneimittelfabrik *Zyma* für ein Produkt gegen Müdigkeit und Zerstreutheit. (SWI)

30, 31 Exemples extraits d'une série d'annonces de conception uniforme, publiées dans la presse professionnelle en faveur d'une fabrique d'encres d'imprimerie. Fig. 30: «La chaise rouge qui est peinte en jaune.» (GER)
32 L'illustration montre William Morris (1834–96), peintre et écrivain d'art anglais, qui inventa la chaise Morris et participa à la renaissance des arts décoratifs – c'est la raison pourquoi *Nevamar* a adopté quelques dessins de Morris pour ses revêtements muraux. (USA)
33 Annonce de presse pour le *Cuir Center.* Vache et canapé bruns sur fond jaune. (FRA)
34, 35 «Les fameux échecs dans l'histoire de l'énergie.» Les annonces d'une fabrique de poêls montrent F. Krell et T. Incline qui ont cherché des sources d'énergie alternatives. (USA)
36 «La tête ailleurs.» Illustration d'une annonce en faveur d'un remède *Zyma* des états de fatigue et de distraction. En polychromie. (SWI)

37

38

Advertisements/Anzeigen/Annonces

37 Double-spread advertisement by *Amoco* for a new diesel-oil additive for locomotives. (USA)
38–40 Illustrations and double-spread advertisement of the Canadian Rehabilitation Council for the Disabled. In black and white. (CAN)
41 Magazine advertisement by *Daon South*, a real estate company planning condominiums, commercial and residential developments and homes in the Dallas-Fort Worth area. (USA)
42, 43 Illustration and complete advertisement for a *Kneipp* herbal shampoo made out of birch, nettles and camomile. In pastel shades. (SPA)

37 «Ein neuer Öl-Zusatz für die lange Fahrt.» Doppelseitige Anzeige eines Chemiekonzerns für einen neuen Diesel-Öl-Zusatz für Lokomotiven. (USA)
38–40 Illustrationen und doppelseitige Anzeige der kanadischen Vereinigung für die Wiedereingliederung der Behinderten mit einem Aufruf, unsere Haltung gegenüber Behinderten zu ändern, da diese für sie die grösste Behinderung darstelle. Schwarzweiss. (CAN)
41 Zeitschriftenanzeige einer Immobiliengesellschaft, die in Dallas-Fort Worth neue Geschäftskomplexe, Wohnüberbauungen und Eigentumswohnungen plant. (USA)
42, 43 Illustration und vollständige Anzeige für ein *Kneipp*-Kräuter-Shampoo aus Birke, Brennessel und Kamille. In feinen Farbtönen. (SPA)

37 «Un nouvel additif pour le long voyage.» Annonce double page publiée par une fabrique de produits chimiques en faveur d'un nouvel additif pour les locomotives diesel. (USA)
38–40 Illustrations et annonce sur page double de l'association canadienne pour la réhabilitation des handicapés. Elle lance un appel que les non-handicapés changent leur attitude à l'égard des handicapés, car l'indifférence représente le plus grand handicap pour eux. (CAN)
41 Annonce de journal d'une société immobilière qui est en train de réaliser un grand complexe réunissant des immeubles à usage de bureaux ou d'habitations et des appartements à vendre. (USA)
42, 43 Illustration et annonce complète pour un shampooing aux herbes de *Kneipp*, contenant des essences du bouleau, de l'ortie et de la camomille. En tons pastel. (SPA)

40

39

THE WORD IS SPREADING. All over the Dallas-Fort Worth metroplex people are talking about us. We're Daon Southwest. ❧ And we're making a name for ourselves. During the next few months we'll be opening many new condominium developments. Planning major new commercial developments. And breaking ground in important new residential developments. So remember our name. ❧ Daon Southwest. We're the people that people are talking about. **⬛ D4ON SOUTHWEST** A DIVISION OF DAON CORPORATION

41

ARTIST / KÜNSTLER / ARTISTE:

37 George Hamblin
38–40 Julius Ciss
41 Jack Unruh
42, 43 Esteve Fort

DESIGNER / GESTALTER / MAQUETTISTE:

37 John Dolby
38–40 Brian Harrod
41 Lance Brown
42, 43 Salvatore Adduci

ART DIRECTOR / DIRECTEUR ARTISTIQUE:

37 John Dolby
38–40 Brian Harrod
41 Lance Brown
42, 43 Salvatore Adduci

AGENCY / AGENTUR / AGENCE – STUDIO:

37 BBDM Advertising
38–40 McCann-Erickson
41 The Richards Group
42, 43 Euroteam

43

42

NOW YOU DON'T HAVE TO GET WET TO GET CLOSE.

PHILISHAVE INTRODUCES THE LIFT AND CUT SYSTEM.

If it were true that only a blade can provide a truly close shave, then we at Philishave would have rested our case years ago.

But Philips technology told us we could make our shaver shave as close or closer than a blade. And persistence is so often, the mother of invention.

May we introduce the 1980 Philishave and a remarkable new shaving principle: lift and cut.

Now every one of our Philishave's 45 rotary-action blades has a unique lifter. The lifter does precisely what its name suggests: it gently lifts the hair, allowing the cutter behind to shave it closer.

The result is a genuine new closeness you can actually feel with your fingertips.

The new Philishave is available in three models: Rechargeable, Exclusive and De Luxe.

You'll notice by their sleek new design and silver/black finish (all black in the case of the De Luxe), that we've spared no detail in making it the perfect shaver in every way. We invite you to try the new Philishave and the lift and cut system for yourself. You'll find the shaver that's always been a cut above the rest, now shaves a cut below the rest.

PHILIPS

Atlas Copco compressed air systems. A force made to serve you.

Air. The very essence of life. Unharnessed, as in a sand storm, totally out of control.

But, through the application of Atlas Copco compressed air systems, a force made to serve you.

The Atlas Copco system is a totally integrated package of compressed air equipment, all designed to help you make better quality products. With faster, more profitable production methods. And in safer, healthier working conditions.

A system which offers you a range of over 3000 products. From compressors and air dryers producing the right quality of air, to hand tools and related airline equipment, to pneumatic controls for automating many industrial processes.

But the system has one other vital component—Service. Which is why we have a network of over 400 Compressed Air Service Centres worldwide – 11 of them in the UK, each staffed by a team of Service Engineers and Systems Specialists, who know compressed air technology and local industrial problems like the backs of their hands. Backed by radio controlled Service vans able to sort out problems on the spot. And able to call on the resources of our Systems Engineering Department at Hemel Hempstead any time they (or you) need to. So if you want advice or the answer to a tricky problem, you couldn't go to a better place.

Training, too, has always been an important and fundamental part of the Atlas Copco operation. Our own staff benefit from it. And our customers their staff do too.

If anyone knows about air systems technology and ways to put it to better use, it's Atlas Copco.

SEND FOR OUR 24-PAGE SYSTEMS GUIDE – JUST PHONE OR WRITE TO THE ADDRESS BELOW.

Atlas Copco

Air systems technology for generations to come.

44

45

44 Double-spread magazine advertisement for the new *Philishave* electric razor which is said to shave as close as a blade. Illustration mainly in shades of blue. (CAN)
45–47 Double-spread advertisement and illustrations showing air "out of control" from a trade magazine campaign in which *Atlas Copco* compressed air systems are advertised as "a force put to work for you". Fig. 45: sand-coloured illustration, the sitting figure is covered by a blue and lilac cloth. (USA)
48–50 Double-spread advertisements from an advertising campaign launched in trade magazines to promote all-weather covering material for terrace roofs, that ice makes neither hot nor cold, that can withstand the pressure of extremely heavy deluges of rain and which doesn't crack open like parched earth. All the illustrations are in full colour. (FRA)

44 Doppelseitige Zeitschriftenanzeige für den neuen *Philishave*-Rasierapparat, der ebenso sauber rasiert wie eine Klinge. Vorwiegend in Blautönen gehaltene Illustration. (CAN)
45–47 Doppelseitige Fachzeitschriftenanzeige und Illustrationen von zwei weiteren Anzeigen aus einer Werbekampagne, in welcher *Atlas Copco* auf dramatische Weise die Kraft ihrer Druckluftsysteme illustriert, die für verschiedene Industriezweige dienstbar gemacht werden kann. Abb. 45: sandfarbene Illustration, sitzende Figur in blaues und lilafarbenes Tuch gehüllt. (USA)
48–50 Doppelseitige Anzeigen aus einer in Fachzeitschriften lancierten Werbekampagne für allwetterfestes Abdeckungsmaterial für Terrassendächer, welchem Eis weder heiss noch kalt macht, das auch sintflutartigen Regenfällen standhält und unter extremer Sonnenbestrahlung nicht wie ausgetrocknete Erde aufspringt. Alle Illustrationen sind mehrfarbig. (FRA)

44 Annonce de magazine sur double page pour le nouveau rasoir *Philishave* qui coupe la barbe au ras de la peau aussi bien qu'une lame. Prédominance de tons bleus. (CAN)
45–47 Annonce de revue professionnelle sur page double et deux illustrations de la même campagne publicitaire montrant l'air «hors contrôle», alors que les systèmes à air comprimé *Atlas Copco* sont «une force faite pour vous servir». Fig. 45: illustration en tons beiges prédominants, figure assise enveloppée dans un châle bleu et lilas. (USA)
48–50 Annonces doubles pages extraites d'une campagne publicitaire lancée dans des revues professionnelles en faveur des matériaux d'étanchéité *Gerland* qui protègent efficacement les toitures-terrasses, là où le froid est le plus brutal, ou la pluie diluvienne et le soleil le plus torride. Toutes les illustrations sont en couleurs. (FRA)

46

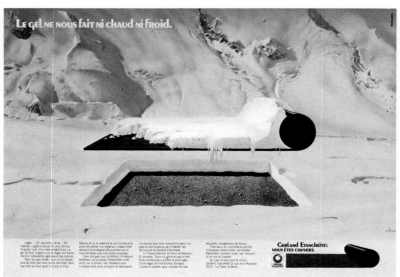

Le gel ne nous fait ni chaud ni froid.

Gerland Etanchéité: VOUS ÊTES COUVERT.

48

Le ciel peut bien nous tomber sur la tête.

Gerland Etanchéité: VOUS ÊTES COUVERT.

49

47

50

51, 52 This advertisement is to make affluent and culturally conscious buyers aware of the new luxury high-rise condominium Four-Leaf Towers in Houston, Texas. The illustration is reproduced in original size. (USA)

53, 54 From a series of magazine advertisements for *Alitalia,* the Italian national airline. Fig. 53 refers to its pilots' expert training; night view of Singapore; Fig. 54 advertises more comfortable flying on the New York route with the Boeing 747. *Alitalia* symbol in green, white and red on a dark sky. (ITA)

55 "Hen-Dollars." The *Bamerindus Bank* encourages more investments for maize cultivation instead of saturated chicken breeding. Cockerel in blue shades. (BRA)

56 Advertisement for *Mexicana Airlines.* Black and white, and blue. (USA)

51

52

La prima volta che il nostro comandante
atterra a Singapore conosce già
perfettamente ogni segreto della pista.

I 5 simulatori di volo del Centro Addestramento Alitalia riproducono esattamente le cabine di pilotaggio dei vari tipi di aerei. Un complesso di computers visualizza su uno schermo, posto dinanzi alla cabina del simulatore, tutte le situazioni di volo che si verificano in conseguenza delle manovre del pilota. Così i piloti Alitalia si addestrano ad effettuare tutte le manovre di volo, dal decollo all'atterraggio, sulle piste degli aeroporti di tutto il mondo. Così i piloti Alitalia diventano quello che sono: piloti perfettamente addestrati. Ma buoni piloti bisogna esserlo sempre: per questo ogni sei mesi sono sottoposti a prove fisiche e verifiche di idoneità, per questo nel Centro

Addestramento Alitalia si tengono periodicamente corsi di aggiornamento dove anche altre compagnie straniere inviano i loro piloti. Ma non basta: l'Alitalia pensa anche ai piloti di domani. Per questo ha acquistato due bimotori Piaggio P166DL3 a turbina e quattro monomotori SIAI-Marchetti SF260 per la scuola di volo creata dalla Compagnia ad Alghero Fertilia.
Quando volate Alitalia,
mettetevi sereni,
efficienza e simpatia
sono nell'aria.

Alitalia
EFFICIENZA E SIMPATIA NELL'ARIA

53

New York è più comoda con i nuovi Boeing 747

Più confortevoli con la **nuova** "Top-Class".
Più comodi con le **nuove poltrone reclinabili** Dreamerette®.

COLLEGAMENTI ITALIA-STATI UNITI

	ROMA	MILANO	NEW YORK
VOLO AZ 1600 LUN. VEN. DOM.	p. 09.50	a. 10.55 p. 12.00	a. 14.40
VOLO AZ 600 SAB. MAR.E		p. 12.00	a. 14.40
VOLO AZ 610 TUTTI I GIORNI	p. 12.15		a. 15.30

	ROMA	MILANO	BOSTON
VOLO AZ 624 MERC. VEN. DOM.	p. 11.15	a. 12.20 p. 13.20	a. 15.50

Tariffe di andata e ritorno a partire da L.511.800

Dal 9 gennaio 1981, New York sarà collegata dai nuovi B747 costruiti dalla Boeing, aerei oggi all'avanguardia tecnologica nel mondo. Su 12 voli settimanali da Roma o Milano per New York, 5 saranno effettuati con i nuovi Boeing, sui quali Alitalia inaugura la "Top-Class". La prima classe ancora più elegante e con un servizio personalizzato, con un supplemento di sole 44.000 lire. A bordo saranno servite specialità della cucina italiana e grandi vini italiani. Nella "Top-Class", Alitalia ha installato un nuovo tipo di poltrone reclinabili, le Dreamerette®, che consentono il massimo comfort per un viaggio di tutto relax. Alitalia ricorda inoltre i tre voli settimanali da Milano e Roma per Boston. Per ulteriori informazioni rivolgetevi al vostro Agente di Viaggio o alle più vicine Agenzie Alitalia. Quando volate a New York, volate con Alitalia: efficienza, simpatia e comodità sono nell'aria.

Alitalia
EFFICIENZA E SIMPATIA NELL'ARIA

54

*Frangodólar.
Com Mais Milho,
Chegaremos
Lá.*

BAMERINDUS
O banco da nossa terra.

55

We give San Antonio a lot more Mexico.

FLY mexicana
More of what you go to Mexico for.

56

ARTIST / KÜNSTLER / ARTISTE:

51, 52 Jean-Michel Folon
55 Miran
56 Nicolas Sidjakov

DESIGNER / GESTALTER:

51, 52 Steven Sessions
53, 54 Otello Fraternale
55 Oswaldo Miranda
56 Sidjakov & Berman Assoc.

ART DIRECTOR:

51, 52 Steven Sessions
53, 54 Silvano Guidone
55 Oswaldo Miranda
56 Jerry Leonhart

AGENCY / AGENTUR / AGENCE:

51, 52 Baxter & Korge, Inc.
53, 54 Armando Testa S. p. A.
55 Umuarama
56 Dailey & Assoc.

51, 52 Mit dieser Anzeige sollen gut situierte und kulturbewusste Käufer auf die neuen, luxuriösen Eigentumswohnungen in den beiden Four-Leaf-Hochhäusern in Houston, Texas, aufmerksam gemacht werden. Illustration in Originalgrösse. (USA)
53, 54 Aus einer Serie von Zeitschriftenanzeigen der italienischen Fluggesellschaft *Alitalia*. Abb. 53 bezieht sich auf die perfekte Ausbildung der Piloten; Nachtansicht von Singapore; Abb. 54 wirbt für bequemere New-York-Flüge mit der Boeing 747. *Alitalia*-Signet in Grün/Weiss/Rot auf dunklem Himmel. (ITA)
55 «Hühner-Dollar.» Eine Bank fordert vermehrte Investitionen für den Maisanbau, da die Hühnerzucht zu stark gefördert wurde. Hahn in Blautönen. (BRA)
56 Mit dieser Anzeige wirbt die mexikanische Fluggesellschaft in den Südstaaten der USA für Flüge ins nahegelegene Nachbarland. Schwarzweiss und blau. (USA)

51, 52 Par moyen de cette annonce on cherche des acheteurs riches et cultivés pour les nouveaux appartements luxueux dans les deux gratte-ciel Four-Leaf Towers à Houston, Texas. Illustration en grandeur originale. (USA)
53, 54 D'une série d'annonces de la compagnie aérienne italienne *Alitalia*. La fig. 53 se réfère à l'entraînement parfait des pilotes; vue de nuit de Singapore; fig. 54: pour les vols confortables à destination de New York à bord la Boeing 747. Symbole de l'*Alitalia* en vert/blanc/rouge dans un ciel sombre. (ITA)
55 Une banque lance un appel en faveur de plus grands investissements dans la culture céréalière, car l'élevage de poules a été trop forcé. Coq bleu. (BRA)
56 La compagnie aérienne méxicaine fait de la publicité dans les Etats frontaliers du Sud des Etats-Unis pour les vols dans le pays voisin. (USA)

57

**Advertisements
Anzeigen
Annonces**

ARTIST / KÜNSTLER / ARTISTE:

57–60 Dietrich Ebert
61, 62 Robert Giusti
63, 64 Al Francekevich

DESIGNER / GESTALTER:

63, 64 Dale Mallie

ART DIRECTOR:

57–60 Uli Weber
61, 62 Ted Curl
63, 64 Lenny Goodman

AGENCY / AGENTUR / AGENCE:

57–60 Leonhardt & Kern
61, 63 Magnus Nankervis & Curl
63, 64 Hoffman York Inc.

58

59

57–60 Complete double-spread advertisement and illustrations from a campaign launched by *Jockey* entitled "*Jockey*. Adam's costume." (GER)
61, 62 Double-spread advertisements for a Bangkok to Los Angeles connection offered as a new route by Thailand's airline. Fig. 61: *Thai* breaks new ground in that it prepares the way to winter-sport resorts in the USA with this connection; Fig. 62: first ad announcing this new quick connection. The motorway crossroads as well as the tracks in the snow form the airline's symbol. (THA)
63, 64 In the middle of the three-dimensional continent (3½ ft. from coast to coast) covered with sheet aluminium, the symbol of *Republic Airlines is* seen. The glowing routes are composed of flexible acrylic tubing wrapped with a light-reflecting material. The product acts as a pliable mirror reflecting any light source directed toward it. Here a blue light was used. (USA)

57–60 Vollständige, doppelseitige Anzeige und Illustrationen aus einer von *Jockey* lancierten Werbekampagne unter dem Titel «*Jockey*. Adam's Kostüm.» (GER)
61, 62 Doppelseitige Anzeigen für eine neue Verbindung der thailändischen Fluggesellschaft von Bangkok nach Los Angeles. Abb. 61: *Thai* zieht neue Spuren, ist also wegbereitend mit dieser Verbindung zu Wintersportorten in den USA; Abb. 62: erste Anzeige für diese neue Schnellverbindung, was durch die Autobahn symbolisiert wird. Das Autobahnkreuz wie auch die Spuren im Schnee zeichnen das Symbol der Fluglinie nach. (THA)
63, 64 In der Mitte des dreidimensionalen, mit Aluminiumblech überzogenen Kontinents (1 m von Küste zu Küste) ist das Symbol der *Republic Airlines* zu sehen. Die Flugverbindungen sind aus beweglichen Acrylröhren, die mit einem lichtreflektierenden Material umwickelt wurden und wie bewegliche Spiegel das auf sie gerichtete Licht zurückwerfen. Hier verwendete der Photograph blaues Licht. (USA)

57–60 Annonce sur page double et illustrations d'une campagne publicitaire intitulée «Costume d'Adam» et lancée en faveur des articles *Jockey*. (GER)
61, 62 Annonces sur doubles pages pour une nouvelle ligne de Bangkok à Los Angeles, desservie par la compagnie aérienne thaïlandaise. Fig. 61: *Thai* trace le chemin par la liaison directe à destination des stations d'hiver des Etats-Unis. Fig. 62: en faveur de la liaison rapide, ce qui est symbolisé par l'autoroute. Les voies d'accès à l'autoroute ainsi que les traces dans la neige représentent le symbole de cette compagnie aérienne. (THA)
63, 64 Au milieu du continent tridimensionnel (1 m de l'est à l'ouest), revêtu de feuilles d'aluminium, on voit le symbole de la compagnie aérienne *Repbulic Airlines*. Les routes aériennes, composées de tubes fléxibles en acrylique, sont couvertes d'un matériel réfléttant la lumière. Elles agissent donc comme des miroirs réfléchissant la lumière braquée vers elles. (USA)

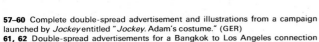

60

63

Our new American run takes us by way of Bangkok and Tokyo, direct to Seattle and Los Angeles. Offering a number of advantages people will delight in exploring.

Seattle Airport is 432 miles closer to Tokyo than other west coast airports, so an hour is saved in flying time.

From Seattle it's just a short jump to some of the best skiing in America, while offering excellent connections to major southern and east coast cities.

And the airport is less congested than others on the west coast, so there's every chance you'll be quicker onto the slopes or with your onward connections.

Choosing this fresh trail is another example of the pioneer spirit that's helped us become one of the most respected airlines in the world today.

Take one of our magnificent 747 flights to America. The run is open, and conditions are perfect.

We're making tracks for America where few have been before.

61

Introducing a fast new route to America.

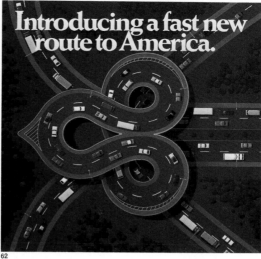

For a great new way to fly to America steer in our direction.

To begin with we take you by way of Bangkok and Tokyo, direct to Seattle and Los Angeles.

A route that offers you a number of advantages.

Like an hour saved in flying time. (Seattle is 432 miles closer to Tokyo than other west coast airports).

Seattle airport is less congested than others on the west coast, too.

So chances are, you'll save time disembarking, going through immigration and making onward connections.

Then there are the other kind of advantages flying to America our way.

Like the smooth ride on our magnificent new 747's. The comfort of our slumber seats in First Class.

The serenity of our Business Class.

And the pleasant surroundings to be found in Economy.

Not to mention the famous Royal Orchid Service wherever you're sitting.

Take route 747 to America. And travel smooth as silk all the way.

62

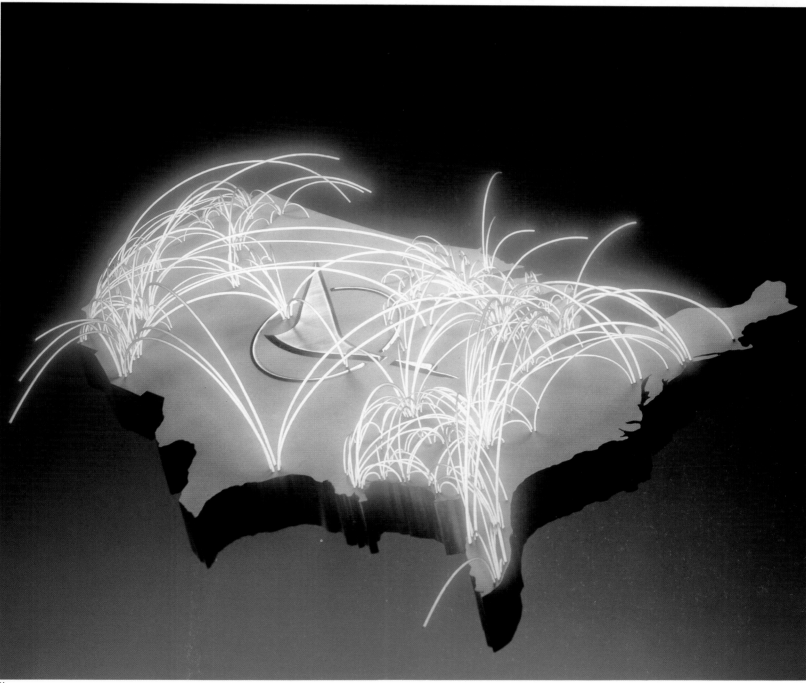

64

le philtre mystérieux
de vos nuits blanches

Magie noire, l'inédit de LANCÔME

65

66

Advertisements
Anzeigen
Annonces

ARTIST / KÜNSTLER / ARTISTE:

65, 66 Ginny Poisson
67–69 Steve Graham

DESIGNER / GESTALTER / MAQUETTISTE:

65 Ginny Poisson
66 Sharon Kennedy
67–69 Barrie Tucker/Ian Kidd
70 Tadanori Yokoo

ART DIRECTOR / DIRECTEUR ARTISTIQUE:

65, 66 Harriet Golfos Santroch
67–69 Barrie Tucker/Ian Kidd
70 Tadanori Yokoo

AGENCY / AGENTUR / AGENCE – STUDIO:

65, 66 T. Eaton Co. Ltd.
67–69 Tucker & Kidd

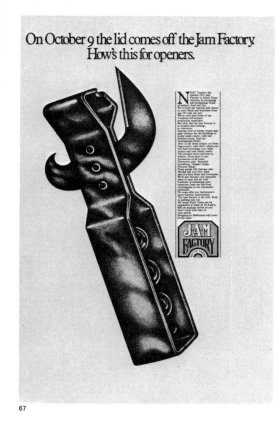

On October 9 the lid comes off the Jam Factory. How's this for openers.

67

The Jam Factory opens tomorrow. An explosion of fashion, food and fun.

68

You like our preserves. You'll love our preserved factory.

69

65, 66 Examples from a campaign launched in daily newspapers by the *Eaton* department store, here for a perfume by *Lancôme* and for the record department as well as to advertise longer opening hours before Christmas. (CAN)
67–69 From a series of newspaper advertisements drawing attention to the opening of a new shopping centre. It is situated in the 125 year-old jam factory in South Yarra, which is why the advertising is done with tins and tin openers. (AUS)
70 *Seibu,* the Tokyo department store, presents five Milanese fashion designers. Black-and-white newspaper ad. (JPN)

65, 66 Beispiele aus einer in der Tagespresse lancierten Kampagne des Warenhauses *Eaton,* hier für ein Parfum von *Lancôme* und für die Plattenabteilung und verlängerte Öffnungszeiten der Läden vor Weihnachten. (CAN)
67–69 Aus einer Serie von Zeitungsanzeigen, die die Eröffnung eines neuen Einkaufszentrums anzeigen. Dieses befindet sich in einer 125jährigen Marmeladenfabrik, weshalb mit Büchsen und Büchsenöffnern geworben wird. (AUS)
70 Das Tokioter Warenhaus *Seibu* präsentiert fünf Milaneser Modeschöpfer. Schwarzweisse Zeitungsanzeige. (JPN)

65, 66 Exemples d'une série d'annonces de presse lancées en faveur des grands magasins *Eaton,* ici pour un parfum *Lancôme* et pour le rayon des disques et des heures d'ouverture prolongées avant la fête de Noël. (CAN)
67–69 Exemples d'une campagne de presse annonçant l'ouverture d'un nouveau supermarché qui se trouve dans une fabrique de confiture construite il y a 125 ans. Les motifs choisis – les boîtes et les ouvre-boîtes – s'y réfèrent. (AUS)
70 Le grand magasin *Seibu* de Tokyo présente cinq couturiers milanais. Annonce de presse en noir et blanc. (JPN)

70

71

ARTIST / KÜNSTLER / ARTISTE:

71 Tina
72 Tadanori Yokoo/
   Tadashi Kurahashi (Photo)
73, 74 Tadanori Yokoo

DESIGNER / GESTALTER:

71 Jacqui Morgan
72–74 Tadanori Yokoo

ART DIRECTOR:

71 Jacqui Morgan
72–74 Tadanori Yokoo

AGENCY / AGENTUR / AGENCE:

71 Jacqui Morgan Studio

72

71 Small-format newspaper advertisement for the dancing *The Ritz* in New York's East Village. (USA)
72–74 With these full-page newspaper advertisements entitled "The Religious Age", the orders of the Nishihonganji Temple in Kyoto wish to encourage the religious consciousness of the Japanese. Fig. 72 shows how the artist imagines extra-terrestrial life; Fig. 73: the texts in the globe are prayers, the circumference shows events in the history of mankind, imposing places from religious and cultural history as well as modern constructions. Fig. 74 points out that despite the conquests of modern science and technology, one cannot survive without faith. (JPN)

71 Kleinformatige Zeitungsanzeige für das Dancing *The Ritz* im Newyorker East Village. (USA)
72–74 Mit diesen ganzseitigen Zeitungsanzeigen, die unter dem Titel «Das religiöse Zeitalter» in der Tagespresse erschienen, will die Tempelgemeinschaft des Nishihonganji-Tempels in Kyoto das religiöse Bewusstsein der Japaner fördern. Abb. 72 zeigt, wie sich der Künstler das ausserirdische Leben vorstellt. Abb. 73: die Texte im Erdball sind Gebete, dem Rand entlang werden Ereignisse in der Menschheitsgeschichte, markante Stätten aus dem Glaubens- und Kulturgeschichte sowie Bauten aus der neuesten Zeit aufgereiht. Abb. 74: der Text erklärt, dass man trotz den Errungenschaften der modernen Wissenschaft und Technik ohne religiösen Glauben nicht auskommen kann. (JPN)

71 Petite annonce de presse pour le dancing *The Ritz* dans le quartier East Village de New York. (USA)
72–74 C'est avec ces annonces pleines pages, intitulées «L'âge religieux» et publiées dans les quotidiens japonais, que la communion du temple Nishihonganji à Kyoto fait appel à la conscience religieuse des Japonais. La fig. 72 montre comment l'artiste imagine la vie après la mort. Fig. 73: les textes dans le globe sont des prières; tout autour on voit des représentations d'importants événements dans l'histoire de l'humanité, des lieux marquants des civilisations occidentales et orientales ainsi que des bâtiments et gratte-ciel construits au cours du 20e siècle. Fig. 74: le texte dit que la foi est d'importance vitale, malgré les conquêtes de la technique et de la science modernes. (JPN)

Advertisements

Anzeigen

Annonces

73

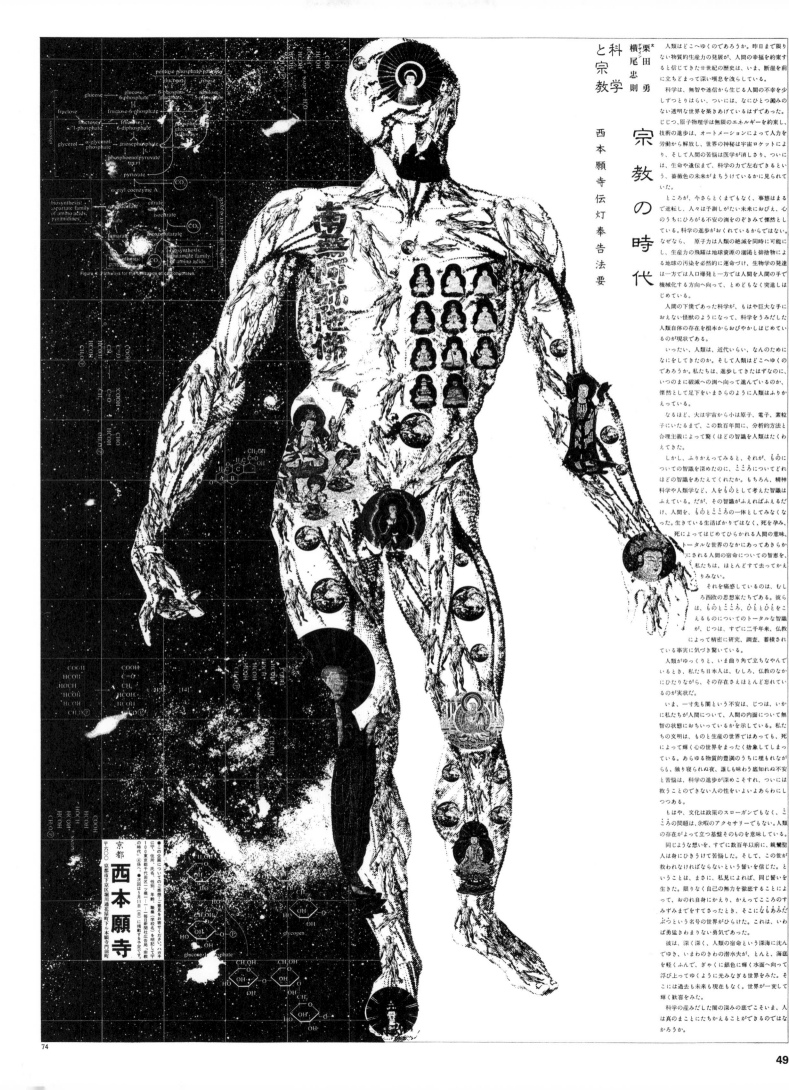

栗田勇
デザイン 横尾忠則

宗教の時代

科学と宗教

西本願寺伝灯奉告法要

人類はどこへゆくのであろうか。昨日まで限りない物質的生産力の発展が、人間の幸福を約束すると信じてきた廿世紀の歴史は、いま、断崖を前に立ちどまって深い嘆息を洩らしている。

科学は、無智や迷信から生じる人間の不幸を少しずつはらい、ついには、なにひとつ濁みのない透明な世界を築きあげているはずであった。じじつ、原子物理学は無限のエネルギーを約束し、技術の進歩はオートメーションによって人力を労働から解放し、世界の神秘は宇宙ロケットにより、そして人間の苦悩は医学が消しさり、ついには、生命や遺伝まで、科学の力で左右できるという、薔薇色の未来がまちうけているかに見られていた。

ところが、今さらとくまでもなく、事態はまるで逆転し、人々は予測しがたい未来におびえ、心のうちにひろがる不安の淵をのぞきみて慄然としている。科学の進歩が「おくれている」からではない。なぜなら、原子力は人類の絶滅を同時に可能にし、生産力の飛躍は地球資源の涸渇と排泄物による地球の汚染を必然的に運命づけ、生物学の発達は一方では人口爆発と一方では人間を人間の手で機械化する方向へ向って、とめどもなく突進しはじめている。

人間の下僕であった科学が、もはや巨大な手におえない怪獣のようになって、科学をうみだした人類自体の存在を根本からおびやかしはじめているのが現状である。

いったい、人類は、近代いらい、なんのためになにをしてきたのか。そして人類はどこへゆくのであろうか。私たちは、進歩してきたはずなのに、いつのまに破滅への淵へ向って進んでいるのか、慄然として足下をいまさらのように人類はふりかえっている。

なるほど、大は宇宙から小は原子、電子、素粒子にいたるまで、この数百年間に、分析的方法と合理主義によって驚くほどの智識を人類はたくわえてきた。

しかし、ふりかえってみると、それが、ものについての智識を深めたのに、こころについてどれほどの智識をあたえてくれたか。もちろん、精神科学や人類学など、人をものとして考えた智識はふえている。だが、その智識がふえればふえるだけ、人間を、ものとこころの一体としてみなくなった。生きている生活ばかりではなく、死を孕み、死によってはじめてひらかれる人間の意味、トータルな世界のなかにあってあきらかにされる人間の宿命についての智恵を、私たちは、ほとんどすて去ってかえりみない。

それを痛感しているのは、むしろ西欧の思想家たちである。彼らは、ものとこころ、ひととひとをこえるものについてのトータルな智識が、じつは、すでに二千年来、仏教によって精密に研究、調査、蓄積されている事実に気づき驚いている。

人類がゆっくりと、いま曲り角で立ちなやんでいるとき、私たち日本人は、むしろ、仏教のなかにひたりながら、その存在さえほとんど忘れているのが実状だ。

いま、一寸先も闇という不安は、じつは、いかに私たちが人間について、人間の内面について無智の状態におちいっているかを示している。私たちの文明は、ものと生産の世界ではあっても、死によって輝く心の世界をまったく捨象してしまっている。あらゆる物質的豊満のうちに埋もれながらも、独り寝られぬ夜、誰しも味わう底知れぬ不安と苦悩は、科学の進歩が深めこそすれ、ついには救うことのできない人の性をいよいよあらわにしつつある。

もはや、文化は政策のスローガンでもなく、こころの問題は、余暇のアクセサリーでもない。人類の存在がよって立つ基盤そのものを意味している。

同じような思いを、すでに数百年以前に、親鸞聖人は身にひきうけて苦悩した。そして、この世が救われなければならないという誓いを信じた。ということは、まさに、私見によれば、同じ誓いを生きた。限りなく自己の無力を徹底することによって、おのれ自身にかえり、かえってこころのすみずみまでをすてさったとき、そこにこそあみだぶつという名号の世界がひらいた。これは、いわば勇猛きわまりない勇気であった。

彼は、深く深く、人類の宿命という深海に沈んでゆき、いまわのきわの潜水夫が、とんと、海底を軽くふんで、ぎゃくに銀色に輝く水面へ向って浮び上ってゆくように光みなぎる世界をみた。そこには過去も未来も現在もなく。世界が一変して輝く歓喜をみた。

科学の産みだした闇の深みの底でこそいま、人は真のまことにたちかえることができるのではなかろうか。

京都
〒六〇〇
京都市下京区堀川通花屋町下ル本願寺門前町
西本願寺

75

ARTIST / KÜNSTLER / ARTISTE:

75–78 Antonio Lopez
79 John Matthews

DESIGNER / GESTALTER / MAQUETTISTE:

75–78 John C. Jay/Charles Banuchi
79 Fred Devito

ART DIRECTOR / DIRECTEUR ARTISTIQUE:

75–78 John C. Jay
79 Fred Devito/John C. Jay

AGENCY / AGENTUR / AGENCE – STUDIO:

75–79 Bloomingdale's

76

Advertisements
Anzeigen
Annonces

75–79 Examples from a series of newspaper advertisements for *Bloomingdale's*, a New York department store. Fig. 75 advertises *Shiseido* cosmetic products; Figs. 76, 77 advertises China-Weeks organized by the store; Fig. 78 invites people to attend a fashion show in which the latest, luxurious winter collection will be displayed; Fig. 79 draws attention to scene-stealing nightclub nylons and panty-hose. (USA)

75–79 Beispiele aus einer Serie von Zeitungsanzeigen des Newyorker Warenhauses *Bloomingdale's*. Abb. 75 wirbt für kosmetische Produkte von *Shiseido;* Abb. 76, 77 laden zu China-Wochen ein, während welcher in der Volksrepublik China hergestellte kunsthandwerkliche Gegenstände, Kleider, Schmuck und Möbel gezeigt und verkauft werden; Abb. 78 lädt zu einer Modeschau ein, an welcher die neueste, luxuriöse Winterkollektion vorgeführt wird; Abb. 79: für die neue Kollektion von aufregenden Strümpfen und Strumpfhosen, die unweigerlich die Blicke auf sich ziehen. (USA)

75–79 Exemples figurant dans une série d'annonces de presse des grands magasins newyorkais *Bloomingdale's.* Fig. 75: en faveur des produits cosmétiques *Shiseido;* fig. 76, 77: annoncent l'ouverture des Semaines Chinoises organisées par ces magasins: exposition et vente d'articles de mode, d'artisanat, de bijoux et de meubles provenant de la République Populaire de Chine; fig. 78: invitation à la présentation de la nouvelle collection luxueuse pour l'hiver; fig. 79 présente la nouvelle collection de bas et de collants qui font fureur. (USA)

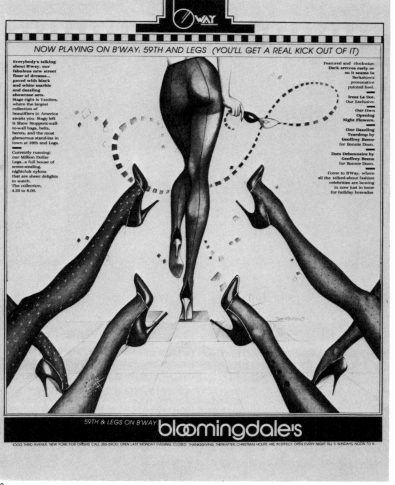

WHY YOU SHOULD SAVE NOW WHILE THE SUN IS STILL SHINING.

If this inflation keeps up, there may be some rainy days ahead.

But there's one way to avoid getting completely soaked. Put your money in a high interest savings plan at Santa Barbara Bank. With credit becoming harder and harder to find, it's nice to have a little something tucked away for emergencies.

Come to one of our 8 offices today. We'll help you decide on the savings program that works best for you. While everyone else is getting wet, you'll be singing in the rain.

SANTA BARBARA BANK & TRUST
The bank that belongs to Santa Barbara.

WHERE TO PUT YOUR MONEY IN AN UPSIDE-DOWN ECONOMY.

In today's topsy-turvy world, a big bank is not necessarily your best bet.

Big banks send your savings home to a big city. Santa Barbara Bank, on the other hand, lends your savings to local borrowers, helping to keep our own economy rightside up.

Come to any one of our 8 offices and choose the savings plan that works best for you. Even if the rest of the world is standing on its ear, you'll be keeping Santa Barbara on its feet.

SANTA BARBARA BANK & TRUST
The bank that belongs to Santa Barbara.

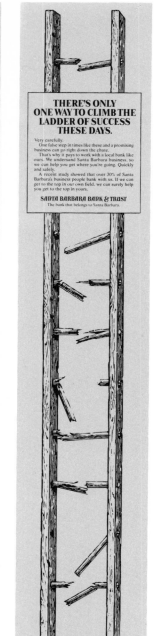

THERE'S ONLY ONE WAY TO CLIMB THE LADDER OF SUCCESS THESE DAYS.

Very carefully.

One false step in times like these and a promising business can go right down the chute.

That's why it pays to work with a local bank like ours. We understand Santa Barbara business, so we can help you get where you're going. Quickly and safely.

A recent study showed that over 30% of Santa Barbara's business people bank with us. If we can get to the top in our own field, we can surely help you get to the top in yours.

SANTA BARBARA BANK & TRUST
The bank that belongs to Santa Barbara.

80

81

82

80–82 Various advertisements conceived to attract prospective savers are shown here in a campaign by the *Santa Barbara Bank & Trust* that announces its new savings programme in daily newspapers. (USA)
83 Black-and-white advertisement of the *Bank of America* that provides the connection to central American states. (USA)
84 Newspaper advertisement for the opening of a new shopping centre called *Santa Monica Place*. With some red. (USA)
85 A *Franklin Park Mall* advertisement for fashion and sports articles and unusual accessories for unusual people. Full-colour illustration. (USA)
86 From a fashion supplement for the new spring collection of a department store promising a rich harvest. In full colour. (USA)
87 For the opening of the *Singing River Mall* shopping centre. In colour. (USA)
88 Advertisement for the 90th anniversary of the *Corpus Christi National Bank* that has served its clients for 47 million minutes. With brown. (USA)

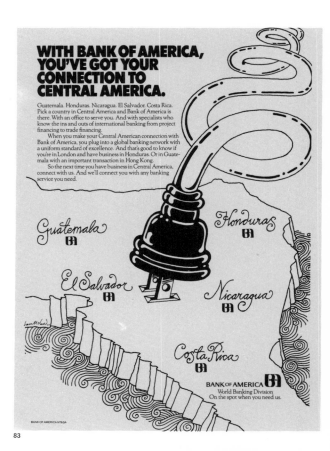

83

84

85

87

86

88

89

90

91

92

Advertisements

Anzeigen

Annonces

89 *Marshall Field's*, the Chicago department store, announces the opening of a new store in Houston, Texas, with a cowboy slogan playing on the company name. (USA)
90 Newspaper advertisement for the new *Sony-Walkman*, a special small cassette recorder. (NLD)
91 Advertisement for *Ultravue* lenses from *American Optical*, manufactured in Brazil. The illustration is in bright colours. (BRA)
92 Black-and-white double-spread magazine advertisement for the *Asian Wall Street Journal*. (USA)
93 Full-page magazine advertisement for *Lacoste* shirts. (GER)
94–96 Examples from a campaign for the opening of the new wing of a Dallas shopping centre. (USA)

89 «Ein neuer Marschall kommt in die Stadt.» Das Chicagoer Warenhaus *Marshall Field's* kündigt die Neueröffnung eines Ladens in Houston, Texas, an. (USA)
90 Zeitungsanzeige für den neuen *Sony-Walkman*, ein speziell kleines Kassettengerät. (NLD)
91 Anzeige für *Ultravue*-Linsen von *American Optical*, die in Brasilien hergestellt werden. Illustration in bunten Farben. (BRA)
92 Doppelseitige Zeitschriftenanzeige, die die Herausgabe des *Asian Wall Street Journal* bekannt gibt und zwar als Tageszeitung und als Wochenblatt. Schwarzweiss. (USA)
93 Ganzseitige Zeitschriftenanzeige für Hemden von *Lacoste*. (GER)
94–96 Beispiele aus einer Kampagne, die anlässlich der Eröffnung des neuen Traktes eines Einkaufszentrums in Dallas lanciert wurde. (USA)

89 «Il y aura un nouveau maréchal en ville.» Le grand magasin *Marshall Field's* de Chicago annonce l'ouverture d'un magasin à Houston, Texas. (USA)
90 Pour le nouveau *Sony-Walkman*, un tout petit magnétophone à cassette. Annonce de presse. (NLD)
91 Annonce en faveur des lentilles optiques *Ultravue* d'*American Optical* qui sont fabriquées au Brésil. Illustration en couleurs vives. (BRA)
92 Annonce de magazine sur page double annonçant la publication de l'*Asian Wall Street Journal* en deux éditions: comme quotidien et comme hebdomadaire. En noir et blanc. (USA)
93 Annonce de magazine pleine page pour les chemises *Lacoste*. (GER)
94–96 Exemples figurant dans une campagne lancée à l'occasion de l'ouverture d'une nouvelle aile d'un supermarché à Dallas. (USA)

ART DIRECTOR / DIRECTEUR ARTISTIQUE:

89 Charles Hively
90 Hans Goedicke
92 John Waters
93 D. & I. Ebert
94–96 Rex Peteet

AGENCY / AGENTUR / AGENCE – STUDIO:

89 Metzdorf Advertising Agency, Inc.
90 KVH/GGK Int. BV
91 Classic Propaganda
92 John Waters Associates
93 Alain Fion
94–96 The Richards Group

93

94   95

96

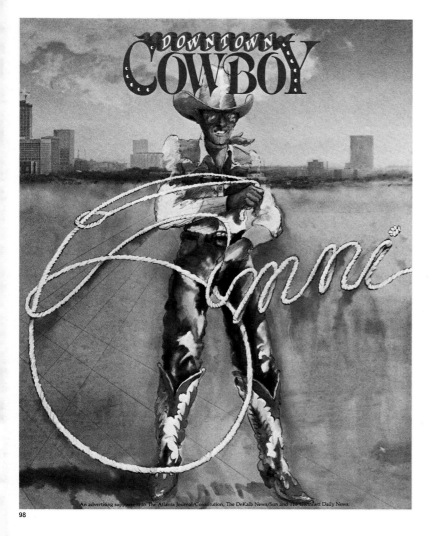

98

99

97, 100 Illustration in actual size and complete magazine advertisement for *Nacona* Western boots. The illustration shows a gila monster. (USA)
98 Front spread of a four-page insert of the *Omni International* chain of hotels announcing a Western Show. Illustration in subdued colours. (USA)
99, 101 From an advertising series for *Liberté* handbags. Yellow shades and red and yellow. (JPN)

97, 100 Illustration in Originalgrösse und vollständige Zeitschriftenanzeige für *Nacona*-Western Boots. Die Illustration zeigt ein Gila-Tier. (USA)
98 Erste Seite einer vierseitigen Beilage, in welcher eine Hotelkette eine Western-Show ankündigt und gleichzeitig für Modeartikel im Western-Stil wirbt, die in den eigenen Läden verkauft werden. Illustration in matten Farben. (USA)
99, 101 Aus einer Anzeigenserie für *Liberté*-Handtaschen. In Gelbtönen, resp. Rot und Gelb. (JPN)

97, 100 Illustration en grandeur originale et annonce de magazine complète pour une marque de bottes Western. L'illustration montre un héloderme dont la morsure est dangereusement venimeuse.(USA)
98 Première page d'un encart de magazine par lequel une chaîne d'hôtels annonce des manifestations style Western et la vente de divers articles de ce genre. En tons pâles. (USA)
99, 101 D'une série d'annonces pour les sacs *Liberté*. En tons jaunes, resp. rouges et jaunes. (JPN)

ARTIST / KÜNSTLER / ARTISTE:

97, 100 Alex Ebel
98 Dan Hobbs
99 Shozo Shinoda
101 Sakumi Hagiwara

100

DESIGNER / GESTALTER:

97, 100 Gail Daniels
98 Dan Hobbs
99, 101 Yasuyuki Uno

ART DIRECTOR:

97, 100 Mark Keller
98 Dan Hobbs
99, 101 Yasuyuki Uno

AGENCY / AGENTUR / AGENCE:

97, 100 Ackerman & McQueen
98 Creative Services, Inc.

101

2

Booklets

Folders

Catalogues

Programmes

Broschüren

Faltprospekte

Kataloge

Programme

Brochures

Dépliants

Catalogues

Programmes

ARTIST / KÜNSTLER / ARTISTE:

102 Heather Cooper/Paul Browning
105–107 David Penney

DESIGNER / GESTALTER / MAQUETTISTE:

102 Scott Taylor
103, 104 Jon Craine
105–107 David Hillman/Nancy Williams

ART DIRECTOR / DIRECTEUR ARTISTIQUE:

102 Robert Burns
103, 104 Jon Craine

AGENCY / AGENTUR / AGENCE – STUDIO:

102 Burns, Cooper, Hynes Ltd.
105–107 Pentagram

102 Four folders in a cardboard portfolio for the *Wood Wilkings* company for a range of services in planning, design, construction and management for the hospitality industry. Root system in chestnut brown and blue, crown in raspberry red on a dark green ground. (CAN)
103, 104 Recto and opened concertina-type folder for IBM business machines. Design in violet, red, black and a dark greenish grey. (USA)
105–107 Broadsheets for the West German Government concerning the conservation of energy and the discovery of alternative energy sources. Full-colour illustrations. (GER)

102 Vier in einem Karton-Portefeuille enthaltene Faltkarten, die über die Dienstleistungen einer Firma Auskunft geben, die auf dem Gebiet des Hotel- und Gastgewerbes von der Planung über die Gestaltung und den Bau bis zum Management alles übernimmt. Wurzelwerk in Goldbraun und Blau, Krone in Hellbraun und Himbeerrot auf dunkelgrünem Hintergrund. (CAN)
103, 104 Vorderseite und geöffneter Leporelloprospekt für IBM-Büromaschinen. Design jeweils in Violett, Rot, Schwarz und dunklem Grüngrau. (USA)
105–107 Aus einer Serie von grossformatigen Blättern, die vom Bundesminister für Forschung und Technologie herausgegeben wurden und Fakten zur Energieforschung enthalten, über alternative Energiequellen, über Energie-Sparmassnahmen und die Förderung herkömmlicher Energiequellen. Mit farbigen Illustrationen. (GER)

102 Quatre dépliants contenus dans un portefeuille en carton. Ils donnent des informations sur les services d'une entreprise qui travaille dans le secteur de l'hôtellerie et de la restauration en assumant tous les travaux, du planning et de la conception générale à la construction et au management. Racines en brun doré et bleu, houppier en brun clair et rose framboise sur fond vert foncé. (CAN)
103, 104 Couverture et dépliant en accordéon pour des machines de bureau IBM. Motifs en violet, rouge, noir et vert grisâtre foncé. (USA)
105–107 D'une série de feuilles à grand format publiées par le ministère ouest-allemand des recherches et de la technologie. Elles sont consacrées à la conservation de l'énergie, à la recherche de sources d'énergie alternatives et à l'exploitation de sources existantes. Illustrations en couleurs. (GER)

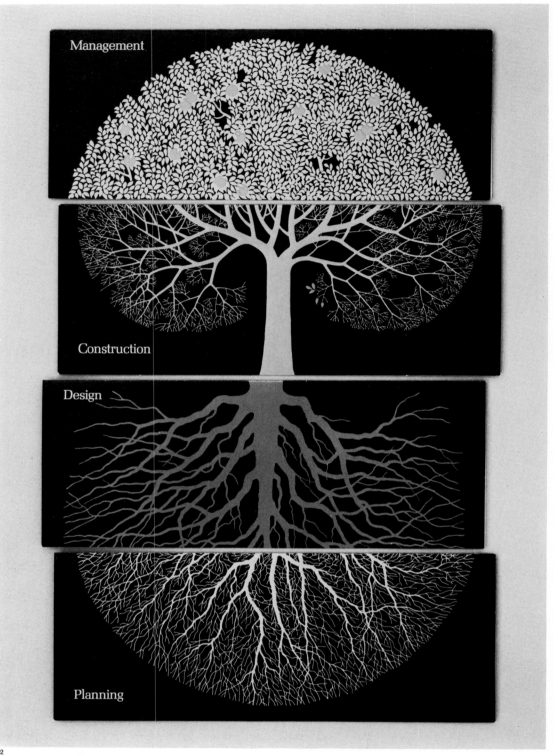

102

103   104

Booklets/Prospekte/Brochures

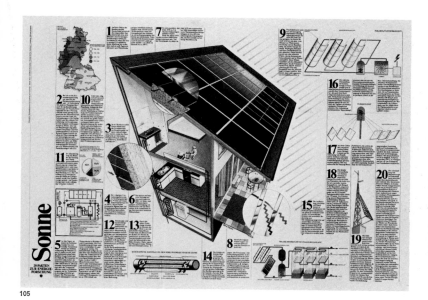

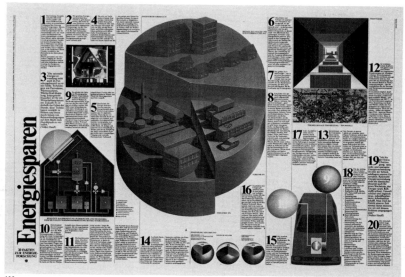

105

106

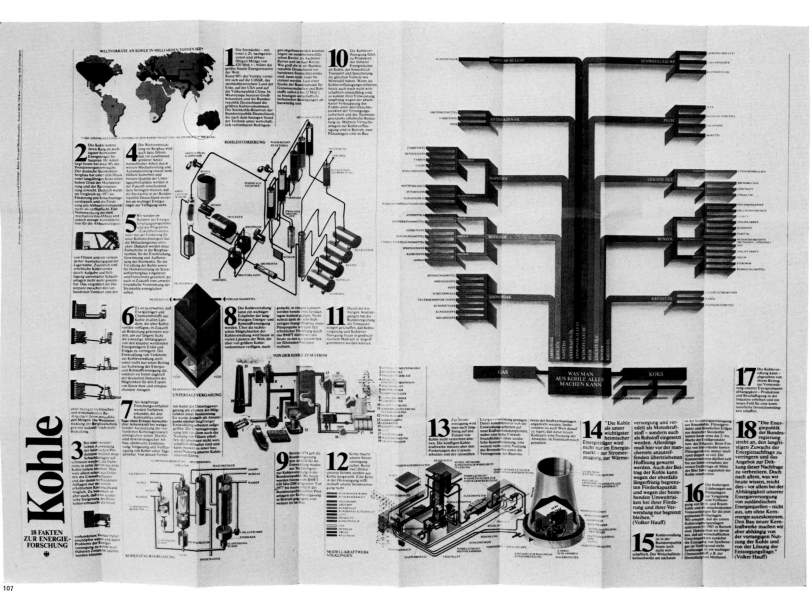

107

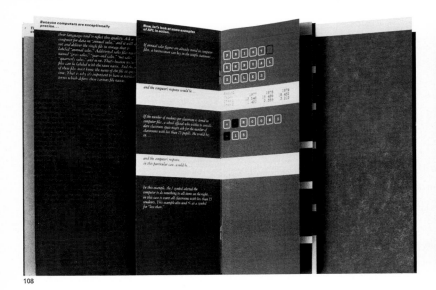

108

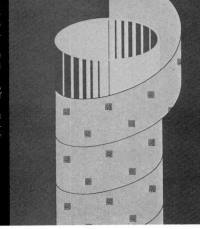

109

ARTIST / KÜNSTLER / ARTISTE:

109 Nicolas Sidjakov/
     Mike Mabry
110, 111 Tom Evans
112 John Thom
114 G. Vittorio Plazzogna

DESIGNER / GESTALTER / MAQUETTISTE:

109 Sidjakov & Berman Associates
112 Fred Witzig
113 Joan Wilking
114 G. Vittorio Plazzogna/D. Nenzi
115 Peter Crockett

AGENCY / AGENTUR / AGENCE – STUDIO:

108 Bonnell & Crosby Inc.
109 Sidjakov & Berman Associates
110, 111 Sanders, Lubinski & Powell
112 Adler, Schwartz Inc.
113 Compugraphic Corp.
114 G. Vittorio Plazzogna
115 Burson Marsteller

110

111

112

113

114

115

ART DIRECTOR / DIRECTEUR ARTISTIQUE:

109 Nicolas Sidjakov/Jerry Berman/Mike Mabry
110, 111 Tom White
112 Peter Adler
113 Joan Wilking
114 G. Vittorio Plazzogna
115 Peter Crockett

Booklets/Prospekte/Brochures

108 Brochure for IBM computers. Narrow interleaved pages in grey and white, other spreads in blue. (USA)
109 Inside spread of a brochure for *Boise Cascade* pipe wrap-kraft paper that can be used for insulating purposes. Beige lettering on black, lilac and light-blue pipe, red printing on beige wrapping paper. (USA)
110, 111 Folder for a *Xerox* customer service. Embossed claws, full-colour monster, russet table, beige wall. (USA)
112 Silver cover of a brochure for VW buses. Embossed with a black grill. (USA)
113 For the large selection of a typesetter's ornaments. Black on silver. Open view. (USA)
114 From a series of folders for a furniture manufacturer. Full-colour illustration. (ITA)
115 Press kit for *Gast* rotary air pumps. When the wheel is turned the piston moves. (USA)

108 Broschüre für IBM-Computer. Schmale Innenseiten in Grau und Weiss, übrige Seiten in Blau. (USA)
109 Innenseite aus einer Broschüre für wasserfestes Packpapier, das auch als Rohr-Isolation verwendet werden kann. Beige Schrift auf Schwarz, Rohr in Hellblau und Lila, beiges Packpapier rot bedruckt. (USA)
110, 111 Faltprospekt für den *Xerox*-Kundendienst. Abb. 110: Vorderseite mit blindgeprägten Tatzen; Abb. 111: mehrfarbiges Ungeheuer, rotbrauner Tisch, beige Wand. (USA)
112 Umschlag (silber) einer Broschüre für VW-Busse. Blindgeprägte Frontansicht mit schwarzem Kühlergitter. (USA)
113 Für die grosse Auswahl an Ornamenten einer Setzerei. Schwarz auf Silber. Geöffnete Ansicht. (USA)
114 Aus einer Serie von Faltprospekten eines Möbelfabrikanten. Mehrfarbige Illustration. (ITA)
115 Pressemappe eines Herstellers von Kreiselpumpen. Beim Drehen des Rades bewegt sich die Pleuelstange. (USA)

108 Brochure pour les ordinateurs IBM. Pages intercalées en gris et blanc, les autres pages sont en bleu. (USA)
109 Page extraite d'une brochure pour un papier d'emballage étanche utilisé aussi pour l'isolation de tuyaux. Typo beige sur noir, tuyau en bleu clair et lilas, papier d'emballage avec marques rouges. (USA)
110, 111 Dépliant vantant le service après-vente mis au pied par *Xerox*. Fig.110: couverture avec pattes gaufrées à sec; fig. 111: monstre en couleurs, table brun rouge, parois beige. (USA)
112 Couverture (argent) d'une brochure pour les camionnettes VW. Gaufrage à sec avec grille noire. (USA)
113 Pour le grand choix d'ornements d'un atelier de composition. Noir sur argent. Vue ouverte. (USA)
114 D'une série de dépliants de *Cadel*, fabricant de meubles. Illustration en couleurs. (ITA)
115 Documentation de presse d'un fabricant de pompes centrifuges. En tournant la roue, la bielle se bouge. (USA)

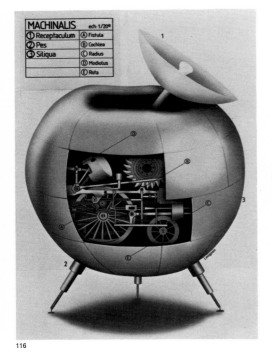

116

117

118

119

120

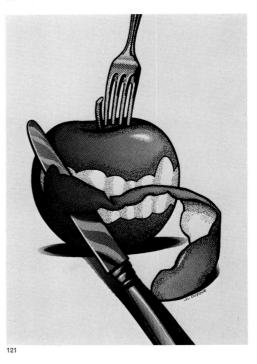

121

ARTIST / KÜNSTLER / ARTISTE:

116 I. Mignon
117 Mediavilla
118, 120 Barraya
119, 121 JL Dufour
123 Milton Glaser

DESIGNER / GESTALTER / MAQUETTISTE:

122, 123 James Miho
124 Mervyn Kurlansky/Sue Horner

ART DIRECTOR / DIRECTEUR ARTISTIQUE:

122, 123 James Miho

AGENCY / AGENTUR / AGENCE – STUDIO:

116–121 Publicis
122, 123 Miho, Inc.
124 Pentagram

116–121 To introduce the various chapters of their latest catalogue, *Graphic Book No. 9,* Mecanorma have chosen the symbol of an apple. They deal with: transfer letters and figures for technical uses, choice of alphabet sheets, tools for graphic designers and retouchers, colouring processes, transfer letters and figures for signage, self-adhesive and transfer-type screen foils. (FRA)
122, 123 Pages from a spiral-bound publication of *Champion Papers* about the history of the catalogue from the 15th century until today. Fig. 122 shows a diagram of the different branches of industry and institutions and their share of the total production of catalogues; Fig.123: full-colour illustration introducing a chapter on printing techniques, here on the web printing presses. (USA)
124 Organigramme for *Esselte,* a Swedish multinational company that manufactures office installations and materials. The organigramme was used at the London headquarters. (GBR)

116–121 Diesmal hat *Mecanorma* den Apfel gewählt, um die verschiedenen Kapitel des *Graphic Book No 9,* des neuesten Katalogs, einzuleiten: Abreibbuchstaben und -ziffern für technische Zwecke, Auswahl der Abreibalphabete, Utensilien für Graphiker und Retoucheure, Verfahren der Farbgebung, Abreibbuchstaben und -ziffern für Signalisierungszwecke, selbstklebende und abreibbare Rasterfolien. (FRA)
122, 123 Aus einer Publikation mit Spiralheftung von *Champion Papers* über die Geschichte des Katalogs vom 15. Jh. bis heute. Abb. 122: zeigt ein Diagramm der verschiedenen Wirtschaftszweige und Institutionen und deren Anteil an der gesamten Katalogproduktion; Abb. 123: farbige Illustration zu einem Kapitel über Druckverfahren, hier den Rollendruck. (USA)
124 Organigramm am Londoner Hauptsitz eines schwedischen multinationalen Konzerns, der hauptsächlich Büroeinrichtungen und -material herstellt. (GBR)

116–121 C'est le thème de la «pomme» que *Mecanorma* a choisi cette fois pour présenter son dernier catalogue, le *Graphic Book No 9:* lettres et chiffres techniques, alphabets transferts, produits pour le montage, le dessin et la retouche et éléments de rangement, procédé de mise en couleur, lettres et chiffres pour la signalisation, trames adhésives et transfert. (FRA)
122, 123 Pages de la publication à reliure spirale d'une papeterie, consacrée à l'histoire du catalogue, du 15e siècle à nos jours. Fig. 122: montre un diagramme des diverses branches industrielles et des institutions et le pourcentage de leur production par rapport à la production totale de catalogues; fig. 123: illustration polychrome introduisant un chapitre sur l'impression, ici l'impression à bobines. (USA)
124 Organigramme d'une entreprise suédoise multinationale qui fabrique des installations et du matériel de bureau. L'organigramme est monté au siège central à Londres. (GBR)

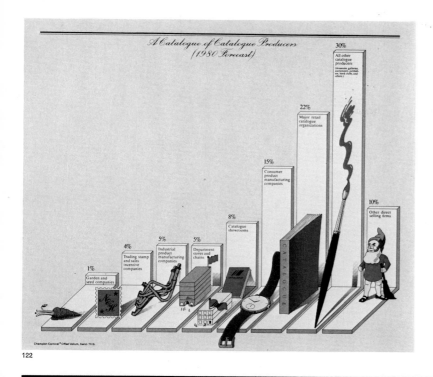

122

123

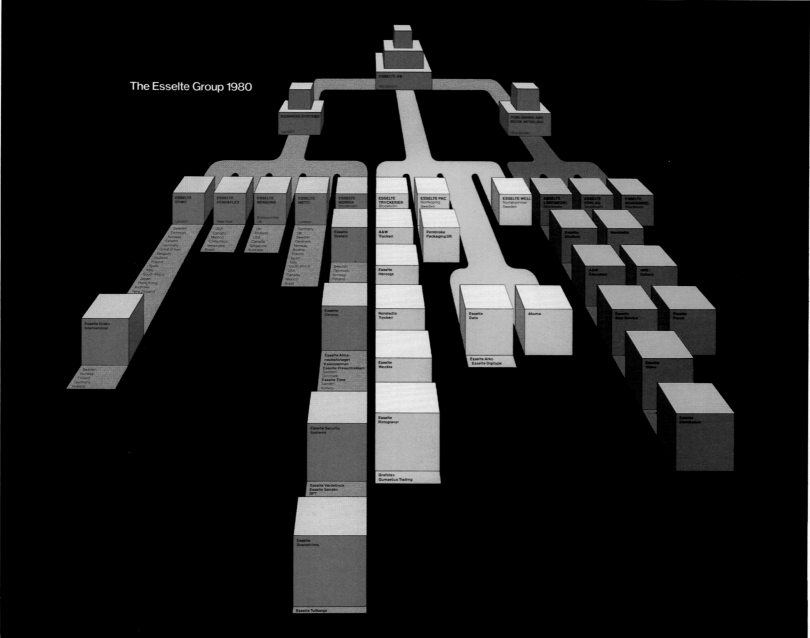

124

125

127

126

130

125, 126 From a series of six brochures for a programme developed by *Participation,* dealing here with the theme of fitness and different aspects of physical training. (USA)

127, 128, 130 From a series of reports about the current problems of higher education as general education, in an interim phase, student programmes and adult education published by the American Association for Higher Education. (USA)

129 Cover illustration of a brochure for the American Hospital Supply Corp. dealing with a programme for reduced costs. (USA)

131 Cover of a monthly catalogue in which the *Ex Libris* publishing company advertises its new publications. In full colour. (SWI)

132 Handbook of the Adelaide College of Arts and Education. (AUS)

128

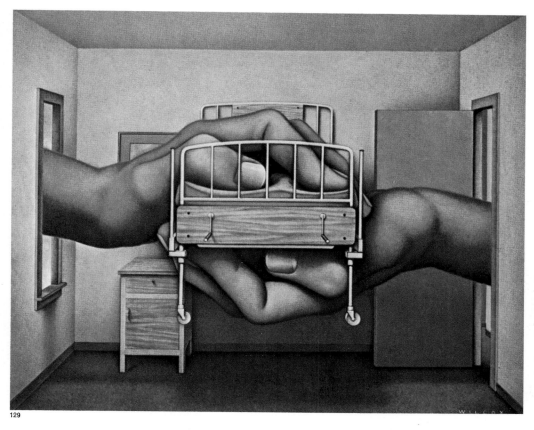

129

131

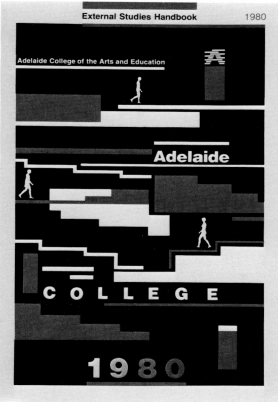

132

ARTIST / KÜNSTLER / ARTISTE:

125 Dennis Noble
126 John Martin
127, 128, 130 Michael David Brown
129 David Wilcox
131 Oskar Weiss

DESIGNER / GESTALTER / MAQUETTISTE:

125, 126 Bruce Mau
127, 128, 130 Michael David Brown
129 Ed Hughes
131 Udo Eschner
132 John Nowland

125, 126 Aus einer Serie von sechs Broschüren zum Thema Fitness, die je einen bestimmten Aspekt beleuchtet, hier zu den Themen «In Form bleiben» und «Der menschliche Bewegungsapparat». (USA)
127, 128, 130 Aus einer Serie von Berichten über aktuelle Probleme der Weiterbildung, wie Allgemeinbildung in einer Übergangsphase, Studienprogramme und Erwachsenenbildung. (USA)
129 Umschlagillustration einer Broschüre, die von einem Unternehmen für Krankenhauseinrichtungen herausgegeben wurde und ein neues Programm zur Senkung der Spitalkosten vorstellt. (USA)
131 Umschlag eines monatlich erscheinenden Katalogs, in welchem der Ex Libris-Verlag seine Neuerscheinungen anzeigt. Mehrfarbig. (SWI)
132 Aus einer Serie von Handbüchern des Adelaide College. (AUS)

125, 126 D'une série de six brochures consacrées au sujet de l'exercice physique. Chacune traite d'un aspect particulier de l'entraînement physique: «comment peut-on rester en forme» et «la motricité de l'homme». (USA)
127, 128, 130 D'une série de rapports sur des problèmes actuels de la formation complémentaire ici p. ex. la formation générale dans une phase transitoire, programmes d'étude et l'éducation permanente. (USA)
129 Illustration de couverture de la brochure d'une association fabriquant des installations d'hôpitaux qui présente un nouveau programme permettant de baisser les frais d'hospitalisation. (USA)
131 Couverture d'un catalogue mensuel par lequel Ex Libris annonce la parution de livres et de disques. Illustration polychrome. (SWI)
132 D'une série de manuels d'une école d'art d'Adelaide. (AUS)

ART DIRECTOR / DIRECTEUR ARTISTIQUE:

127, 128, 130 Charlotte Marson
129 Kerry Bierman
131 Oswald Dubacher
132 John Nowland

AGENCY / AGENTUR / AGENCE – STUDIO:

125, 126 Fifty Fingers Inc.
127, 128, 130 Michael David Brown, Inc.
129 American Hospital Supply Corp./Design Dept.
132 John Nowland Graphic Design

134

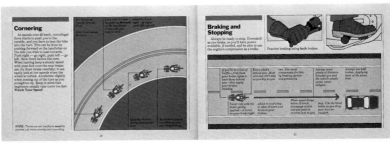

135

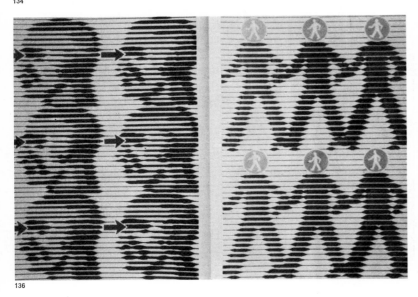

136

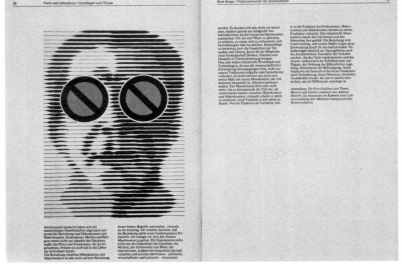

137

ARTIST / KÜNSTLER / ARTISTE:

134, 135 Guy Hubert/Robert Dosil
140, 141 Gottfried Helnwein

DESIGNER / GESTALTER / MAQUETTISTE:

134, 135 Roberto Dosil
136, 137 Andreas Henrich
138, 139 Alan Peckolick

ART DIRECTOR / DIRECTEUR ARTISTIQUE:

134, 135 Roberto Dosil
136, 137 Wolfgang Sprang
138, 139 Alan Peckolick

AGENCY / AGENTUR / AGENCE – STUDIO:

134, 135 Kent Allan Design Group
138, 139 Lubalin Peckolick Assoc. Inc.

134, 135 Safe Riding Guide brochure of the Ministry of Transportation and Highways in the Province of British Columbia informing motor cyclists how to avoid accidents in critical situations. (CAN)
136, 137 Publication of the University of Applied Art in Offenbach/M on a discussion on form and lifestyle, here for «Functional change in the world of design». Screened photograph. (GER)
138, 139 About the *Chase Manhattan Bank's* approach to corporate responsability. White on red. (USA)
140, 141 Complete cover and illustration in actual size for the catalogue of the AT publishing company. The same illustration is used for the book entitled «Wonderful Water.» (SWI)

134, 135 Broschüre des Verkehrsministeriums von British Columbia, die den Motorradfahrer darüber informiert, wie er sich in kritischen Situationen verhalten soll um Unfälle zu verhüten. (CAN)
136, 137 Publikation der Hochschule für Gestaltung, Offenbach/M, zu einem Kolloquium über Form und Lebensform, hier zu «Funktionswandel der Zeichenwelten». In Linienraster aufgelöstes Photo. (GER)
138, 139 Broschüre über das Firmenbewusstsein einer Bank. Umschlag weiss auf Rotbraun. (USA)
140, 141 Vollständiger Umschlag und Illustration in Originalgrösse für den Katalog des *AT-Verlags*. Die selbe Illustration diente als Umschlag für das Buch *Wunderbares Wasser*. (SWI)

134, 135 Brochure du Ministère des Transports de la Colombie Britannique contenant des règlements de sécurité pour les motocyclistes. Illustration en couleurs. (CAN)
136, 137 Publication de la Hochschule für Gestaltung, Offenbach/M, consacrée à un colloque sur les enseignes et le changement de leur fonction. Photos tramées à lignes. (GER)
138, 139 D'une brochure sur le sens de responsabilité sociale d'une banque. 138: blanc/bordeaux. (USA)
140, 141 Couverture complète et illustration en grandeur originale du catalogue d'une maison d'édition. La même illustration a servi de couverture d'un ouvrage sur les eaux médicinales. (SWI)

138

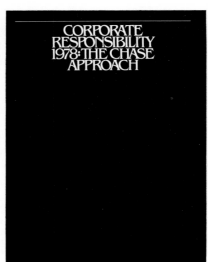

139

140

141

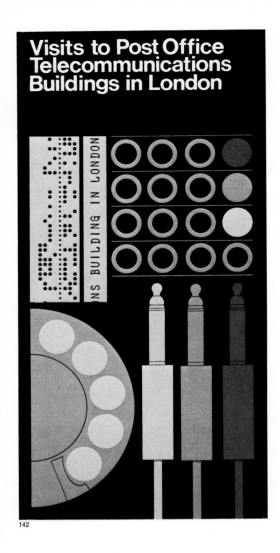

142

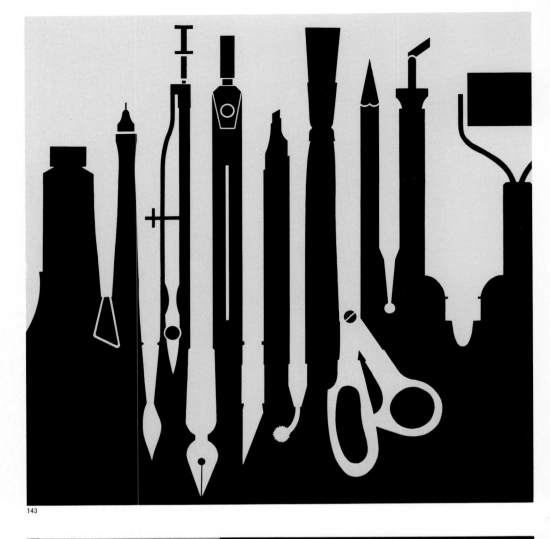

143

ARTIST / KÜNSTLER / ARTISTE:

142 Brian Denyer
143 Herny Brimmer
147 Olle Eksell
148 Joseph Argenziano
149 John McConnell/Mark Biley

DESIGNER / GESTALTER / MAQUETTISTE:

142 Brian Denyer
143 Herny Brimmer
144 Jon Craine
145, 146 Fritz Gottschalk/Stefan Wassmer
147 Olle Eksell
148 Richard Walukanis
149 John McConnell/Mark Biley

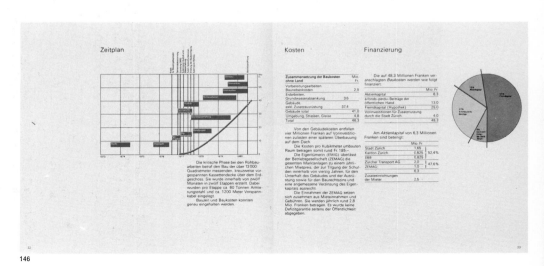

144

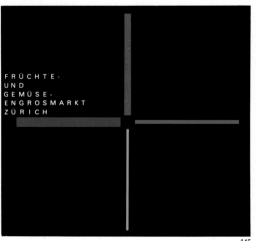

145

146

ART DIRECTOR / DIRECTEUR ARTISTIQUE:

142 Brian Denyer
143 Michel Dattel
144 Jon Craine
147 Olle Eksell
148 Richard Walukanis

142 Cover of a small prospectus for visitors to the Post Office Telecommunications Buildings in London. Light blue, raspberry red and lilac on black. (GBR)
143 Opened inside spread for the semester programme of the Academy of Art College, San Francisco. (USA)
144 Cover of a small-format brochure for an IBM system for customer order servicing to handle last minute changes. Dun, lilac and green on black. (USA)
145, 146 Cover and inside spread of a brochure for the new fruit and vegetable wholesale market in Zurich, showing a timetable as well as a costs and financing plan. (SWI)
147 Folder with information about the association of civil servants. (SWE)
148 Information folder for tourism advertising in *Fortune* magazine. (USA)
149 Series of three specimen-lettering catalogues of the Face Photosetting Ltd. (GBR)

142 Umschlag eines kleinen Prospektes über Fernmeldezentralen in London mit den Öffnungszeiten für Besucher. Hellblau, Himbeerrot und Lila auf Schwarz. (GBR)
143 Geöffnete Innenseite des Semesterprogramms einer Kunsthochschule. (USA)
144 Umschlag einer kleinformatigen Broschüre für ein IBM-System, das eine termingerechte Ausführung von Bestellungen garantiert, auch wenn in letzter Minute noch Änderungen nötig sind. Graubraun, Lila und Grün auf Schwarz. (USA)
145, 146 Umschlag und Innenseite einer Broschüre über den neuen Früchte- und Gemüse-Engrosmarkt in Zürich. Graphik: Zeitplan, Kosten und Finanzierung. (SWI)
147 Faltprospekt mit Angaben über den Verein der Verwaltungsangestellten. (SWE)
148 Informationsmappe über Tourismuswerbung in der Zeitschrift *Fortune*. (USA)
149 Serie von drei Schriftmusterkatalogen der Face Photosetting Ltd. (GBR)

142 Couverture d'un petit prospectus sur les centrales de télécommunication à Londres avec les heures d'ouverture pour les visiteurs. Bleu, rose et lilas. (GBR)
143 Page intérieure du programme des cours d'une école des beaux-arts. (USA)
144 Couverture d'une petite brochure présentant un nouveau système IBM permettant l'exécution des ordres à terme, même si le client désire changer son ordre à la dernière minute. Brun grisâtre, lilas et vert sur fond noir. (USA)
145, 146 Couverture et page intérieure d'une brochure consacrée au nouveau marché aux légumes et aux fruits de Zurich. Diagrammes: horaire, frais et financement. (SWI)
147 Dépliant d'information de l'association des employés de l'administration. (SWE)
148 Documentation sur la publicité touristique dans le magazine *Fortune*. (USA)
149 Série de trois catalogues des caractères d'un atelier de composition. (GBR)

148

147

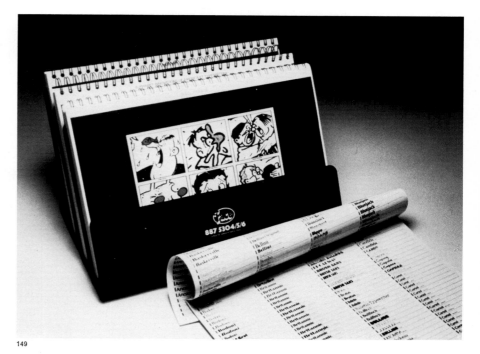

149

AGENCY / AGENTUR / AGENCE – STUDIO:

142 Denyer Design Associates
143 Brimmer Design
144 IBM
145, 146 Gottschalk & Ash Intl.
147 Marianne Pihlgren
149 Pentagram

Booklets/Prospekte/Brochures

150

Booklets/Prospekte/Brochures

"Itchcruciating"
(allergic itch
causing great discomfort
or anguish)

151

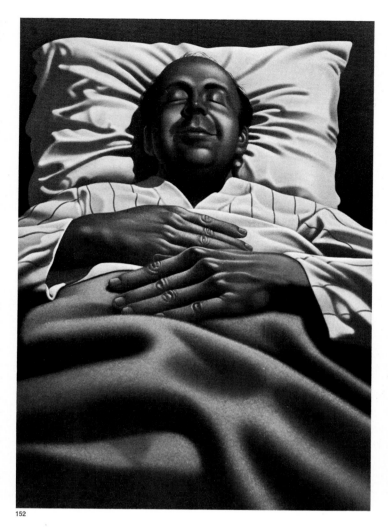

152

153

ART DIRECTOR / DIRECTEUR ARTISTIQUE:

150–152 Julien Jarreau/Jim McFarland
153 Larry Stires
154 Rolf Harder

AGENCY / AGENTUR / AGENCE – STUDIO:

150–152 Sudler & Henessey, Inc.
153 Ciba-Geigy Design
154 Rolf Harder & Assoc.

150–152 Cover illustration, complete cover and inside spread of a folder for *Benadryl,* a *Parke-Davis* medicament that provides relief of allergic urticaria. The same motif was used for a double-spread trade magazine advertisement. (USA)
153 This full-colour illustration for the antidepressant *Tofranil* by *Ciba-Geigy* was inserted in an information folder sent to doctors. (USA)
154 Recto of a folder for *Bactrim,* a wide-ranging antibiotic manufactured by *Roche.* The illustrations are in light blue and white on darker blue. (CAN)

150–152 Umschlagillustration, vollständiger Umschlag und Innenseite eines Faltprospektes für ein Mittel gegen Nesselsucht. Das selbe Motiv wurde auch für eine doppelseitige Fachzeitschriftenanzeige verwendet. (USA)
153 Diese mehrfarbige Illustration wurde einer an Ärzte versandten Informationsmappe über das Antidepressivum *Tofranil* von *Ciba-Geigy* beigelegt. (USA)
154 Vorderseite eines Faltprospektes für das Breitspektrum-Antibiotikum *Bactrim* von *Roche.* Die Illustrationen in Hellblau und Weiss auf dunklerem Blau zeigen mit roten Punkten die hauptsächlichsten Wirkungsbereiche. (CAN)

150–152 Illustration de couverture, couverture complète et page intérieure d'un dépliant pour un médicament de l'urticaire. Le même motif a été utilisé pour une annonce double page publiée dans la presse professionnelle. (USA)
153 Cette illustration polychrome fait partie d'une documentation sur *Tofranil,* un antidépresseur de *Ciba-Geigy.* Elle est destinée au corps médical. (USA)
154 Couverture d'un dépliant en faveur de *Bactrim,* un bactéricide à large spectre de *Roche.* L'illustration en bleu clair et blanc sur un fond bleu foncé montre à l'aide de points rouges le domaine d'action de ce médicament. (CAN)

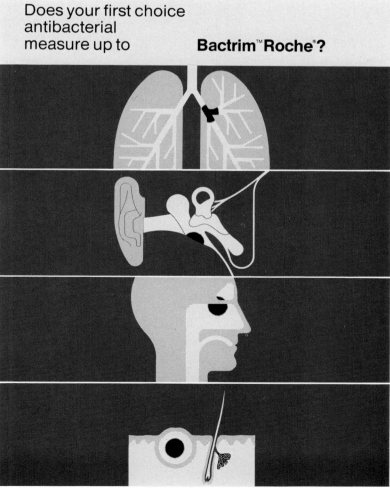

Does your first choice antibacterial measure up to **Bactrim™Roche®?**

154

155–158 As a self-promotion piece, Gordon Mortensen sent nine envelopes at one day intervals to prospective clients, each envelope containing one part of the illustration (Figs. 157, 158) and one chapter from a dime novel type mystery (Fig. 155) until the client knew who and what his company does. Fig. 156 shows the complete illustration of the whole mystery put together in poster form. (USA)
159, 160 Cover and inside spread of a small-format self-promotional brochure by *Pentagram*. (GBR)
161 Call for entries for the annual *Laus* competition. (SPA)

155–158 Gordon Mortensen schickte angehenden Kunden während 9 Tagen einen Briefumschlag, am 10. eine Kartonrolle. Die Umschläge enthielten jeder einen Teil einer Illustration (157, 158) und ein Kapitel einer als Groschen-Roman aufgemachten Kriminalgeschichte (155), die langsam das Geheimnis lüftete: eine gekonnte Eigenwerbungskampagne. Abb. 156: vollständiges Blatt. (USA)
159, 160 Umschlag und Innenseite einer kleinformatigen Eigenwerbungsbroschüre von *Pentagram* mit Beispielen von Finger-Fadenspielen. (GBR)
161 Einladung zur Unterbreitung von Arbeiten für den jährlichen Wettbewerb von *Laus*. (SPA)

155–158 Pendant neuf jours de suite, Gordon Mortensen adressait des enveloppes à ses clients futurs, le dixième jour c'était une tube qu'ils recevaient. Chacune des enveloppes contenait une partie d'une illustration (157, 158) qui dévoilait pas à pas le secret: il s'agissait d'une campagne autopromotionnelle très originale. Fig. 156: feuille complète. (USA)
159, 160 Couverture et page intérieure d'une petite brochure autopromotionnelle de *Pentagram* avec plusieurs exemples de jeux à ficelles. (GBR)
161 Invitation à soumettre des travaux pour le concours annuel de *Laus*. (SPA)

155

156

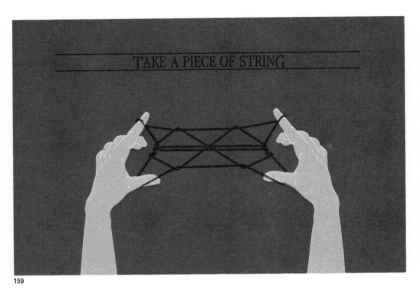

159

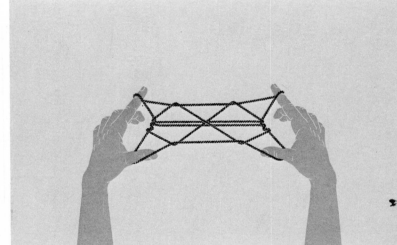

160

Booklets/Prospekte/Brochures

161

74

ARTIST / KÜNSTLER / ARTISTE:

155–158 Charles Shields/Eraldo Carugati/
Ed Soyka/Christine Mortensen/John Lykes/
Franz Altschuler/Ignacio Gomez/
Jösef Sumichrast/Roger Huyssen/
V. Courtlandt Johnson/Barrie Schwortz (Photo)
159, 160 David Penney
161 Ferrándiz

DESIGNER / GESTALTER / MAQUETTISTE:

155–158 Gordon Mortensen
159, 160 David Hillman/Nancy Williams

ART DIRECTOR / DIRECTEUR ARTISTIQUE:

155–158 Gordon Mortensen

AGENCY / AGENTUR / AGENCE – STUDIO:

155–158 Mortensen Design
159, 160 Pentagram

157

158

162

163

164

ARTIST / KÜNSTLER / ARTISTE:

162, 163 Norman Green
164 K. Endrikat AG
165 Charles White
166 Bruce Mau

DESIGNER / GESTALTER / MAQUETTISTE:

162, 163 Norman Green
164 K. Endrikat AG
166 Bruce Mau

ART DIRECTOR / DIRECTEUR ARTISTIQUE:

162, 163 Norman Green
164 K. Endrikat AG
166 Bruce Mau

AGENCY / AGENTUR / AGENCE – STUDIO:

162, 163 Jerry Anton Associates
164 K. Endrikat AG
165 Willardson & White, Inc.
166 Fifty Fingers Inc.

Booklets/Prospekte/Brochures

162, 163 Examples from a series of self-promotional cards by the illustrator Norman Green. In shades of green and orange. (USA)
164 Opened, large-format greetings card of the printers *Gebr. Achilles*. (GER)
165 Charles White III's self promotion. Illustration in dark colours. (USA)
166 First spread from a self-promotional brochure by the *Fifty Fingers* agency. The illustration symbolizes the studio's work. (USA)

162, 163 «Die Gemüse-Frauen.» Beispiele aus einer Serie von Eigenwerbungskarten des Illustrators Norman Green. In Grün-, resp. Orangetönen. (USA)
164 Geöffnete, grossformatige Glückwunschkarte der Druckerei *Gebr. Achilles*. (GER)
165 Dieser Humpty-Dumpty wird von Charles White III als Eigenwerbung verschickt. Illustration in dunklen Farbtönen. (USA)
166 Erste Seite aus einer Eigenwerbungsbroschüre der Agentur *Fifty Fingers*. Die Illustration soll die Arbeit des Studios symbolisieren, das die einzelnen Teile einer Werbekampagne oder einer Image Werbung sorgfältig zusammenbaut. (USA)

162, 163 «Les femmes-légumes.» Exemples d'une série de cartes autopromotionnelles de l'illustrateur Norman Green. En tons verts, resp. orange. (USA)
164 Carte de vœux à grand format d'une imprimerie. (GER)
165 Carte autopromotionnelle de Charles White III avec une illustration de Humpty-Dumpty. En tons foncés. (USA)
166 Première page d'une brochure autopromotionnelle de l'agence publicitaire *Fifty Fingers*. L'illustration devrait symboliser le travail du studio qui «monte» soigneusement les «pièces» d'une campagne publicitaire ou d'un programme global de marque. (USA)

165

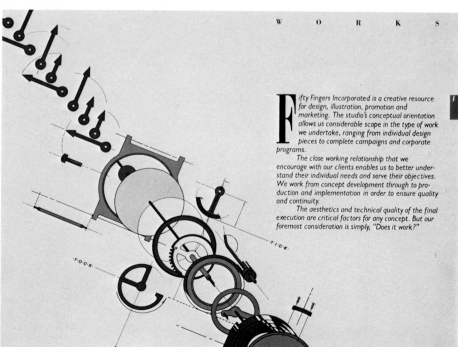

W O R K S

Fifty Fingers Incorporated is a creative resource for design, illustration, promotion and marketing. The studio's conceptual orientation allows us considerable scope in the type of work we undertake, ranging from individual design pieces to complete campaigns and corporate programs.

The close working relationship that we encourage with our clients enables us to better understand their individual needs and serve their objectives. We work from concept development through to production and implementation in order to ensure quality and continuity.

The aesthetics and technical quality of the final execution are critical factors for any concept. But our foremost consideration is simply, "Does it work?"

166

ARTIST / KÜNSTLER / ARTISTE:

167 Charles Goslin
168 Braldt Bralds
169, 170 Bob Matthijsen
171 Steve Jenkins

DESIGNER / GESTALTER / MAQUETTISTE:

167 Charles Goslin
168 Manfred Riediger
169, 170 Bob Matthijsen
171 Steve Jenkins

167 Cover of a brochure distributed by Charles Goslin for self-promotional purposes. Grey illustration. (USA)
168 Space promotion of the magazine *Mein schöner Garten* (My lovely garden) addressed to potential advertisers and illustrated by famous artists. In full colour. (GER)
169, 170 Pink pig on the recto of a greetings card that *Theo Bauwens,* ham specialists in Holland, sent for the New Year. His business has been running for four years. (NLD)
171 Inside spread of a self-promotional brochure by the designer Steve Jenkins. Offset and silkscreen. (USA)

167 Titelbild einer Broschüre, die Charles Goslin als Eigenwerbung verschickte. Illustration in Grautönen. (USA)
168 Die Zeitschrift *Mein schöner Garten* wirbt mit berühmten Künstlern bei potentiellen Inserenten. Mehrfarbige Illustration. (GER)
169, 170 «Ausgezogenes» und «zusammengefaltetes» rosa Schwein auf der Vorderseite einer Glückwunschkarte, die ein holländischer Schinkenproduzent zum Neuen Jahr verschickte. Sein Geschäft besteht seit vier Jahren. (NLD)
171 Innenseite einer Eigenwerbungsbroschüre eines Designers. Gedruckt in Offset und Siebdruck. (USA)

167 Couverture d'une brochure autopromotionnelle de Charles Goslin. Illustration en tons gris. (USA)
168 Le magazine *Mein schöner Garten* (Mon beau jardin) fait de la publicité autopromotionnelle avec des artistes célèbres. En polychromie. (GER)
169, 170 Cochon rose «déplié» et «plié» sur une carte de vœux d'un producteur hollandais de jambon. (NLD)
171 Page intérieure d'une brochure autopromotionnelle d'un graphiste. Imprimée en offset et en sérigraphie. (USA)

167

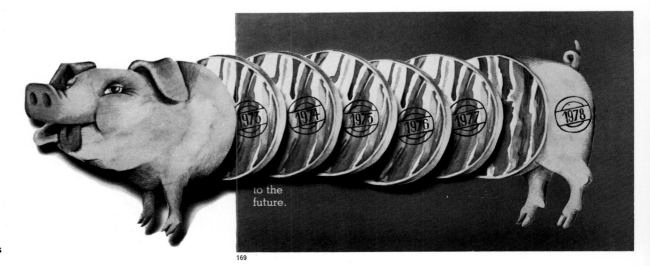

169

Booklets/Prospekte/Brochures

»MEIN SCHÖNER GARTEN«
IST DAS PARADIES FÜR IHRE WERBUNG
Ihre Anzeigenwerbung fällt auf fruchtbaren Boden
in diesem natürlichen Umfeld, dieser Welt der Natur-
und Gartenfreunde und ihrer positiven Grundein-
stellung zu allen schönen und praktischen Dingen des
Lebens. ——— Da befruchtet die Zeitschriften-Umwelt,
das Interesse an der Werbung, am besten natürlich,
wenn Ihre Anzeigen mediengerecht angelegt sind:
als ein natürlicher Teil von »Mein schöner Garten«.

168

ART DIRECTOR / DIRECTEUR ARTISTIQUE:

167 Charles Goslin
168 Robert Pütz
169, 170 Bob Matthijsen
171 Steve Jenkins

AGENCY / AGENTUR / AGENCE – STUDIO:

168 Robert Pütz GmbH & Co.
169, 170 BM Graphic Design
171 Steve Jenkins

170

171

172

173

172 Recto of a folder for a *Space* system – the computerized packaging evaluation service of the Container Corporation of America. Lilac dots, ground in blue turning into white. (USA)

173 Cover of an Indiana Credit Union League annual with addresses of credit institutions in the state of Indiana. Their services are as numerous as the patches on the quilt. (USA)

174 Title spread of a report analysing the characteristics of *Fortune* subscribers. Light and dark blue chequered ground, white lettering. (USA)

175, 176 "The world's games of chance" is the title of this small cultural history about such games, published by a German lottery organization. Fig. 175: Games of dice: painting by J. G. Edlinger and game of fox and geese; Fig. 176: Miniature of manuscript by Alfons der Weise. (GER)

177–179 Cover in the rich yellow company colours and double spreads from the railway guide of the Dutch National Railways. (NLD)

180 For a new model of an IBM computer. Yellow, green, blue, red and beige. (USA)

172 Vorderseite eines Faltprospektes für ein neues System, das elektronisch die geeignetste Verpackungsart (Grösse, Material etc) austüftelt. Lila Punkte, Grund blau in Weiss auslaufend. (USA)

173 Umschlag eines Jahrbuches mit Adressen von Kreditinstituten im Staate Indiana. Ihre Dienstleistungen sind so verschieden, wie die einzelnen Teile des abgebildeten Quilts. (USA)

174 Titelblatt eines Berichts, der die Eigenschaften der *Fortune*-Abonnenten analysiert. Dunkel- und hellblau karrierter Grund, weisse Schrift. (USA.)

175, 176 «Glücksspiele der Welt» ist der Titel dieser kleinen Kulturgeschichte des Glücksspiels, die von Nordwestlotto in Nordrhein-Westfalen herausgegeben wurde. Abb. 175: Würfelspiele: Gemälde von J. G. Edlinger und Gänsespiel; Abb. 176: Miniatur aus der Handschrift Alfons des Weisen. (GER)

177–179 Umschlag (tiefgelber Grund: Hausfarbe) und Doppelseiten aus dem Kursbuch der Niederländischen Staatsbahnen mit Liste der Bahnhöfe, Informationen und Erklärungen der Piktogramme. (NLD)

180 Für ein neues Computer-Modell von IBM. Gelb, Grün, Blau, Rot und Beige. (USA)

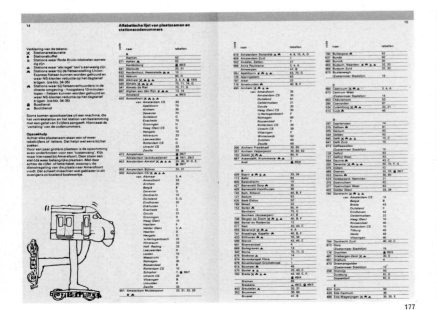

177

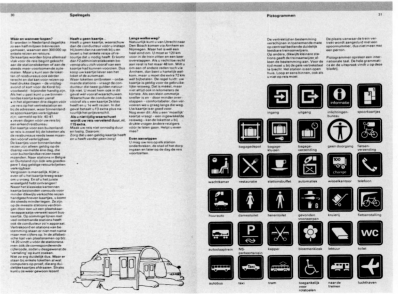

178

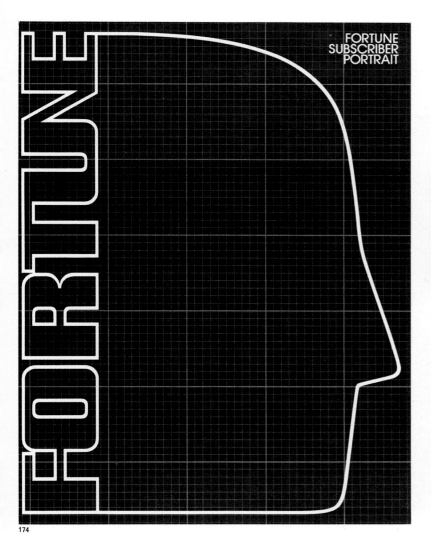

174

175

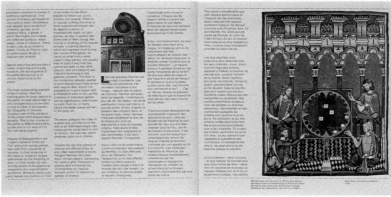

176

172 Couverture d'un dépliant pour un nouveau système électronique permettant de calculer en un tourne-main l'emballage le plus approprié pour n'importe quel produit. (USA)
173 Couverture d'une publication annuelle contenant les adresses des banques de crédit de l'Indiana. Leurs services sont aussi diversifiés que les dessins du quilt. (USA)
174 Couverture d'une analyse des caractéristiques des abonnés du magazine *Fortune*. Fond carré en bleu foncé et bleu clair, typographie blanche. (USA)
175, 176 D'une petite histoire culturelle intitulée «Les jeux de hasard dans le monde» et publiée par la lotterie de la Rhénanie-du-Nord-Westphalie. Fig. 175: Les jeux de dé: peinture de J. G. Edlinger et jeu de l'oie; fig. 176: miniature d'un manuscrit d'Alphonse le Sage. (GER)
177–179 Couverture (jaune foncé: couleur type) et pages doubles de l'indicateur des Chemins de fer Néerlandais avec liste des gares, renseignements généraux et explications des pictogrammes. (NLD)
180 Pour un nouveau modèle d'un ordinateur IBM. Jaune, vert, bleu, rouge et beige. (USA)

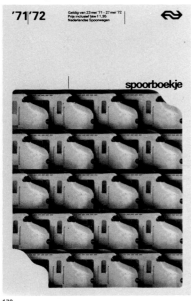

179

ARTIST / KÜNSTLER / ARTISTE:

172 Jim Matusik
173 Jemerson
174 Joseph Argenziano

DESIGNER / GESTALTER / MAQUETTISTE:

172 Jeff Barnes
173 Jemerson
174 Richard Walukanis
175, 176 Hans-Jürgen Rau
177–179 Tel Design
180 Bob Salpeter

ART DIRECTOR / DIRECTEUR ARTISTIQUE:

172 Jeff Barnes
173 Jemerson
174 Richard Walukanis
175, 176 Hans-Jürgen Rau
177–179 S. Wijsenbeek
180 Bob Salpeter

AGENCY / AGENTUR / AGENCE – STUDIO:

172 CCA Communications
175, 176 Studio Rau
180 Bob Salpeter, Inc.

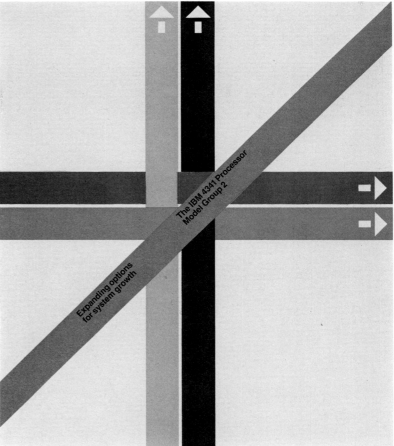

180

181

ARTIST / KÜNSTLER / ARTISTE:

181 Elwyn Mehlman/Bob Grigg
182, 183 Richard Mantel/Push Pin Studios
184 Joe Salina
185 Lisbeth Lindgren
186 Rodica Prato

DESIGNER / GESTALTER / MAQUETTISTE:

181 Petter Thoen
182, 183 Donette Reil/Wes Keebler
184 David Menear
186 Ira Teichberg

182

183

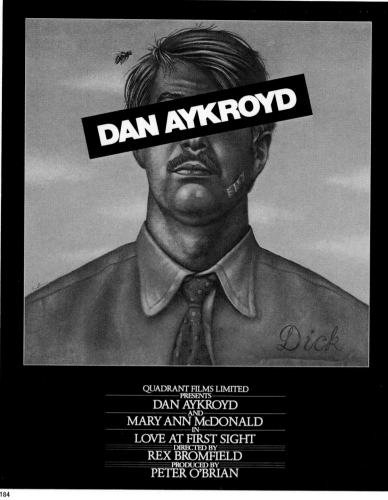

Booklets/Prospekte/Brochures

ART DIRECTOR / DIRECTEUR ARTISTIQUE:

181 Petter Thoen
182, 183 Donette Reil/Wes Keebler
184 David Menear
185 Marita Anderson
186 Lou Dorfsman/Ira Teichberg

AGENCY / AGENTUR / AGENCE – STUDIO:

181 Dancer Fitzgerald Sample
182, 183 Webb Silberg Companies
184 Momentum Design
185 Reklamteam AB
186 CBS/Broadcast Group

181 Double spread from a brochure for *Premiere,* a Californian TV station using the cable system. (USA)
182, 183 Two black-and-white illustrations from a Reinsurance Facilities Corp. brochure dealing with "Definitive statements" and "Opening new business opportunities". (USA)
184 Quadrant Films Ltd. advertises the film *Love at first sight.* (CAN)
185 Catalogue for *Lee* jeans sent to jeans shops. Olive-green jeans suit. (SWE)
186 Folder for CBS agents about television commercials and the target public. (USA)

181 Doppelseite aus der Broschüre einer kalifornischen TV-Station, die vor allem Filme von amerikanischen Filmstudios und Theateraufführungen über Kabel-Fernsehen anbietet. (USA)
182, 183 Zwei Schwarzweiss-Illustrationen aus der Broschüre einer Rückversicherungs-Anstalt, hier zu den Themen definitive Abschlüsse und neue Geschäftsmöglichkeiten. (USA)
184 Eine Film-Vertriebsgesellschaft bietet den Film *Liebe auf den ersten Blick* an. (CAN)
185 An Jeans-Geschäfte versandter Katalog für *Lee*-Jeans. Olivegrüner Jeansanzug. (SWE)
186 Mappe für CBS-Aquisiteure über Fernseh-Werbespots und Zielpublikum. (USA)

181 Page double de la brochure d'une station TV californienne annonçant un vast programme de films américains et de représentations de théâtre par télédistribution. (USA)
182, 183 Deux illustrations noir-blanc extraites de la brochure d'une compagnie de réassurance, intitulées «détermination définitive» et «entamer de nouvelles relations commerciales.». (USA)
184 Une société de distribution de films offre le film *Le coup de foudre.* (CAN)
185 Catalogue de la nouvelle collection de jeans *Lee,* distribué aux magasins. Vert olive. (SWE)
186 Documentation pour les agents de CBS sur la publicité télévisée et le public visé. (USA)

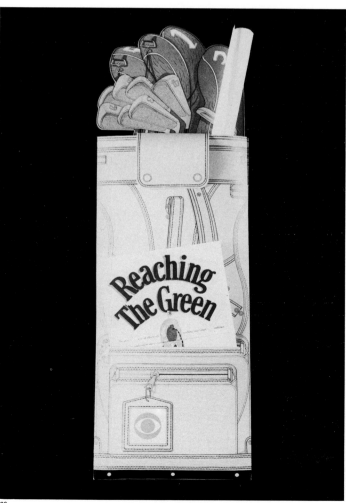

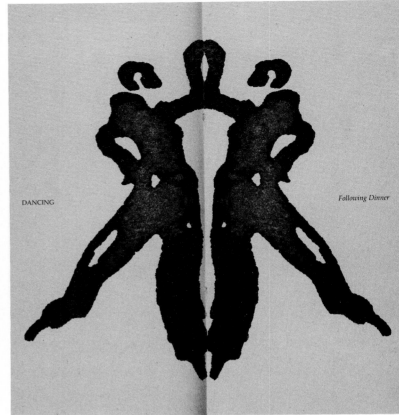

MUSIC   *By Kal Kalloday*

187

DANCING   *Following Dinner*

188

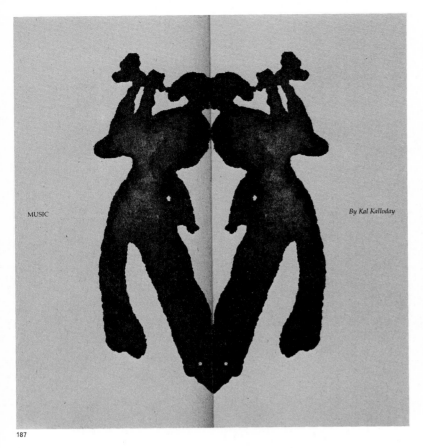

189

190

187, 188 Small-format invitation brochure for a dinner organized by the Mental Health Association of Texas in honour of a professor. (USA)
189, 190 Invitation issued by the Columbus Society of Communicating Arts. Red and yellow. (USA)
191, 192 The *Escher Wyss* machine factory presents a company portrait for its 125th anniversary. (SWI)
193 Invitation to an exhibition of Heinz Jost's theatre posters. In black and white. (SWI)
194 Invitation of the *Bobst* machine factory to an open-house day. In full colour. (SWI)

187, 188 Kleinformatige Broschüre als Einladung zu einem Diner, das von einer Nervenheilanstalt zu Ehren eines Professors organisiert wurde. Die Illustrationen erinnern an den Rorschach-Test. (USA)
189, 190 Einladung zu einem Meeting einer Gesellschaft für Kommunikationsgraphik. Rot/Gelb. (USA)
191, 192 Die Maschinenfabrik *Escher Wyss* zeigt ein Firmenporträt zum 125jährigen Bestehen. (SWI)
193 Einladung zu einer Ausstellung der Theaterplakate von Heinz Jost. Schwarzweiss. (SWI)
194 Einladung zu einem Tag der offenen Tür bei der Maschinenfabrik *Bobst*. Mehrfarbig. (SWI)

187, 188 Petite brochure servant d'invitation à un dîner organisé par une clinique psychiatrique en honneur d'un professeur. Les illustrations rappellent le test de Rorschach. (USA)
189, 190 Invitation à la réunion d'une société de communication graphique. Rouge et jaune. (USA)
191, 192 *Escher Wyss,* important atelier de constructions mécaniques, présente une rétrospective, en coopération avec la ville de Zurich, à l'occasion de son 125e anniversaire. (SWI)
193 Invitation à l'exposition des affiches de théâtre de Heinz Jost. En noir et blanc. (SWI)
194 Invitation à la journée des portes ouvertes des Usines Bobst SA. En polychromie. (SWI)

ARTIST / KÜNSTLER / ARTISTE:

187, 188 Terry Widener
191, 192 Herbert Leupin
193 Heinz Jost
194 Béat Brüsch

DESIGNER / GESTALTER / MAQUETTISTE:

187, 188 Steve Gibbs
189, 190 Mark Ulrich
193 Heinz Jost
194 Béat Brüsch

ART DIRECTOR / DIRECTEUR ARTISTIQUE:

187, 188 Steve Gibbs
189, 190 Mark Ulrich
191, 192 Rainer Stahel
194 J.-H. Francfort

Booklets/Prospekte/Brochures

AGENCY / AGENTUR / AGENCE – STUDIO:

187, 188 The Richards Group
189, 190 Salvato & Coe
194 Béat Brüsch

175 JAHRE
ESCHER WYSS
ZÜRICH

Ausstellung im Stadthaus Zürich

191

192

HEINZ JOST
Theaterplakate
Eine Ausstellung
im Personalrestaurant
von Radio Bern
Schwarztorstrasse 21
Bern Oktober 1980

193

BOBST
PORTES OUVERTES
25 & 26 OCTOBRE
1980

194

195

197

196

199

195 Catalogue of an exhibition of American colour photography shown on the occasion of American cultural weeks in Porto. (POR)
196 Cover of a publication of an organization of evangelical journalists entitled "The message as poster. The poster as message". (GER)
197–200 From a small publication realized on the occasion of the E. A. Poe Festival at the University of Maryland. Printed in dark blue on beige paper. (USA)
201 Greetings card of the Zurich school and museum of arts and crafts. (SWI)

195 Katalog zu einer Ausstellung über amerikanische Farbphotographie, die im Rahmen amerikanischer Kulturwochen in Porto veranstaltet wurde. (POR)
196 Titelblatt einer Publikation des Gemeinschaftswerks evang. Publizistik mit dem Titel «Die Botschaft als Plakat. Das Plakat als Botschaft». (GER)
197–200 Aus einer kleinformatigen Publikation zum E. A. Poe Festival der Universität Maryland. Dunkelblau gedruckt auf beigem Papier. (USA)
201 Glückwunschkarte der Kunstgewerbeschule und des Kunstgewerbemuseums Zürich. Sie zeigt einen grossen Pfeil von oben nach unten, kleinere Pfeile von rechts nach links, sowie im Hochformat einen Kopf aus noch kleineren Pfeilen. (SWI)

195 Catalogue d'une exposition de la photographie couleur américaine, organisée dans le cadre des semaines culturelles américaines à Porto. (POR)
196 Couverture de la publication d'une organisation évangélique de journalisme sur l'interaction du message et de l'affiche. (GER)
197–200 Pages et doubles pages d'une petite publication pour un festival que l'Université du Maryland avait consacré à E. A. Poe. Bleu foncé sur beige. (USA)
201 Carte de vœux de l'Ecole des Arts et Métiers et du Musée des Arts Décoratifs de Zurich. Elle montre une grande flèche de haut en bas, plusieurs petites flèches de droit à gauche, ainsi qu'une tête en flèches (en verticale). (SWI)

The Westminster Church was built in 1852 by The Presbytery of Baltimore on a cemetery known as The Western Burial Ground. The catacombs created by the construction are now thought to hold as many as two thousand tombs. The graveyard, founded in 1792, is perhaps best known as the burial place of Edgar Allan Poe. The church housed an active congregation until 1977.

A committee of interested Marylanders has been formed in conjunction with The University of Maryland School of Law to guide the efforts to restore and preserve this important landmark. The committee, The Westminster Preservation Trust, is a private non-profit corporation bringing together individuals willing to work toward the restoration and adaptive use of the building.

198

He was discovered semi-conscious outside a polling place on East Lombard Street and taken to what is now Church Home and Hospital. There he died on October 7, 1849 without recovering sufficiently to explain what had happened to him. There is no evidence to indicate that Poe was a drug addict, but apparently he had little tolerance for alcohol. This weakness may have contributed to his death.

200

ARTIST / KÜNSTLER / ARTISTE:

195 João Machado
197–200 Jerry Dadds/Gary Yealdhall/
Cameron Gerlach/Nancy Urbanski/
Richard Waldrep

DESIGNER / GESTALTER / MAQUETTISTE:

195 João Machado
196 Peter v. Kornatzki
197–200 Jerry Dadds
201 Emilio Paroni

ART DIRECTOR / DIRECTEUR ARTISTIQUE:

195 João Machado
197–200 Jerry Dadds

AGENCY / AGENTUR / AGENCE – STUDIO:

197–200 Eucalyptus Tree Studio

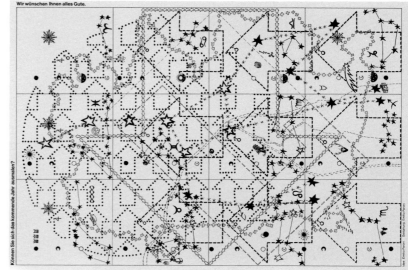

201

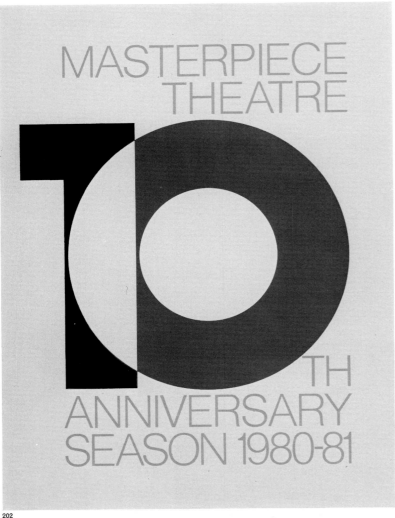

202

ARTIST / KÜNSTLER / ARTISTE:

203 Béat Brüsch
204 Kenzo Nakagawa/Norio Innami (Photo)
208 Geoffrey Moss

DESIGNER / GESTALTER / MAQUETTISTE:

202 Ivan Chermayeff
203 Béat Brüsch
204 Kenzo Nakagawa/Satch Morikami
205 V. Barl/W. Slansky
206, 207 Jean Widmer

203

ART DIRECTOR / DIRECTEUR ARTISTIQUE:

202 Ivan Chermayeff
204 Kenzo Nakagawa
205 V. Barl/W. Slansky
208 Melanie Roher

AGENCY / AGENTUR / AGENCE – STUDIO:

202 Chermayeff & Geismar Assoc.
203 Béat Brüsch
204 Nippon Design Center
208 Melanie Roher Design

204

205

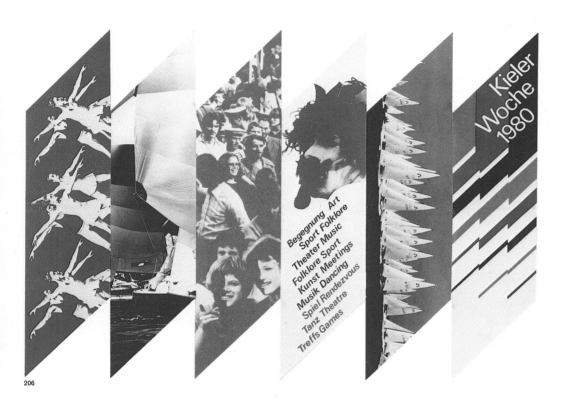

206

207

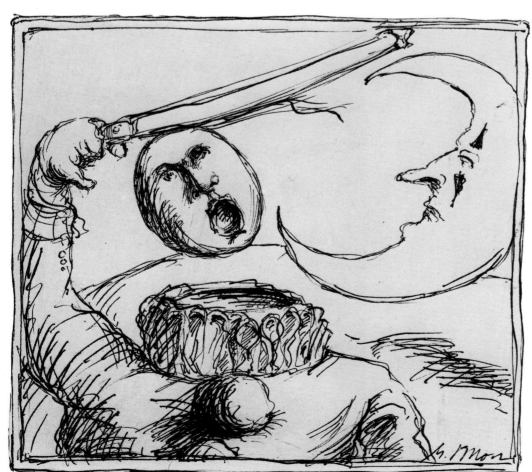

208

Booklets/Prospekte/Brochures

202 Press kit for the 10th anniversary of the *Masterpiece Theatre*. "10" in blue and red, light grey lettering. (USA)
203 Invitation to an exhibition of work by Beat Brüsch. Light green and pink dash of colour painted by hand. (SWI)
204 Opened folder for the Kyoto fair. Full-colour objects on red, gold and blue. (JPN)
205 Double spread from a brochure for the 75th anniversary of the design department at the Niederrhein University. (GER)
206, 207 Programme for the 1980 Kiel Week. (GER)
208 Cover illustration of the catalogue for the "Pierrot Lunaire" exhibition at the Guggenheim Museum, New York. (USA)

202 Pressemappe zum 10jährigen Jubiläum des *Masterpiece Theatre*. «10» in Blau und Rot, hellgraue Schrift. (USA)
203 Einladung zu einer Ausstellung von Werken von Beat Brüsch. Hellgrüner und rosa Farbstrich von Hand gemalt. (SWI)
204 Geöffneter Faltprospekt für die Messe in Kyoto. Mehrfarbige Gegenstände auf Rot, Gold und Blau. (JPN)
205 Doppelseite aus einer Broschüre, die zum 75jährigen Jubiläum des Fachbereichs Design der Fachhochschule Niederrhein in Krefeld erschien. (GER)
206, 207 Programm der Kieler Woche 1980. (GER)
208 Umschlagillustration des Katalogs zur Ausstellung «Pierrot Lunaire» im Guggenheim Museum in New York. (USA)

202 Documentation publiée à l'occasion des dix ans d'existence du *Masterpiece Theatre*. Chiffre en bleu et rouge. (USA)
203 Invitation à l'exposition de l'œuvre de Beat Brüsch. Traits en rose et vert pâle ajoutés à la main. (SWI)
204 Dépliant ouvert pour la foire de Kyoto. Objets polychromes sur des bandes en rouge, or et bleu. (JPN)
205 Page double d'une brochure publiée à l'occasion des 75 ans d'existence du département de design graphique de l'Université de Krefeld. (GER)
206, 207 Programme du festival de Kiel 1980. (GER)
208 Illustration de couverture du catalogue de l'exposition «Pierrot Lunaire» au Musée Guggenheim à New York. (USA)

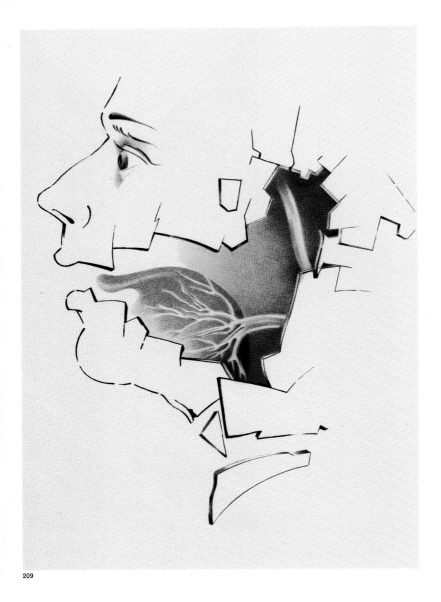

209

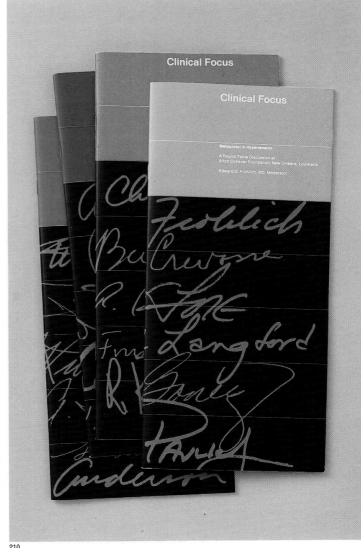

210

Booklets/Prospekte/Brochures

ARTIST / KÜNSTLER / ARTISTE:

209 Christian Lang
211 Cheryl Griesbach/Stanley Martucci
212 Roy Carruthers
213, 214 William Charmatz

209 Cover illustration of a prospectus from a series for *Tegretol* manufactured by *Geigy,* a medicament for the treatment of Trigeminus neuralgia and other spasmodic conditions. (SWI)
210 Series of publications for discussions in various hospitals about *Lopressor* by *Geigy,* a medicament for high blood pressure. Upper border in yellow, blue, red or green. (USA)
211 Illustration of a regularly printed publication about the sterile treatment of injuries. (USA)
212 Cover illustration for a booklet on *Benadryl* by *Parke-Davis,* a medicament for allergic colds. (USA)
213, 214 From a prospectus for *Magel,* a medicine for the treatment of digestive disorders. (USA)

209 Umschlagillustration eines Prospektes aus einer Serie für *Tegretol* von *Geigy,* ein Medikament zur Behandlung der Trigeminus-Neuralgie und anderer krampfartiger Zustände. (SWI)
210 Serie von einheitlich gestalteten Publikationen über Diskussionen an verschiedenen Krankenhäusern über *Lopressor* von *Ciba-Geigy,* ein Mittel gegen zu hohen Blutdruck. Oberer Rand in Gelb, Blau, Rot oder Grün, im unteren Teil finden sich die Unterschriften der Diskussionsteilnehmer. (USA)
211 Illustration einer regelmässig erscheinenden Publikation über keimfreie Wundbehandlung. (USA)
212 Umschlagillustration eines Prospektes für *Benadryl* gegen allergischen Schnupfen. (USA)
213, 214 Aus einem Prospekt für *Magel,* ein Mittel gegen Verdauungsstörungen. (USA)

209 Couverture d'un dépliant d'une série consacrée au *Tégrétol,* un médicament *Geigy* contre la névralgie du trijumeau et d'autres douleurs convulsives. (SWI)
210 D'une série de publications de conception uniforme consacrées à des discussions tenues dans divers hôpitaux sur *Lopressor* de *Ciba-Geigy,* un médicament contre l'hypertension. En haut avec bande rouge, jaune, bleue ou verte, en bas avec les signatures des participants. (USA)
211 Illustration d'une publication régulière sur le soin aseptique de plaies. (USA)
212 Illustration de couverture d'un dépliant pour un médicament conre la rhinite allergique. (USA)
213, 214 Pour les comprimés et la suspension *Magel* combattant l'indigestion. (USA)

212

211

DESIGNER / GESTALTER / MAQUETTISTE:

209 Christian Lang
210 Bob Paganucci
211 Cheryl Griesbach/Stanley Martucci
212 Jim McFarland
213, 214 Fred Acker

ART DIRECTOR / DIRECTEUR ARTISTIQUE:

209 Christian Lang
210 Bob Paganucci
211 Robert Derling
212 Jim McFarland
213, 214 Fred Acker

AGENCY / AGENTUR / AGENCE – STUDIO:

209 Ciba-Geigy/Zentrale Werbung
210 Bob Paganucci
211 J. R. Druid Assoc.
212 Sudler & Hennesey, Inc.
213, 214 Acker Design

firefighter...

213

214

215

216

215, 216 Teil der Illustration und Doppelseite aus dem grosszügig aufgemachten Saison-Programmheft der Canadian Opera Company, hier zur Oper *Norma* von Vincenzo Bellini. (CAN)
217 Umschlag des Katalogs zur Ausstellung «Besucher in Arizona 1846–1980», an welcher Werke von Malern gezeigt werden, die Arizona während diesen Jahren besucht haben. Mehrfarbig. (USA)
218 Aus dem Programm des Kunstfestivals in State College, PA, hier zu den Ausstellungen. (USA)
219–222 Aus dem Katalog zur Mailänder Ausstellung über Majakowski, Meyerhold und Stanislawski, die unter Mitwirkung des sowjetrussischen Kultusministeriums zusammengestellt wurde. (ITA)

215, 216 Part of the illustration and double spread from a generously conceived seasonal programme of the Canadian Opera Company, here for the opera *Norma* composed by Vincenzo Bellini. (CAN)
217 Cover of the catalogue for the exhibition "Visitors to Arizona 1846–1980" at the Phoenix Art Museum. Shown are works by painters who visited Arizona during this period. In full colour. (USA)
218 From the programme for exhibitions at the Central Pennsylvania Festival of the Arts. (USA)
219–222 From the catalogue of the Milan exhibition about Mayakovski, Meyerhold and Stanislavski, prepared with the co-operation of the Russian Ministry of Culture. (ITA)

215, 216 Partie de l'illustration et page double du programme-souvenir luxueux de la Canadian Opera Company, ici pour l'opéra *Norma* de Vincenzo Bellini. (CAN)
217 Couverture du catalogue de l'exposition «Visiteurs de l'Arizona 1846–1980». On y présente des œuvres des artistes ayant visité cette région pendant cette période. En polychromie. (USA)
218 Du programme du festival des arts de State College en Pennsylvanie. (USA)
219–222 Du catalogue d'une exposition consacrée à Maïakovski, Meyerhold et Stanislavski, organisée à Milan avec le concours du Ministère soviétique de la Culture. (ITA)

Visitors to Arizona 1846 to 1980

217

218

ARTIST / KÜNSTLER / ARTISTE:

215, 216 Miro Malish
217 David Hockney
218 Lanny Sommese
219–222 V. P. Kiselëv

DESIGNER / GESTALTER / MAQUETTISTE:

215, 216 Louis Fishauf
217 Larry Yang/Kurt Gibson
218 Lanny Sommese
219–222 Bruno Monguzzi

ART DIRECTOR / DIRECTEUR ARTISTIQUE:

215, 216 Louis Fishauf
218 Lanny Sommese
219–222 Roberto Sambonet/Bruno Monguzzi

AGENCY / AGENTUR / AGENCE – STUDIO:

217 IBM Design Center
218 Lanny Sommese Design
219–222 Studio Sambonet

Booklets/Prospekte/Brochures

219

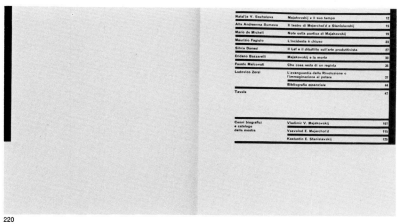

220

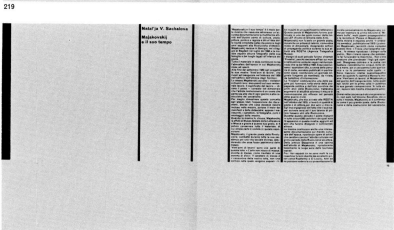

221

222

SCHAUSPIEL IM ZDF 1981
ÖDIPUS DER STURM EIN
MITTSOMMERNACHTSTRAUM
DER MENSCHENFEIND
DIE WILDENTE TORQUATO
TASSO LIEBER GEORG DER
WELTVERBESSERER
DIE LOKOMOTIVE
VARIATIONEN DAS
KLEINE HOTEL
PYGMALION DIE LIEBEN
KINDER LIEBLING, ICH
LASS MICH SCHEIDEN
DER SCHÜTZLING

223

Niki de Saint Phalle
Retrospektive

224

KÜNSTLER GESELL-
SCHAFT

225

FOLK- & VOLKS-
STÜCKE

226

227

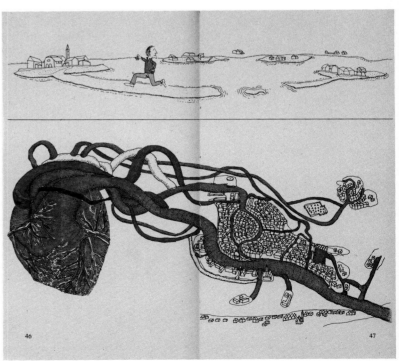

228

94

ARTIST / KÜNSTLER / ARTISTE:

227–229 Pietro Ricca
230 K. Endrikat AG

DESIGNER / GESTALTER / MAQUETTISTE:

223, 225, 226 Christof Gassner
224 Helmut M. Schmittsiegel/
Gisela Büchelmaier
230 K. Endrikat AG

ART DIRECTOR / DIRECTEUR ARTISTIQUE:

224 Helmut M. Schmittsiegel
230 K. Endrikat AG

AGENCY / AGENTUR / AGENCE – STUDIO:

224 Institut für Communication
230 K. Endrikat AG

223, 225, 226 From the programme publication "Plays on the ZDF 1981", the second channel of German Television. Cover in black and white and gold; the double spreads introduce texts and brief information on the plays put together under these headings. (GER)
224 Catalogue for a retrospective of the works of Niki de Saint Phalle, shown in West Germany and Austria. In bright colours. (GER)
227–229 Illustrations from a tourist guide for Venice, here about Venice's problems, its monuments and its gods. (ITA)
230 This catalogue reviews the last decade at the New Gallery— Ludwig Collection in Aachen. (GER)

223, 225, 226 Aus dem Programmheft «Schauspiel im ZDF 1981» des Zweiten Deutschen Fernsehens. Titelblatt in Schwarzweiss und Gold; die Doppelseiten leiten jeweils kurze Inhaltsangaben über die Stücke ein, die unter diesem Titel zusammengefasst wurden. (GER)
224 Katalog für eine in der Bundesrepublik und Österreich gezeigte retrospektive Werkschau von Niki de Saint Phalle. Bunte Farben. (GER)
227–229 Illustrationen aus einem Fremdenführer über Venedig, hier über Venedigs Probleme, seine Steine und seine Götter. (ITA)
230 Der Katalog bringt einen Rückblick über die letzten 10 Jahre der Neuen Galerie – Sammlung Ludwig in Aachen. (GER)

223, 225, 226 Extraits du programmes des représentations de théâtre par la deuxième chaîne de la TV allemande. Couverture en noir-blanc et or; les pages doubles introduisent des comptes rendus des pièces réunies sous cette catégorie. (GER)
224 Catalogue pour une exposition rétrospective de l'œuvre de Niki de Saint Phalle présentée en Allemagne fédérale et en Autriche. (GER)
227–229 Illustrations figurant dans un guide de Venise, ici sur les problèmes de la ville, ses pierres et ses saints. (ITA)
230 Ce catalogue présente une rétrospective des dernières dix années d'une galerie et collection d'Aix-la-Chapelle. (GER)

230

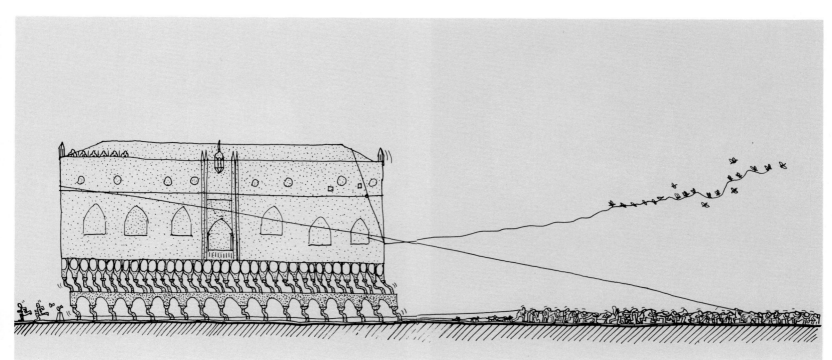

229

231

232

233

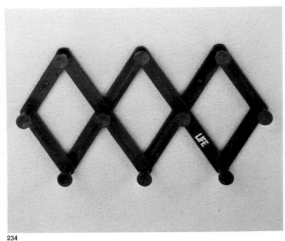

234

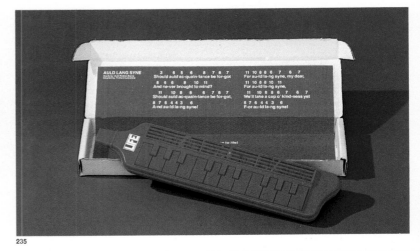

235

236

237

LIFE Direct Mailings
LIFE Direktwerbung
LIFE Publicité directe

238

DESIGNER / GESTALTER / MAQUETTISTE:

231–240 Gilbert Lesser

ART DIRECTOR / DIRECTEUR ARTISTIQUE:

231–240 Gilbert Lesser

239

231–240 Examples from a series of advertising gimmicks that *Life* magazine sent to potential advertisers and which cover all possible and impossible occasions. Fig. 231: "A big kiss from *Life*" on Valentine's Day, a greeting sent in chocolate form; Fig. 232: a huge pencil that can be used to note certain pithy comments; Figs. 233, 234: a rack made out of red plastic, showing that in many ways its versatility is analogous to that of *Life* as a means of communicating advertising; Fig. 235: instrument as a New Year's greeting; Fig. 236: an invitation to a New Year's party in a restaurant called *The Underground*; Fig. 237: *Life* and the *J. Walter Thompson* advertising agency are "making a big splash": invitation to cruise the Chicago shoreline advertised with a straw hat; Fig. 238: "Something too hot to handle" – a Valentine dedicated to the hottest print advertising in the world, in other words for the art directors and copywriters who create it. Grill glove in the shape of a red heart; Fig. 239: chimes packed in a silver packing tube so that one can make a joyful noise – sent as holiday greetings from the *Life* team; Fig. 240: by means of this red rake, *Life* praises itself as a communicator of advertising in the food industry. The red brochure in the form of a menu gives details of advertising procedures, etc. (USA)

231–240 Beispiele aus einer Serie von Werbemitteln, welche die Zeitschrift *Life* zu allen möglichen und unmöglichen Anlässen an potentielle Inserenten verschickte. Abb. 231: «Einen herzlichen Kuss von *Life*» – zum Valentins-Tag wird ein süsser Gruss aus Schokolade verschickt; Abb. 232: überdimensionierter Bleistift für «einige spitze Bemerkungen»; Abb. 233, 234: Aufhängevorrichtung aus rotem Plastik, die ebenso vielseitig ist, wie *Life* als Werbeträger; Abb. 235: Melodika als Neujahrsgruss; Abb. 236: Einladung zu einer Silvester-Party im Restaurant *The Underground*; Abb. 237: *Life* und *J. W. Thompson* laden mit diesem Strohhut zu einer Boots-Party an den Gestaden Chicagos ein; Abb. 238: «Zu heiss um anzufassen.» Rotes Herz als Grillhandschuh für «heisse» Werbung am Valentins-Tag; Abb. 239: dieses in einer silbernen Kartonröhre verpackte Glockenspiel für «ein fröhliches Gebimmel» wurde von der *Life*-Equipe als Weihnachtsgruss verschickt; Abb. 240: mit dieser roten Raffel preist sich *Life* in der Nahrungsmittelbranche als Werbeträger an; die als Menue-Karte aufgemachte rote Broschüre enthält Angaben über Auflage, Leseranalysen, Redaktionsteam, Kaufgewohnheiten etc. (USA)

231–240 Exemples d'une série d'objets de publicité que le magazine *Life* distribue aux annonceurs éventuels chaque fois qu'une occasion se présente. Fig. 231: «Un grand baiser de *Life*» en chocolat pour le jour du Saint-Valentin; fig. 232: immense crayon pour «quelques remarques piquantes»; fig. 233, 234: support de plastique rouge qui sert à de mulitples fins, de même que *Life* sert de support de publicité à de multiples branches; fig. 235: instrument de musique apportant les bons vœux de Nouvel An; fig. 236: invitation à la fête du Saint-Sylvestre au restaurant *The Underground*; fig. 237: invitation à une croisière organisée par *Life* et l'agence *J. W. Thompson*; fig. 238: «Trop chaud pour tenir.» Gant molletonné en forme d'un cœur rouge pour la publicité «brûlante» du Saint-Valentin; fig. 239: pour un «joyeux tintement» à Noël, *Life* envoie ce jeux de cloches dans une tube en carton argenté; fig. 240: râpe rouge adressée aux annonceurs éventuels de l'industrie alimentaire; la petite brochure rouge, évoquant une carte des mets, contient des indications sur le tirage, la circulation, les collaborateurs, les abonnés, etc. (USA)

240

241

242

243

ARTIST / KÜNSTLER / ARTISTE:

241 Bill Farley
242 Robert Lerner
243 Bob Haberfield
244 Gerdi Mader

DESIGNER / GESTALTER / MAQUETTISTE:

241 C. W. Axon
242 Richard Rogers
243 Ken Cato
244 Mader's Design

ART DIRECTOR:

241 C. W. Axon
242 Jack Reich
243 Ken Cato
244 Kurt F. Steiner

AGENCY / AGENTUR / AGENCE:

241 Axon Garside & Co Ltd
242 Richard Rogers Inc.
243 Cato Hibberd Design Pty Ltd
244 PS-Marketing GmbH

241 Recto of a folder for a weapon performance recorder system made by *Ferranti*. (GBR)
242 Cover of a prospectus for an IBM electronic memory system. Ground in red and ruby-red, cubes in blue, green and white. (USA)
243 The illustration on the inside spread of a Pulp & Paper Mills folder shows The Banjo, a ballad singer. The other side is filled with information about postage stamps. (AUS)
244 Christmas card from a textile manufacturer. When the 24 miniature doors are opened, a "Happy Christmas" greetings appears. In full colour. (GER)

241 Vorderseite eines Faltprospektes für Computer-Systeme für Fernlenkwaffen. (GBR)
242 Titelblatt eines Prospektes für neue elektronische Speichersysteme von IBM. Grund in Rot und Weinrot, Kuben in Blau, Grün und Weiss. (USA)
243 Die Illustration auf der Innenseite des Faltprospektes einer Papierfabrik zeigt den Bänkelsänger The Banjo. Auf der Rückseite finden sich Informationen über Briefmarken. (AUS)
244 Weihnachtskarte des Stoffabrikanten *Zell-Schönau*. Wenn die 24 Türchen geöffnet sind, erscheint der Wunsch «Ein frohes Weihnachtsfest». Mehrfarbig. (GER)

241 Dépliant pour un nouveau système électronique de guidage par télécommande. (GBR)
242 Couverture d'un prospectus pour un nouveau système électronique de mémoire IBM. Fond en rouge et bordeaux, cubes en bleu, vert et blanc. (USA)
243 L'illustration à l'intérieur du dépliant d'une papeterie montre le chanteur des rues The Banjo. Au verso on trouve des informations et des illustrations de timbres australiennes. (AUS)
244 Carte de Noël d'un fabricant de textiles. Dès que les 24 portes sont ouvertes, le vœux «joyeux Noël» apparaît en allemand. En polychromie. (GER)

3

Magazine Covers
Magazine Illustrations
Newspaper Illustrations
Trade Magazines
House Organs
Corporate Publications
Annual Reports
Book Covers

Zeitschriften-Umschläge
Zeitschriften-Illustrationen
Zeitungs-Illustrationen
Fachzeitschriften
Hauszeitschriften
Firmenpublikationen
Jahresberichte
Buchumschläge

Couvertures de périodiques
Illustrations de périodiques
Illustrations de journaux
Revues professionnelles
Journaux d'entreprise
Publications d'entreprise
Rapports annuels
Couvertures de livres

245–247 Covers from various issues of the magazine *TV Guide*. The illustrations refer to a programme about situation comedies, a baseball series and how one can win with knowledge and a bit of cunning, and an article about the shooting of the film *Shogun*. The illustrations are in full colour. (USA)
248 Cover from an edition of the *Junior League Review* referring to an article about Pope John Paul's Asia tripentitled *Papal Pageantry comes to Asia*. (USA)
249 First edition of *Asiaweek*, a newly formed magazine, with an article about Pope John Paul's Asia tripentitled *Papal Pageantry comes to Asia*. Coloured stripes on a yellow ground. (HKG)
250 Cover from *New West* magazine, this edition being completely devoted to the subject of water. (USA)
251–254 Cover from a Sunday magazine for articles dealing with umpires at sports events, the terrifying experience some people have when making speeches, and Cleveland's leftists. (USA)

245–247 Titelblätter einer Fernsehzeitschrift. Die Illustrationen beziehen sich auf eine Sendung über Situationskomik, eine Serie über Baseball und wie man mit Können und Schlauheit gewinnen kann und einen Artikel über die Dreharbeiten des Films *Shogun*. Mehrfarbige Illustrationen. (USA)
248 Umschlag einer Ausgabe der Zeitschrift der Vereinigung von Jugendverbänden, hier zu einem Artikel über die Verbesserung der Situation des Kindes. (USA)
249 Erste Ausgabe der neugestalteten Zeitschrift *Asiaweek*, hier zu einem Artikel über die Asienreise von Papst Johannes Paul II. Farbige Streifen auf gelbem Grund. (HKG)
250 Titelblatt einer Ausgabe der Zeitschrift *New West*, die vollständig dem Thema Wasser gewidmet ist. (USA)
251–254 Titelblätter eines Sonntags-Magazins, hier zu Artikeln über den Schiedsrichter und die Publikumsreaktionen, das Halten von Reden und über Linksgruppierungen in Cleveland. (USA)

245–247 Couvertures d'un programme de TV. Les illustrations se réfèrent à une émission sur le comique de la situation, à une série sur le baseball et comment l'équipe peut gagner grâce au savoir-faire et à l'habileté, et enfin à un rapport sur le tournage du film *Shogun*. Illustrations polychromes. (USA)
248 Couverture d'un numéro du magazine des associations des unions de la jeunesse, ici avec référence à un article sur l'amélioration de la situation de l'enfant. (USA)
249 Premier numéro d'*Asiaweek*, dont la conception est entièrement nouvelle. L'illustration se rapporte à la visite du Pape Jean Paul II en Asie. Bandes polychromes sur fond jaune. (HKG)
250 Couverture d'un numéro du magazine *New West* qui est entièrement consacré au sujet de l'eau. (USA)
251–254 Couvertures d'un magazine dominical, ici sur l'arbitre et la réaction du public à l'égard de ses décisions, sur les discours qui énervent souvent les deux côtés et sur la gauche à Cleveland. (USA)

Magazine Covers
Zeitschriftenumschläge
Couvertures de périodiques

245

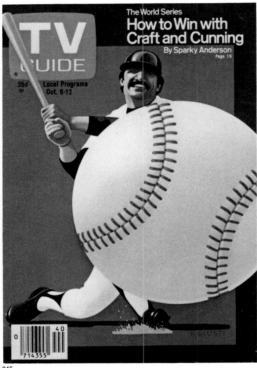

246

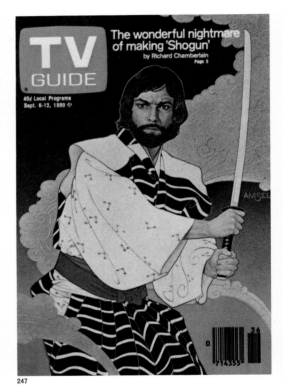

247

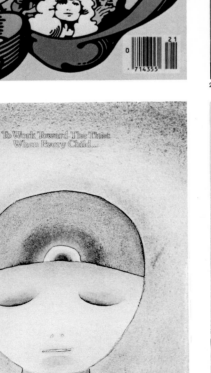

248

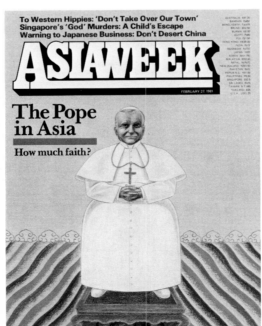

249

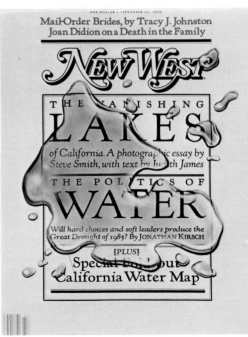

250

251

ARTIST / KÜNSTLER / ARTISTE:

245 Don Weller
246 Robert Giusti
247 Richard Amsel
248 Jean-Michel Folon
249 John Shramenko
250 Joe Heiner / Ed Scarisbrick
251, 252 Ray Domingo
253 Mary Lynn Blasutta
254 Mark Andresen

DESIGNER / GESTALTER / MAQUETTISTE:

245–247 Jerry Alten
248 Elaine Crawford
249 Henry Steiner
250 Mike Salisbury
251–254 Greg Paul

ART DIRECTOR / DIRECTEUR ARTISTIQUE:

245–247 Jerry Alten
248 Elaine Crawford
249 Henry Steiner
250 Roger Black
251–254 Greg Paul

AGENCY / AGENTUR / AGENCE – STUDIO:

249 Graphic Communication Ltd.
251–254 Greg Paul & Associates

PUBLISHER / VERLEGER / EDITEUR:

245–247 Triangle Publications Inc.
248 Association of Junior Leages, Inc.
249 Asiaweek Ltd.
250 Joe Gravitt Armstrong
251–254 Plain Dealer Publishing Co.

252

253

254

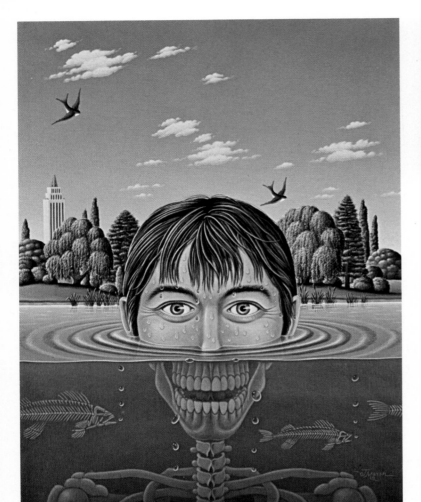

255

256

Magazine Covers
Zeitschriftenumschläge
Couvertures de périodiques

255–262 Covers of various issues of *Time* magazine. Figs. 255, 256: *The poisoning of America*—this article deals with the problem of poisonous industrial waste. Figs. 257, 258: *Who'll fight for America?*—article on the manpower crises in the American army. Fig. 259 refers to an article entitled *Storm over the Alliance*—cover story on the Carter Administration's open dismay over the lack of its allies' backing in the crises of the American hostages in Iran and the Soviet invasion in Afghanistan. The heading and the cover illustration allude to a famous Western by Zinneman. Fig. 260: article on one of Reagans election events in Detroit with an allusion to *Superman*. Fig. 261: for a preview of the film *The Empire Strikes Back!* Fig. 262: inquiry on Billy Carter's Libyan connections and the role the White House played in this affair. (USA)

255–262 Titelblätter von verschiedenen Ausgaben des Nachrichtenmagazins *Time.* Abb. 255, 256: «Wie Amerika vergiftet wird» bezieht sich auf einen Artikel über giftige Industrie-Abfälle. Abb. 257, 258: «Wer wird für Amerika kämpfen?» – Leitartikel über Rekrutierungsschwierigkeiten bei der Armee. Abb. 259: zu einem Artikel mit dem Titel «Sturm über der Allianz» – die Geiselaffäre im Iran und der russische Einmarsch in Afghanistan verschärften die Spannungen zwischen Amerika und seinen Alliierten. Schlagzeile und Umschlagillustration beziehen sich auf den Film *Zwölf Uhr mittags.* Abb. 260: Reportage über eine Wahlveranstaltung Reagans in Detroit mit dem Symbol von *Superman.* Abb. 261: zu einer Besprechung des Science-Fiction-Films *Das Imperium schlägt zurück.* Abb. 262: zu einer Untersuchung, ob Billy Carter im Auftrag des Weissen Hauses nach Libyen reiste. (USA)

255–262 Couvertures de divers numéros du magazine d'information *Time.* Fig. 255, 256: «L'empoisonnement de l'Amérique» se réfère à un article sur les déchets industriels toxiques; fig. 257, 258: «Qui va se battre pour l'Amérique?» – article de fond sur les difficultés dans la levée de troupes; fig. 259: pour un article intitulé «L'alliance est fortement scouée» – la prise d'ôtages en Iran et l'intervention soviétique en Afghanistan ont aggravé le désaccord entre les Etats-Unis et ses alliés. La manchette et l'illustration de couverture font allusion au film *Le train sifflera trois fois.* Fig. 260: manifestation électorale de Reagan à Detroit avec allusion au *Superman;* fig. 261: compte-rendu du film *L'empire contre-attaque;* fig. 262: enquête sur les voyages secrets de Billy Carter en Libye et le rôle qu'avait joué la Maison Blanche dans cette affaire. (USA)

258

ARTIST / KÜNSTLER / ARTISTE:

255, 256 James Marsh
257, 258 Marvin Mattelson
259 Edward Sorel
260 Eraldo Carugatti
261 Marshall Arisman
262 David Levine

DESIGNER / GESTALTER / MAQUETTISTE:

255, 256, 260, 262 Rudolph Hoglund
257, 258, 261 Walter Bernard

ART DIRECTOR / DIRECTEUR ARTISTIQUE:

255, 256, 260, 262 Rudolph Hoglund
257, 258 Walter Bernard / Rudolph Hoglund
259, 261 Walter Bernard

PUBLISHER / VERLEGER / EDITEUR:

255–262 Time, Inc.

257

APRIL 28, 1980 $1.25

TIME

High Noon for America's Allies

HELMUT'S HOTEL

FRENCHIE'S DANCE HALL

JULY 21, 1980 $1.25

TIME

Feeling Super in Detroit

Iran Frees A Hostage

I'M FOR REAGAN

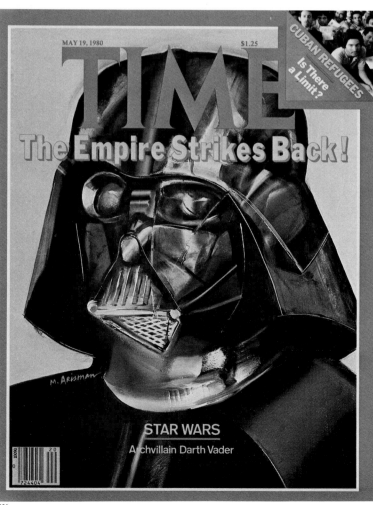

MAY 19, 1980 $1.25

TIME

The Empire Strikes Back!

CUBAN REFUGEES
Is There a Limit?

STAR WARS
Archvillain Darth Vader

M. Arisman

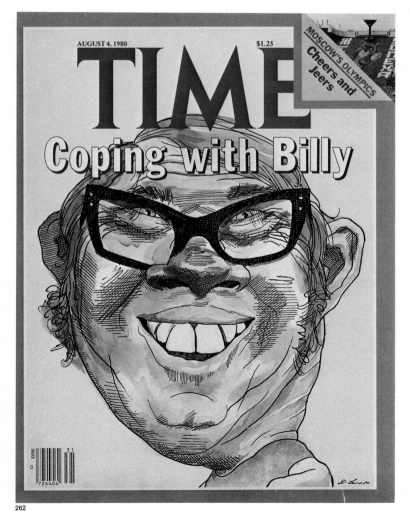

AUGUST 4, 1980 $1.25

TIME

Coping with Billy

MOSCOW'S OLYMPICS
Cheers and Jeers

263

264

265

ARTIST / KÜNSTLER / ARTISTE:

263 Renee Klein
264 Patrick Blackwell
265 Charles Waller
266 Milton Glaser
267 Robert Grossman
268, 269 Yoji Kuri

DESIGNER / GESTALTER / MAQUETTISTE:

263–265 Ronn Campisi
266 Milton Glaser
268, 269 Yoji Kuri

ART DIRECTOR / DIRECTEUR ARTISTIQUE:

263–265 Ronn Campisi
266, 267 Ruth Ansel
268, 269 Yoji Kuri

AGENCY / AGENTUR / AGENCE – STUDIO:

266 Milton Glaser, Inc.
268, 269 Gallery Art Kuri Jikken Kobo

PUBLISHER / VERLEGER / EDITEUR:

263–265 Boston Globe Magazine
266, 267 New York Times Magazine
268, 269 Pigeon Corp.

Magazine Covers
Zeitschriftenumschläge
Couvertures de périodiques

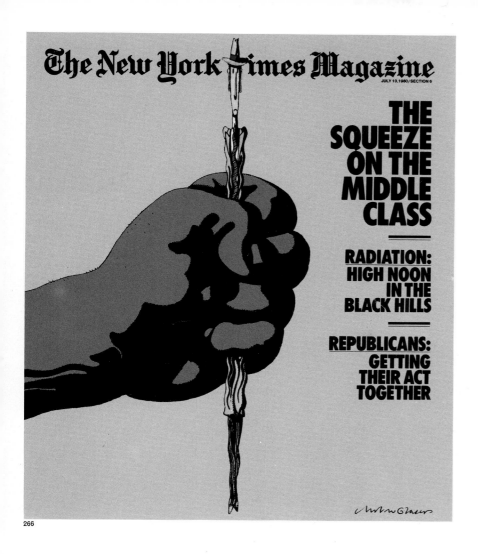

266

263–265 Covers of the weekly magazine of the *Boston Globe*. Fig. 263 refers to the pros and cons of sex education; Fig. 264: for a review of the new *Bartlett's* dictionary of quotations; Fig. 265: from an article entitled *Inventing Life;* it deals with the research on DNA (deoxyribo-nucleic acid) and the profits that can be made in the field of genetics. All illustrations are in full colour. (USA)
266, 267 Covers of the week-end magazine of the *New York Times*. Fig. 266: the middle class is being squeezed out by taxation (green fist on a yellow ground); Fig. 267 refers to an article about Ed Koch, the man behind New York's Mayor (light blue ground, red lettering). (USA)
268, 269 Covers of *Bébé*, a magazine for parents of new-born and young children and the problems involved. Fig. 268: vase in deep blue; Fig. 269: sun in red and yellow. (JPN)

263–265 Titelblätter des wöchentlich erscheinenden Magazins des *Boston Globe*. Abb. 263: «Die Fakten des Lebens lehren» – dieser Artikel bezieht sich auf das Für und Wider des Sexualunterrichts an Schulen; Abb. 264: zu einer Besprechung eines neuen Zitatenlexi-kons; Abb. 265: «Leben erfinden» – hier geht es um die Forschung auf dem Gebiet der Übertragung von Erbeigenschaften durch DNS (Desoxyribonucleinsäure) und die Ge-schäfte, die damit gemacht werden. Alle Illustrationen sind mehrfarbig. (USA)
266, 267 Umschläge des Wochenendmagazins der *New York Times*. Abb. 266: der Mittel-stand wird durch die Steuerbelastung ausgequetscht (grüne Faust auf gelbem Grund); Abb. 267: über Ed Koch, den Mann hinter dem Rücken des New Yorker Bürgermeisters (hellblauer Grund, roter Schriftzug). (USA)
268, 269 Titelblätter einer Zeitschrift für Eltern über Probleme mit Neugeborenen und Kleinkindern. Abb. 268: Vase in kräftigem Blau; Abb. 269: Sonne in Rot und Gelb. (JPN)

263–265 Couvertures du supplément illustré du *Boston Globe*. Fig. 263: «Enseigner les faits de la vie» – cet article discute le pour et le contre de l'enseignement sexuel à l'école, fig. 264: se rapporte à un compte-rendu d'un nouveau dictionnaire de citations; fig. 265: «Inventer la vie» – référence à un rapport sur l'A. D. N. (acide désoxyribonucléique), les recherches génétiques et les profits qui en résultent. Illustrations en couleurs. (USA)
266, 267 Couverture du supplément week-end du *New York Times*. Fig. 266: la classe moyenne est la plus frappée par les charges fiscales (poignée verte sur fond jaune); fig. 267: rapport sur Ed Koch, l'homme derrière le Maire de New York (illustration sur un fond en bleu clair, en-tête en rouge). (USA)
268, 269 Couvertures d'une revue destinée aux parents. Fig. 268: vase en bleu vif; fig. 269: soleil en rouge et jaune. (JPN)

267

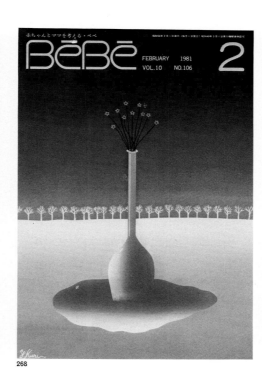

268

269

ARTIST / KÜNSTLER / ARTISTE:

270, 272, 273, 275 Barth
271 Gloor
274 Jüsp
276, 277 Beate Brömse

ART DIRECTOR / DIRECTEUR ARTISTIQUE:

270–275 Franz Mächler
276, 277 Gunnar Larsen

PUBLISHER / VERLEGER / ÉDITEUR:

270–275 Nebelspalter-Verlag
276, 277 Gunnar Larsen

276

270–275 Covers of various issues of *Nebelspalter*, a humorous and satirical weekly. The illustrations show how the world has changed, how a horse gets on a jockey's nerves, how precarious the situation in the energy sector could become, how Mr. X eavesdrops on nature by sneaking upon it, how house owners can protect themselves in their mountain resort from hang-gliders, and how Switzerland, despite the Olympic boycott, rushed to take part in Moscow. Full-colour illustrations. (SWI)
276, 277 Complete cover and illustration in actual size from a fashion magazine. (FRA)

270–275 Titelblätter verschiedener Ausgaben des humoristisch-satirischen Wochenblattes *Nebelspalter*. Die Illustrationen zeigen, wie sich die Welt verändert hat, wie das Pferd den Jockey nervt, wie prekär die Lage auf dem Energiesektor werden kann, wie Herr X auf leisen Sohlen die Natur belauscht, wie man sich in seinem Ferienhaus auch gegen Deltasegler vorsehen muss, wie die Schweiz trotz Teilnahmeboykott an die Olympischen Spiele nach Moskau eilt. Mehrfarbige Illustrationen. (SWI)
276, 277 Vollständiges Titelblatt einer Modezeitschrift und Illustration in Originalgrösse. (FRA)

270–275 Couvertures de divers numéros de l'hebdomadaire humoristique *Nebelspalter*. Les illustrations montrent comment les temps ont changé, comment le cheval se moque du jockey, combien la situation énergétique est précaire, comment M. X. observe la nature à pas feutré, qu'il faut se méfier aussi du delta-plane, et comment la Suisse se rendait à la hâte aux Jeux Olympiques de Moscou, nonobstant le boycottage des Jeux décidé par les autres nations. Illustrations en polychromie. (SWI)
276, 277 Couverture complète et illustration en grandeur nature du magazine *Mode Avantgarde*. (FRA)

270

271

272

273

274

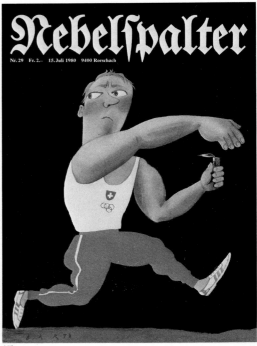

275

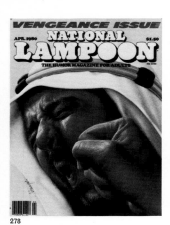

278

ARTIST / KÜNSTLER / ARTISTE:

278, 279 Eraldo Carugati
280 George I. Parrish
281, 282 Mark Hess
283 Béat Brüsch
284, 285 Tsutomu Toguchi

DESIGNER / GESTALTER / MAQUETTISTE:

278–282 Skip Johnston
283 Béat Brüsch
284, 285 Tsutomu Toguchi

ART DIRECTOR / DIRECTEUR ARTISTIQUE:

278–282 Skip Johnston
283 Jean Parmentier

279

Fun Takes a Holiday
DEC. 1980
NATIONAL LAMPOON
OR MAGAZINE FOR ADULTS
$1.50
WPS 34490

TATTOOS
FOR FUN PARTS
OF YOUR BODY
DESPERATE FUN
FUNNY FARM
PLUS
SOME FUN
BENEATH THE
MISTLETOE WITH
A "SURPRISE
ENDING"

280

The Past and How It Got There
SEPT. 1980
NATIONAL LAMPOON
THE HUMOR MAGAZINE FOR ADULTS
$1.50
WPS 34490

Remember the Alamo?

281

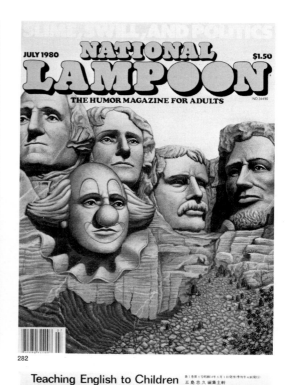

SLIME, SWILL, AND POLITICS
JULY 1980
NATIONAL LAMPOON
THE HUMOR MAGAZINE FOR ADULTS
$1.50
IND 34490

282

OKAPI
209

GUIDE DES REGIONS DE FRANCE,
VOYAGE AU PAYS DU CANTAL

283

Teaching English to Children
児童英語教育
特集 ● 私のくふうした指導法
第5号
児童英語技能 児童英語技能 合格者発表
検定試験 合格者発表

284

Teaching English to Children
児童英語教育
特集 ● 現代子どもロジー
第4号

285

AGENCY / AGENTUR / AGENCE – STUDIO:

283 Béat Brüsch
284, 285 Toguchi Art Studio

PUBLISHER / VERLEGER / EDITEUR:

278–282 National Lampoon
283 Bayard Presse
284, 285 Japec

278–282 Covers and illustration in actual size from *National Lampoon*, a humorous monthly magazine. Figs. 278, 279: this edition is entirely devoted to the subject of revenge; Fig. 280: for an edition about fun, also under the Christmas tree or mistletoe; Fig. 281: from an edition dealing with the glorious history of the United States of America and the resistance of 180 Texans in Alamo during the Texan independence war; Fig. 282: from an edition about shady intrigues that take place in the world of politics and election campaigning. The headings are in yellow. (USA)
283 Cover of an edition of the youth magazine *Okapi*. This edition contains tips for hiking holidays. Full colour. (FRA)
284, 285 Covers in bright colours from two series of an English course for children. (JPN)

278–282 Titelblätter und Illustration in Originalgrösse der humoristischen Monatsschrift *National Lampoon*. Abb. 278, 279: diese Ausgabe ist ausschliesslich dem Thema Rache gewidmet; Abb. 280: für eine Ausgabe über «Spass», auch unter dem Weihnachtsbaum, bzw. dem Mistelzweig; Abb. 281: zu einer Nummer über die glorreiche Vergangenheit der USA, als 180 Texaner in Alamo einer mexikanischen Übermacht standhielten; Abb. 282: zu einer Nummer über schmierige Machenschaften in der Politik. Der Namenszug ist jeweils in Gelb. (USA)
283 Titelbild einer Nummer der Jugendzeitschrift *Okapi*. Diese Ausgabe enthält Tips für Wanderferien. Mehrfarbig. (FRA)
284, 285 Umschläge in bunten Farben von zwei Folgen eines Englisch-Kurses für Kinder. (JPN)

278–282 Couvertures et illustration en grandeur nature du mensuel humoristique *National Lampoon*. Fig. 278, 279: ce numéro est consacré entièrement au sujet de la «vengeance»; fig. 280: pour un numéro sur l'amusement, même sous l'arbre de Noël, resp. sous une branche du gui; fig. 281: sur le passé glorieux des E.-U. – Alamo jouait un rôle important dans la guerre entre le Texas et le Mexique, où 180 Texans avaient résisté longtemps à des forces mexicaines; fig. 282: numéro sur les machinations sordides dans la politique. En-tête toujours en jaune. (USA)
283 Couverture d'un numéro d'*Okapi*, magazine pour les jeunes, ici avec des conseils pour des excursions. En polychromie. (FRA)
284, 285 Couvertures en couleurs vives de deux suites d'un cours d'anglais pour enfants. (JPN)

ARTIST / KÜNSTLER:

286, 287 Shigeo Fukuda
288 Sue Llewellyn
289, 290 Fred-Jürgen Rogner
291 Gilda Belin
292 Beate Brömse

DESIGNER / GESTALTER:

286, 287 Shigeo Fukuda
288 Sue Llewellyn

ART DIRECTOR:

286, 287 Shigeo Fukuda
288 Stan McCray
289, 290 Frank DeVino
291 Gerhard Berger
292 Gunnar Larsen

PUBLISHER / VERLEGER:

286, 287 Itoki Co., Ltd.
288 Dallas Morning News
289, 290 Omni Publications
    International Ltd.
291, 292 Mode International

286

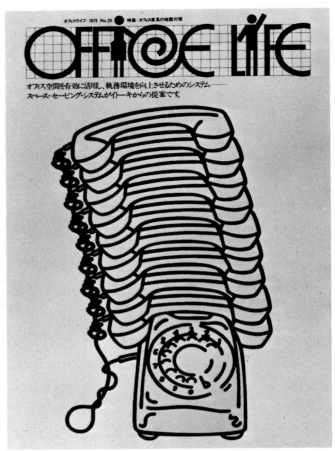

287

289

290

288

286, 287 Covers of two editions of the magazine *Office Life*. (JPN)
288 Cover of the illustrated week-end supplement of the *Dallas Morning News*. (USA)
289, 290 Two covers of *Omni* magazine. Fig. 289: anniversary edition for two years of publication. The original painting (mostly in luminous paint in shades of blue) is available as poster in a limited edition. Fig. 290: dark figure in front of a green background. Titles in red. (USA)
291, 292 Covers of a fashion magazine. Fig. 291 in pink and light blue; Fig. 292 in dark lilac with red, pink and greenish blue. (FRA)

286, 287 Titelblätter von zwei Ausgaben der Zeitschrift *Office Life*. (JPN)
288 Titelblatt der farbigen Wochenendbeilage der *Dallas Morning News*. Im Artikel, auf welchen sich die Illustration bezieht, geht es um Streben nach Perfektion. (USA)
289, 290 Zwei Titelblätter der Zeitschrift *Omni*. Abb. 289: Jubiläumsnummer zum zweijährigen Bestehen. Das Originalgemälde (vorwiegend in Blautönen) wurde in Leuchtfarben ausgeführt und ist in einer limitierten Auflage als Poster erhältlich. Zu einem Artikel über die Zukunft der Menschheit. Abb. 290: dunkle Figur vor grünem Hintergrund. Titel jeweils in Rot. (USA)
291, 292 Umschläge einer Mode-Zeitschrift. Abb. 291 in Rosa und Hellblau; Abb. 292 in dunklem Lila mit Rot, Rosa und Grünblau. (FRA)

286, 287 Couvertures de deux numéros du magazine *Office Life*. (JPN)
288 Couverture du supplément de la fin de semaine de *Dallas Morning News*. Dans l'article, auquel l'illustration se réfère, on discute l'aspiration à la perfection. (USA)
289, 290 Deux couvertures du magazine *Omni*. Fig. 289: numéro publié à l'occasion des deux ans d'existence du magazine. La peinture originale (en bleu prédominant) a été réalisée en couleurs phosphoréscentes et un tirage limité est en vente comme poster. L'illustration se réfère à un article sur l'avenir de l'humanité. Fig. 290: figure sombre sur fond vert. (USA)
291, 292 Couvertures du magazine *Mode International*. Fig. 291 en rose et bleu pâle, fig. 292 en lilas foncé avec rouge, rose et bleu verdâtre. (FRA)

291

292

293

295

294

296

293, 294 Two double spreads in bright colours from a magazine published by *Sanrio*. (JPN)
295 Cover of *Vorwärts* (Forward), a weekly publication addressed to Social Democrats. This issue is devoted to the subject: money, credit, insurance. In dark colours on yellow. (GER)
296 Article about burnt-out businessmen before retirement age, from *Dynamic Years Magazine*. (USA)
297 Cover in pastel colours for an issue of *The New Yorker* magazine. (USA)
298 Full-page illustration for an article published in *Cue* magazine. (USA)
299, 300 Cover and illustration in actual size of the initial issue of the weekly magazine *Die Woche*, referring to an investigation on power in Switzerland. (SWI)

293, 294 Zwei Doppelseiten in bunten Farben aus einer von *Sanrio* herausgegebenen Zeitschrift. (JPN)
295 Titelblatt des *Vorwärts*, einer Wochenzeitschrift für Sozialdemokraten. In dunklen Tönen. (GER)
296 Mehrfarbige Illustration zu einem Artikel in der Zeitschrift *Dynamic Years Magazine* über Geschäftsleute, deren Energie schon vor dem Pensionsalter ausgebrannt ist. (USA)
297 Titelblatt in Pastellfarben für eine Ausgabe des Wochenmagazins *The New Yorker*. (USA)
298 Ganzseitige Illustration zu einem in der Zeitschrift *Cue* erschienenen Artikel. (USA)
299, 300 Umschlag und Illustration (in Originalgrösse) der Null-Nummer des Wochenmagazins *Die Woche* von *Ringier*, hier zu einer Untersuchung über die Macht in der Schweiz. (SWI)

293, 294 Pages doubles en couleurs vives figurant dans un magazine publié par *Sanrio*. (JPN)
295 Couverture d'un hebdomadaire qui s'adresse essentiellement aux Sociaux-démocrates. Ce numéro est entièrement consacré au sujet: argent, crédit, assurance. En couleurs sombres. (GER)
296 Article sur les hommes d'affaire qui sont épuisés bien avant l'âge de la retraite. (USA)
297 Couverture en couleurs pastel du magazine hebdomadaire *The New Yorker*. (USA)
298 Illustration pleine page accompagnant un article paru dans le magazine *Cue*. (USA)
299, 300 Couverture et illustration (en grandeur originale) du numéro initial du magazine *Hebdo*, se référant ici à une enquête sur la répartition du pouvoir en Suisse. (SWI)

ARTIST / KÜNSTLER / ARTISTE:

293, 294 Yoji Kuri
295 Dieter Wiesmüller
296, 298 Geoffrey Moss
297 Eugene Mihaesco
299, 300 Béat Brüsch

DESIGNER / GESTALTER / MAQUETTISTE:

293, 294 Yoji Kuri
299, 300 Béat Brüsch

297

ART DIRECTOR / DIRECTEUR ARTISTIQUE:

293, 294 Yoji Kuri
295 Hans-Jürgen Gotta/Joachim Widmann
296 Laura Doss
297 Lee Lorenz
298 Judy Garlan
299, 300 Günter Halden

AGENCY / AGENTUR / AGENCE – STUDIO:

293, 294 Gallery Art Kuri Jikken Kobo
299, 300 Béat Brüsch

PUBLISHER / VERLEGER / EDITEUR:

293, 294 Sanrio Co.
295 Neuer Vorwärts Verlag Nau & Co.
296 Dynamic Years Magazine
297 The New Yorker Magazine, Inc.
298 Cue Magazine
299, 300 Ringier Verlag

299

300

298

301

Magazine Illustrations
Zeitschriften-Illustrationen
Illustrations de périodiques

301–305 These full-page illustrations have appeared in a novel about a movie, entitled *Bigeiko* and published in *Goro* magazine by *Shogakukan Ltd.* All illustrations are in strong colours. (JPN)

301–305 Diese ganzseitigen Illustrationen sind in der Zeitschrift *Goro* erschienen. Sie stammen aus einem Roman mit dem Titel *Bigeiko,* der von einem Film handelt. Alle Illustrationen in bunten Farben. (JPN)

301–305 Ces illustrations pleines pages ont paru dans le magazine *Goro* accompagnant un roman intitulé *Bigeiko* qui traite d'un film. Les illustrations sont en couleurs vives. (JPN)

ARTIST / KÜNSTLER / ARTISTE:
301–305 Tadanori Yokoo

DESIGNER / GESTALTER / MAQUETTISTE:
301–305 Tadanori Yokoo

ART DIRECTOR / DIRECTEUR ARTISTIQUE:
301–305 Tadanori Yokoo

PUBLISHER / VERLEGER / EDITEUR:
301–305 Shogakukan Ltd.

302

303

304

305

306

307

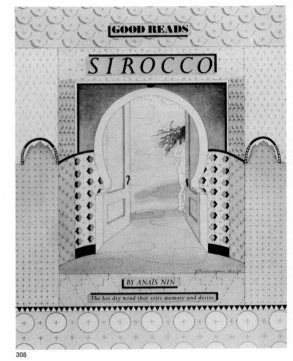

308

306, 307 Full-page illustrations from *Inc.* magazine. Fig. 306: this article explains why hasty decisions do not lead to the solving of problems (beige and black); Fig. 307: business people are made aware of the fact that any kind of information can be obtained directly from Washington (George Washington dressed in the uniform of his days). (USA)
308 Cover of the story *Sirocco* by Anaïs Nin that appeared in *Self*, a women's magazine. The story takes place on Mallorca. Light shades of colour. (USA)
309, 310 Illustrations from the magazine *Harrowsmith*. Fig. 309: *The sinking Ark*—article dealing with the extermination of certain animals, for example the Bengal tiger; Fig. 310: a short story entitled *Some kind of Piggery Jokery*. (USA)
311 *Shocking news.* Illustration for an article on the pros and cons of electric-shock therapies. In full colour. (USA)
312 One-and-a-half page illustration in yellow, light blue and pink for an article in the magazine *Vital* about sleep and what happens during this time. (FRA)

306, 307 Ganzseitige Illustrationen aus der Zeitschrift *Inc.* Abb. 306: in diesem Artikel wird ausgeführt, weshalb überstürzte Entscheide Probleme nicht lösen (beige und schwarz); Abb. 307: Geschäftsleute werden darüber aufgeklärt, dass sie jede Art von Information direkt von Washington erhalten können (George Washington in der Uniform seiner Zeit). (USA)
308 Titelseite der Erzählung *Schirokko* von Anaïs Nin, die in der Frauenzeitschrift *Self* erschien. Die Handlung spielt auf Mallorca. Helle Farbtöne. (USA)
309, 310 Illustrationen aus der Zeitschrift *Harrowsmith*. Abb. 309: «Die sinkende Arche» – hier geht es um die Ausrottung von Tierarten, z. B. des bengalischen Tigers; Abb. 310: zu einer Kurzgeschichte über schmutzige Witzeleien. (USA)
311 Illustration zu einem Artikel über das Für und Wider von Elektroschock-Therapien. Mehrfarbig. (USA)
312 Eineinhalbseitige Illustration in Gelb, Hellblau und Rosa zu einem Artikel in der Zeitschrift *Vital* über den Schlaf und was sich während dieser Zeit ereignet. (FRA)

306, 307 Illustrations pleines pages tirées du magazine *Inc.* Fig. 306: dans cet article on discute pourquoi les décisions précipitées ne résolvent pas les problèmes (beige et noir); fig. 307: cet article s'adresse aux hommes d'affaire et aux industriels les informant qu'ils peuvent se procurer toute sorte de renseignement directement de Washington (George Washington dans l'uniforme de son temps). (USA)
308 Page de titre du récit «Sirocco» d'Anaïs Nin, qui a paru dans la revue féminine *Self*. Le cadre évoqué est celui de Deyà dans l'île de Majorque. Prédominance de tons clairs. (USA)
309, 310 Illustrations initiales extraites du magazine *Harrowsmith*. Fig. 309: «L'arche coule» – dans cet article il est question de l'extinction de certains animaux, p. ex. du tigre royal; fig. 310 accompagne un récit sur des plaisanteries de mauvais goût. (USA)
311 Illustration figurant dans un article sur le pour et le contre de la thérapeutique par électrochoc. En polychromie. (USA)
312 Illustration sur une page et demie (jaune, bleu, rose) introduisant un article du magazine *Vital*, sur les découvertes bouleversant les idées traditionnelles. intitulé *Vous dormez: ce qui se passe*. (FRA)

309

310

311

ARTIST / KÜNSTLER / ARTISTE:

306 Karen Watson
307 Cheryl Roberts
308 Barbara Nessim
309 Terry Shoffner
310 Maureen Paxton
311 Bruce Mau
312 Serge Fenech

DESIGNER / GESTALTER / MAQUETTISTE:

306, 307 Ken Silvia

ART DIRECTOR / DIRECTEUR ARTISTIQUE:

306. 307 Ken Silvia
308 Bea Feitler / Paula Greif
309, 310 James M. Lawrence
311 Stephen Costello
312 Jacques Marcy

AGENCY / AGENTUR / AGENCE – STUDIO:

311 Fifty Fingers Inc.

PUBLISHER / VERLEGER / EDITEUR:

306, 307 INC. Magazine
308 SELF Magazine
309, 310 Camden House Publishing Ltd.
311 Comac Communications Ltd.
312 Medi-Media

Magazine Illustrations
Zeitschriften-Illustrationen
Illustrations de périodiques

312

313 Illustration for an article about face-lifting that appeared in *City Magazine*. Red bricks. (USA)
314 Full-page black-and-white illustration that introduces a story in *Westermanns Monatshefte* entitled *Der erste Kuss* (The first Kiss). (GER)
315, 317 Illustrations from the news magazine *L'Espresso*. Fig. 315 preview of a work of diary notes, to be published on the occasion of the 100th anniversary of Dostoevsky's death; Fig. 317: for an article on Italian patriotism, how it is expressed in literature, songs, television and in sport. All objects in green, white and red. (ITA)
316 Part of a magazine pull-out as a visual editorial relating all the articles and stories which have a single theme. (USA)

313 Illustration aus der Zeitschrift *City Magazine* zu einem Artikel über Facelifting. Rote Backsteine, weiss gekleidete Handwerker. (USA)
314 Ganzseitige Schwarzweiss-Illustration, die eine Erzählung in *Westermanns Monatshefte* mit dem Titel *Der erste Kuss* einleitet. (GER)
315, 317 Illustrationen aus dem Nachrichtenmagazin *L'Espresso*. Abb. 315: Vorabdruck aus einem zum 100. Todestag Dostojewskis erschienenen Werk mit bisher unveröffentlichten Tagebuchnotizen; Abb. 317: zu einem Artikel über Patriotismus in Italien, wie er in der Literatur, den Chansons, am Fernsehen und im Sport zum Ausdruck kommt. Alle Gegenstände in den Landesfarben Grün/Weiss/Rot. (ITA)
316 Teil eines Auslegers, in welchem die verschiedenen Artikel und Beiträge visualisiert wurden, die in einer Nummer der Zeitschrift erschienen. (USA)

313 Illustration parue dans le magazine *City Magazine* dans un article sur le lissage. Tête en rouge brique, ouvriers en manteaux blancs. (USA)
314 Illustration pleine page en noir et blanc en regard de la page initiale d'un récit dans *Westermanns Monatshefte*, intitulé «Le premier baiser». (GER)
315, 317 Illustrations du magazine d'information *L'Espresso*. Fig. 315: extrait d'un ouvrage publié à l'occasion du centenaire de la mort de Dostoïevski et rassemblant des notes inédites des ses journaux. Fig. 317: première page double introduisant un article sur le patriotisme en Italie et comment il s'exprime dans la littérature, les chansons, à la TV et dans le sport. Tous les objets dans les couleurs italiennes vert/blanc/rouge. (ITA)
316 Partie d'un encart en accordéon qui relate visuellement les articles et commentaires d'un numéro du magazine qui ont un seul sujet. (USA)

314

313

315

ARTIST / KÜNSTLER / ARTISTE:

313 John Martin
314 Dietrich Lange
315, 317 Tullio Pericoli
316 David Battle

"I suspect they have nightmare fantasies," she said, giggling, "of my baring my notorious torso for their scrutiny. Wouldn't that be a theatrical flourish, a farewell to the academic world no one would ever forget." page 311

"And, of course, most deans, provosts, and presidents themselves were once professors, and a coward cannot be remade overnight. There is no evidence that "Jaws" got his start as a jellyfish." page 317

316

317

ART DIRECTOR / DIRECTEUR ARTISTIQUE:

313 Rob Melbourne
314 Jürgen Peters
316 David Battle

AGENCY / AGENTUR / AGENCE – STUDIO:

313 Fifty Fingers Inc.

PUBLISHER / VERLEGER / EDITEUR:

313 City Magazine
314 Westermanns Monatshefte
315, 317 L'Espresso
316 Antioch Review

318

319

320

Magazine Illustrations
Zeitschriften-Illustrationen
Illustrations de périodiques

318 Black-and-white illustration from an Ode to Heraclitus entitled "Song from the depth of the world, the depth of the eye and the brevity of life". (SWE)
319, 320 Spread and illustration from *Zeit-Magazin* from a long-running series published by the since deceased art critic and journalist Manuel Gasser entitled "My Aunt Mélanie's cooking" with selected recipes—here for a Coq au vin de Bourgogne. (GER)
321 Black-and-white illustration on the introducing double spread of an article called *Men's Mythology*. (JPN)
322 Full-page illustration from *Zeit-Magazin,* the colour supplement of the weekly newspaper *Die Zeit,* for a new series that appeared with the title *Im Dickicht der Gefühle* (In the thicket of emotions). (GER)

318 Schwarzweiss-Illustration zu einer Ode an Heraklit mit dem Titel «Lied von der Tiefe der Welt, der Tiefe des Auges und der Kürze des Lebens». (SWE)
319, 320 Seite und Illustration aus dem *Zeit-Magazin.* In einer langen Folge veröffentlichte der inzwischen verstorbene Kunstkritiker und Publizist Manuel Gasser unter dem Titel *Die Küche meiner Tante Mélanie* ausgewählte Rezepte, hier für einen Coq au vin de Bourgogne. (GER)
321 Schwarzweiss-Illustration zu einem Artikel über die Mythologie des Menschen. (JPN)
322 Ganzseitige Illustration aus dem *Zeit-Magazin,* dem farbigen Supplement der Wochenzeitung *Die Zeit,* hier zu einer neuen Folge, die unter dem Titel *Im Dickicht der Gefühle* erschien. (GER)

318 Illustration en noir et blanc accompagnant une Ode à Héraclite, intitulée «Cantique de la profondeur du monde, de la profondeur de l'œil et du passage de la vie». (SWE)
319, 320 Page et illustration du magazine illustré de l'hebdomadaire *Die Zeit.* Dans une longue série, feu Manuel Gasser, critique d'art et journaliste, avait publié sous le titre «La cuisine de ma Tante Mélanie» des recettes choisies, ici pour un coq au vin de Bourgogne. (GER)
321 Illustration noir-blanc en regard de la page initiale d'un article sur la mythologie de l'homme. (JPN)
322 Illustration pleine page du *Zeit-Magazin,* le supplément illustré du journal hebdomadaire *Die Zeit,* introduisant ici une nouvelle suite d'articles intitulée «L'impénétrabilité des émotions». (GER)

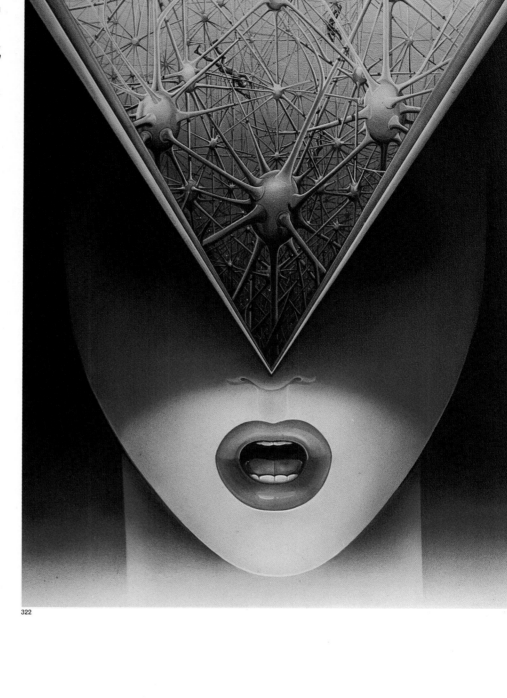

322

321

ARTIST / KÜNSTLER / ARTISTE:

318 Dan Jonsson
319, 320, 322 Ute Osterwalder
321 Shin Matsunaga

ART DIRECTOR / DIRECTEUR ARTISTIQUE:

319, 320, 322 Marcus Osterwalder

PUBLISHER / VERLEGER / EDITEUR:

318 Tidningen Vi
319, 320, 322 Zeitverlag Gerd Bucerius KG

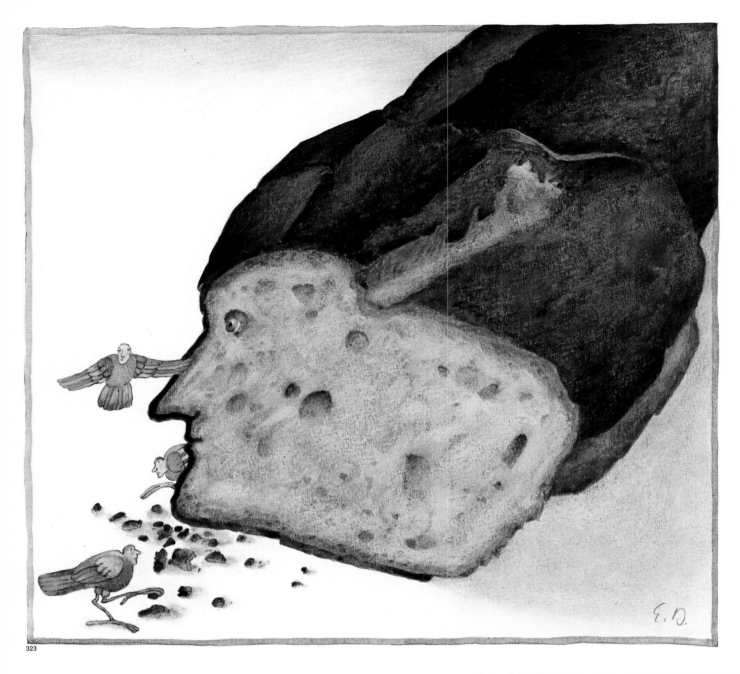

323

Magazine Illustrations
Zeitschriften-Illustrationen
Illustrations de périodiques

323–325 Illustrations from a regular series in the youth magazine *Okapi* with the title "15 Gestures of Jesus", interpreted by Etienne Delessert. Here for the parts in the Bible where he breaks bread, where he walks on the Sea of Galilee, and how he left the temple. (FRA)
326, 327 Full-page illustrations from the magazine *New Realities*. Fig. 326: the author states that it is now possible to reveal the seat of human physical ailments by using the divining-rod method; Fig. 327: the article asks if the physical body, the conscious, or the subconscious mind is in charge of our being. Illustrations in full colour. (USA)
328 Caricature on the *Federal Reserve* that appeared in *Time* magazine. (USA)

323–325 Illustrationen aus einer regelmässigen Folge in der Jugendzeitschrift *Okapi* mit dem Titel «15 Gesten von Jesus», die von Etienne Delessert interpretiert werden. Hier zu den Bibelstellen: Jesus, wie er das Brot bricht, wie er über den See Genezareth geht und wie er den Tempel verlässt. (FRA)
326, 327 Ganzseitige Illustrationen aus der Zeitschrift *New Realities*. Abb. 326: der Autor behauptet, dass es möglich ist, Krankheiten nach der selben Methode zu erkennen, wie man früher mit der Wünschelrute Wasser fand; Abb. 327: zu einer Diskussion über die Frage, ob der Körper, das Bewusstsein oder das Unterbewusstsein den Menschen lenken. Mehrfarbig. (USA)
328 Karikatur aus dem Nachrichtenmagazin *Time* über die Bundesbank, die wie ein zweijähriges Kind seine Katze die Nation bis zum letzten Blutstropfen auswindet, ohne es zu merken. (USA)

323–325 Au moyen de ces illustrations, Etienne Delessert interprète des écrits de la Bible dans une série intitulée *15 Gestes de Jésus*, parue dans le magazine pour la jeunesse *Okapi:* Jésus donne du pain, il marche sur les eaux, il quitte le Temple. (FRA)
326, 327 Extraits du magazine *New Realities*. Fig. 326: l'auteur prétend que les maladies peuvent être découvertes selon la méthode de la baguette devinatoire pour découvrir des sources d'eau cachées; fig. 327: on discute dans cet article si le corps, la conscience ou le subconscient font agir l'homme. (USA)
328 Caricature du magazine d'information *Time:* la Banque Nationale tord la Nation pareil à un gamin qui tord son chat jusqu'à la dernière goutte de sang sans s'en apercevoir. (USA)

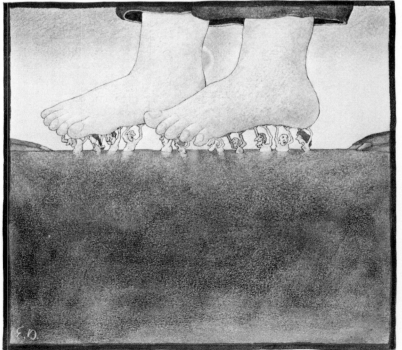

324

ARTIST / KÜNSTLER / ARTISTE:

323–325 Etienne Delessert
326 Ed Soyka
327 John Lykes
328 Frances Jetter

DESIGNER / GESTALTER / MAQUETTISTE:

326, 327 Gordon Mortensen

ART DIRECTOR / DIRECTEUR ARTISTIQUE:

323–325 Jean Parmentier
326, 327 Gordon Mortensen
328 Anthony Libardi

AGENCY / AGENTUR / AGENCE – STUDIO:

326, 327 Mortensen Design

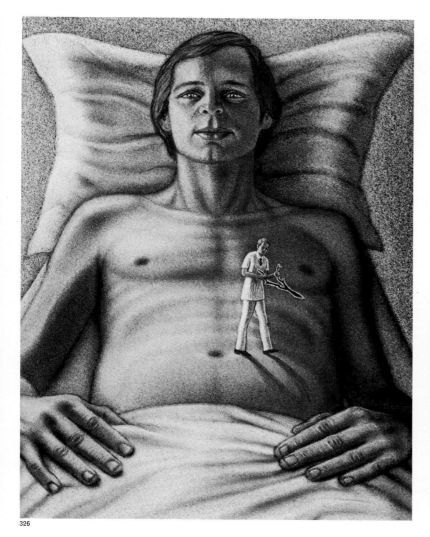

326

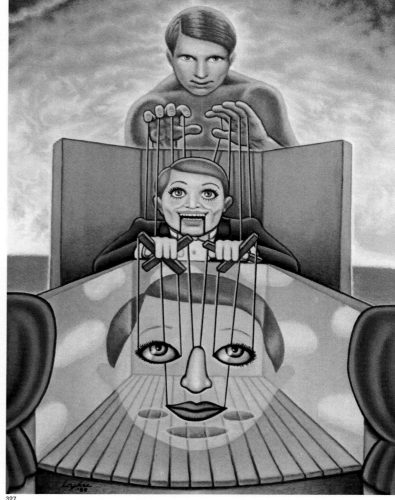

327

325

328

PUBLISHER / VERLEGER / EDITEUR:

323–325 Bayard Presse
326, 327 New Realities Magazine
328 Time, Inc.

ARTIST / KÜNSTLER / ARTISTE:

329 Zbigniew Lengren
330 Wieslaw Rosocha
331 Jan Sawka
332 Stefan Wielgus
333 Dagmar Frinta
334 Seymour Chwast
335 Jean Claude Suarès

329

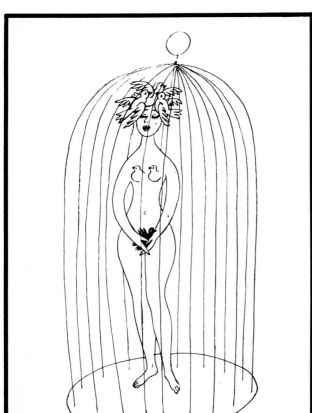

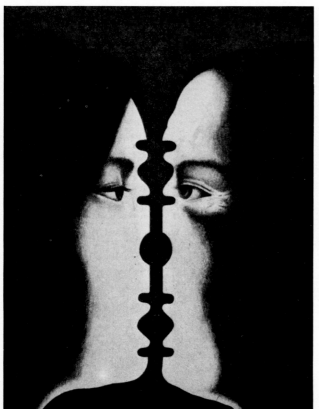

330

331

332

ART DIRECTOR / DIRECTEUR ARTISTIQUE:

329, 330, 332 Witold Filler
331, 333, 334 Chris Austopchuk
335 Paul Hardy

333

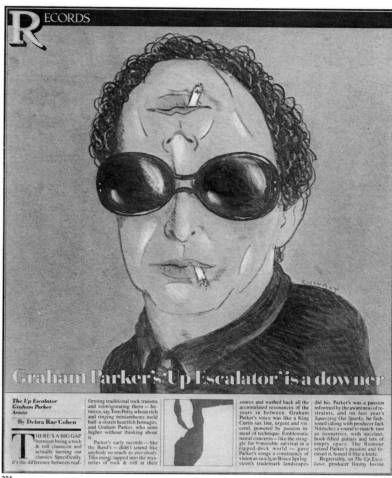

334

329, 330, 332 Cartoons from the satirical weekly *Szpilki*. Fig. 332 alludes to the American boycott of the Olympic Games in Moscow. (POL)
331 Illustration from an article published in the magazine *Rolling Stones* on the American economy in the throes of the recession. (USA)
333 Illustration from an article in *Rolling Stones* dealing with a fifty-year-old housewife who hears the voice of the Virgin Mary and is in the habit of announcing, on the eve of Catholic feasts, the disasters that are about to overtake humanity. The roman Catholic Church is all the more alarmed by this because Veronica Lueken already has hundreds of adherents. (USA)
334 Illustration for a review of the record *Up Escalator* by pub-rock singer Graham Parker. (USA)
335 Pen drawing for the monthly letter page of *Attenzione* magazine. (USA)

329, 330, 332 Karikaturen aus der satirischen Wochenzeitschrift *Szpilki*. Abb. 332 bezieht sich auf den Olympiaboykott der amerikanischen Sportler in Moskau. (POL)
331 Illustration aus einem in der Zeitschrift *Rolling Stones* erschienenen Artikel über die von der Rezession geplagte amerikanische Wirtschaft. (USA)
333 Illustration zu einem Artikel in der Zeitschrift *Rolling Stones*. Es geht hier um eine 50jährige Hausfrau, die offenbar die Stimme der Jungfrau Maria hört und jeweils am Vorabend katholischer Feiertage das Unheil voraussagt, das die Menschheit heimsuchen wird, worüber die katholische Kirche natürlich besorgt ist, da Veronica Lueken Hunderte von Anhängern hat. (USA)
334 Zu einer Besprechung der Platte *Up Escalator* des Pub-Rock-Sängers Graham Parker. (USA)
335 Federzeichnung zur monatlichen Leserbriefseite der Zeitschrift *Attenzione*. (USA)

329, 330, 332 Caricatures de l'hebdomadaire satirique *Szpilki*. La fig. 332 se réfère au boycottage des Jeux Olympiques de Moscou par l'équipe américaine. (POL)
331 Illustration figurant dans un article sur l'économie américaine ébranlée par la récession et l'inflation qui a paru dans le magazine *Rolling Stones*. (USA)
333 Illustration en regard de la page initiale d'un article de *Rolling Stones* où il est question des visions d'une femme de 50 ans qui communique, à la veille de fêtes catholiques, le message de châtiment et de la rédemption qu'attendent de l'humanité et l'irritation de l'Eglise Catholique à l'égard de cet évangile de Veronica Lueken. (USA)
335 Page initiale d'un article sur le disque *Up Escalator* de Graham Parker, chanteur rock. (USA)
336 Dessin à la plume illustrant la page mensuelle des Lettres du magazine *Attenzione*. (USA)

PUBLISHER / VERLEGER / EDITEUR:

329, 330, 332 Szpilki
331, 333, 334 Rolling Stone
335 Attenzione Magazine

335

Magazine Illustrations
Zeitschriften-Illustrationen
Illustrations de périodiques

ARTIST / KÜNSTLER / ARTISTE:

336, 337 Peter Lloyd
338 Ignacio Gomez
339 Stan Watts
340 Jeff Cummins

DESIGNER / GESTALTER / MAQUETTISTE:

336, 337 Michael Brock
338 James Kiehle
340 Roger Carpenter

ART DIRECTOR / DIRECTEUR ARTISTIQUE:

336–340 Michael Brock

PUBLISHER / VERLEGER / EDITEUR:

336–340 Playboy Enterprises, Inc.

336

337

338

340

339

336–340 Double spread and illustrations from *Oui* magazine. Fig. 336, 337: for an article on new scientific knowledge about how one can heighten intelligence, stimulate the imagination and improve memory (in bright colours); Fig. 338: information about reporters who have no access to women's changing rooms (in mat colours); Fig. 339: an interview with Gregg Almond, who later died in a motor-bicycle accident; Fig. 340: interview with Pete Townshend, a guitarist with The Who group (dark shades, green armchair). (USA)

336–340 Doppelseite und Illustrationen aus der Zeitschrift *Oui*. Abb. 336, 337: zu einem Artikel über neue wissenschaftliche Erkenntnisse, wie die Intelligenz gesteigert, die Phantasie angeregt und das Gedächtnis verbessert werden können (in grellen Farben); Abb. 338: über Reporter, die zu Damen-Umkleideräume keinen Zutritt haben (matte Farben); Abb. 339: Interview mit Gregg Almond, der bei einem Motorradunfall ums Leben kam; Abb. 340: Interview mit Pete Townshend, dem Guitarristen der Gruppe The Who (dunkle Farbtöne, grüner Sessel). (USA)

336–340 Page double et illustrations extraites du magazine *Oui*. Fig. 336, 337: article sur les découvertes scientifiques les plus récentes permettant d'augmenter l'intelligence, d'animer la fantaisie et d'améliorer la mémoire (en couleurs vives); fig. 338: sur les reporters qui n'ont pas accès aux vestiaires des dames (en tons mats); 339: interview avec Gregg Almond, qui avait perdu sa vie dans un accident de moto; fig. 340: interview avec Pete Townshend, guitarriste du groupe The Who (tons foncés, chaise verte). (USA)

341

342

343

344

341 Illustration in actual size from *The Dial* magazine, for a discussion on the BBC production of the Shakespeare play *The Taming of the Shrew*. (USA)
342 Full-colour illustration from *Financial Post Magazine* for an investigation on opinion polls and their influence on politicians. (USA)
343 An old poster reproduced in the magazine of the *National Football League* illustrates an article on a well-known game that took place in 1921. (USA)
344 Collage from *The Nation* for an article on the decline of personal freedoms. (USA)

341 Illustration in Originalgrösse zu einer Besprechung der BBC-Produktion des Shakespeare-Stücks *Der Widerspenstigen Zähmung*. (USA)
342 Mehrfarbige Illustration aus *Financial Post Magazine* zu einer Untersuchung über Meinungsumfragen und deren Einfluss auf die Politiker. (USA)
343 Dieses alte Plakat illustriert einen Artikel über ein Fussballspiel, das im Jahre 1921 ziemlich Staub aufgewirbelt hatte. (USA)
344 Collage zu einem Artikel über den Abbau der persönlichen Freiheiten. (USA)

341 Illustration en grandeur nature accompagnant un rapport sur la mise en scène par la BBC de la pièce *la Mégère apprivoisée* de Shakespeare. (USA)
342 Illustration polychrome du *Financial Post Magazine* extraite d'une enquête sur les sondages d'opinion et leur influence sur les hommes politiques. (USA)
343 Cette vieille affiche illustre un article sur un match de football qui semble avoir échauffé les esprits en 1921. (USA)
344 Collage accompagnant un article sur le déclin des libertés personnelles. (USA)

ARTIST / KÜNSTLER / ARTISTE:

341 Milton Glaser
342 John Martin
343 Steve Carver
344 Jean Claude Suarès

ART DIRECTOR / DIRECTEUR ARTISTIQUE:

341 Susan Reinhardt
342 Jackie Young
343 David Boss
344 Jean Claude Suarès

AGENCY / AGENTUR / AGENCE – STUDIO:

341 Milton Glaser, Inc.
342 Fifty Fingers Inc.

PUBLISHER / VERLEGER / EDITEUR:

341 The Dial
342 Financial Post Magazines
343 National Football League
344 The Nation

345

346

ARTIST / KÜNSTLER / ARTISTE:

345 Theo Rudnak
346 Mark Ulrich
347 Dominique Blondeau
348 Jacob Knight
349, 350 Michael Foreman
351 Daniel Mafia
352 David Schleinkofer

349

347

Magazine Illustrations

DESIGNER / GESTALTER / MAQUETTISTE:
345–347 Greg Paul

ART DIRECTOR / DIRECTEUR ARTISTIQUE:
345–347 Greg Paul
348–352 Jerry Alten

AGENCY / AGENTUR / AGENCE – STUDIO:
345–347 Greg Paul & Associates

PUBLISHER / VERLEGER / EDITEUR:
345–347 Plain Dealer Publishing
348–352 Triangle Publications Inc.

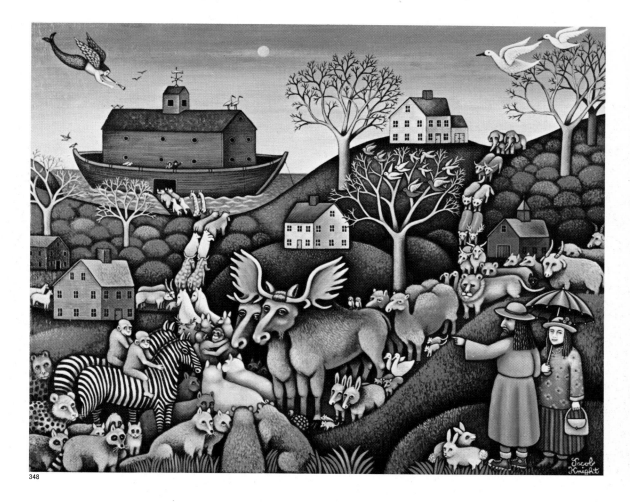

348

345–347 Full-page illustrations from the Sunday magazine *The Plain Dealer*. Fig. 345: about women left alone by death or divorce who are helped to seek new lives in a special "displaced homemaker" programme at a community college; Fig. 346: presents a selfhelp programme for former mental patients to acquire control and confidence; Fig. 347: about the "science" that aids munchers in their quest for the perfect potato chip. (USA)
348–352 Illustrations from *TV Guide* for programmes on the filming of parts of the Bible, bootleggers who sell illegal video-cassettes are becoming the scourge of the movie business, the conflict between tough reporting and station profits, how American TV reporters had trouble in providing an objective coverage of the hostage crisis in Iran, and the role pay-TV is now playing in the world of sport. (USA)

345–347 Ganzseitige Illustrationen aus dem Sonntagsmagazin *The Plain Dealer*. Abb. 345: über ein neues Programm, das Frauen, die nach dem Tod ihres Mannes oder nach der Scheidung Schwierigkeiten haben, neu ins Berufsleben einführt; Abb. 346: über eine Selbsthilfegruppe für ehemalige Psychiatrie-Patienten; Abb. 347: über Kartoffel-Chips und die Industrie, die dahinter steckt. (USA)
348–352 Illustrationen aus einer Fernseh-Programmzeitschrift, hier über die Verfilmung von Bibel-Stellen, über Bootlegger, deren illegale Überspielungen von Videokassetten für die Filmindustrie eine Plage werden, über seriöse Berichterstattung oder profitable Sensationspresse, über die Bemühungen von TV-Reportern, objektiv über die iranische Geiselaffäre zu berichten und eine Kabel-TV-Station, die vor allem Sportveranstaltungen sendet. (USA)

345–347 Illustrations pleines pages du magazine dominicale *The Plain Dealer*. Fig. 345: pour un nouveau programme qui réintègre ces femmes-là dans la vie professionnelle qui ne savent plus se débrouiller après la mort du mari ou après le divorce; fig. 346: sur un groupe d'entraide pour des anciens patients psychiatriques; fig. 347: l'industrie alimentaire en quête des chips parfaites. (USA)
348–352 Illustrations d'un programme de TV, ici sur l'adaptation cinématographique de quelques parties de la Bible, sur les enregistrements illégaux sur vidéocassette qui menacent l'industrie cinématographique, sur le journalisme sérieux ou la presse à sensation profitable, sur les efforts des reporters da la TV en faveur de rapports objectifs sur la prise d'ôtages en Iran et sur une station de télédistribution pour des événements sportifs. (USA)

350

351

352

133

De strakke lijnen van deze ruime woonkeuken worden versoepeld door vier cirkelvormen: een groot rond eetblad op een stenen zuil; een kast voor jassen en kruiden; een stookruil met barbecue-haard en als laatste een kast waarin een grote koelkast met vrieskast passen. De kamerboge zuilen staan zo dat ze kookrommel vanaf de eettafel aan het oog onttrekken. Het basisonderwerp is van wit geschilderde baksteentjes, maar kan ook uitgevoerd worden in strak stucwerk of glanzend plaatmateriaal van kunststof.

353

Magazine Illustrations
Zeitschriften-Illustrationen
Illustrations de périodiques

353–357 Double spreads and full-page illustrations from *Avenue* magazine. Fig. 353: from an article about kitchens and kitchen installations (in blue shades with brown leaves); Fig. 354: for a medical article about psoriasis; Fig. 355: for a review in the literary part of the magazine on a book by Antonio Porta; Fig. 356: for an interview series about women in Europe, here in England; Fig. 357: from a report on Italian furniture design (in mat shades with blue, red and reddish ochre). (NLD)
358 Illustration in sepia from a magazine for criminal thrillers. (JPN)

353–357 Doppelseiten und ganzseitige Illustrationen aus der Zeitschrift *Avenue*. Abb. 353: aus einem Artikel über Küchen und Kücheneinrichtungen (in Blautönen, braune Blätter); Abb. 354: zu einem medizinischen Artikel über Schuppenflechten; Abb. 355: zu einer Besprechung eines Werks von Antonio Porta im Literaturteil der Zeitschrift; Abb. 356: zu einer Interviewserie über die Frau in Europa, hier in England; Abb. 357: aus einem Beitrag über italienisches Möbel-Design (in matten Farbtönen mit Blau, Rot und Braunrot). (NLD)
358 Ilustration in Sepia aus einer Kriminalroman-Zeitschrift. (JPN)

353–357 Pages doubles et illustrations pleines pages du magazine *Avenue*. Fig. 353 accompagne un article présentant des aménagements de cuisines (tons bleus, feuilles brunes); fig. 354: pour un article médicale sur la psoriasis; fig. 355: illustre un compte-rendu de l'œuvre d'Antonio Porta dans le supplément littéraire; fig. 356: pour une série d'interviews sur la position de la femme en Europe, ici en Angleterre, fig. 357: extrait d'un rapport sur le design de meubles en Italie (tons mats avec bleu, rouge et brun rouge). (NLD)
358 Illustration en sépia tirée d'un magazine consacré exclusivement aux romans policiers. (JPN)

354

355

357

ARTIST / KÜNSTLER / ARTISTE:

353, 357 Martijn van der Jagt
354 Braldt Bralds
355 Frans Evenhuis
356 Erhard Göttlicher
358 Tadami Yamada

DESIGNER / GESTALTER / MAQUETTISTE:

353 Yoke Westerman
357 Carla Goossens

ART DIRECTOR / DIRECTEUR ARTISTIQUE:

353–357 Dick de Moei
358 Tadami Yamada

PUBLISHER / VERLEGER / EDITEUR:

353–357 De Geillustreerde Pers NV
358 Hayakawa Publishing, Inc.

356

358

359

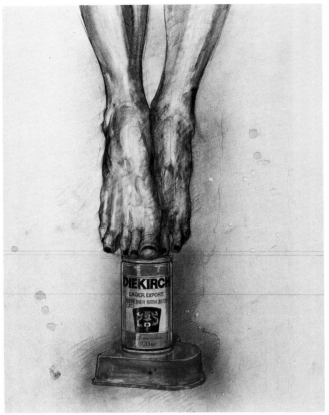

360

362

359 Full-colour illustration introducing an article on the scapegoat which appeared in the women's magazine *Brigitte*. (GER)
360 Another illustration from the interview series in *Avenue* magazine dealing with women in Europe, here in Luxembourg (see Fig. 356). (NLD)
361 Full-page illustration from a trilogy that appeared in *Avenue* magazine about the Antilles: "We just want to have a look around". (NLD)
362 Cover illustration for an article in *The Financial Post Magazine* entitled *How to cope with office stress*. (USA)
363 Double-spread illustration from *McCall's* magazine, for autumn menus. (USA)

359 Mehrfarbige Illustration zu einem Artikel in der Frauenzeitschrift *Brigitte: Paar sucht Sündenbock. Wer spielt mit?* (GER)
360 Eine weitere Illustration zur Interviewserie der Zeitschrift *Avenue* zum Thema Frauen in Europa, hier in Luxembourg (s. Abb. 356). (NLD)
361 Ganzseitige Illustration aus einer Trilogie über die Antillen aus der Zeitschrift *Avenue:* «Wir kommen uns mal umsehen». (NLD)
362 Umschlagillustration einer Finanzzeitschrift zu einem Artikel über Stress im Büro und wie man damit fertig wird. (USA)
363 Doppelseitige Illustration aus der Zeitschrift *McCall's* mit Menuvorschlägen für Herbstgemüse. (USA)

359 Illustration polychrome introduisant un article dans le magazine féminin *Brigitte* sur un couple en quête d'un bouc émissaire. (GER)
360 Une autre illustration de la série d'interviews sur la position de la femme en Europe, ici on parle du Luxembourg (v. fig. 356). (NLD)
361 Illustration pleine page extraite d'une trilogie sur les Antilles intitulée «Nous venons jeter un simple coup d'œil». Du magazine *Avenue*. (NLD)
362 Illustration de couverture d'un périodique économique se référant à un article sur le stress dans le bureau. (USA)
363 Illustration sur page double introduisant un article du magazine *McCall's* avec des recettes pour les légumes d'automne. (USA)

Magazine Illustrations
Zeitschriften-Illustrationen
Illustrations de périodiques

ARTIST / KÜNSTLER / ARTISTE:

359 Anne Brosi
360 Erhard Göttlicher
361 Mariet Numan
362 John Martin
363 Wendell Minor

DESIGNER / GESTALTER / MAQUETTISTE:

359 Heide Winds
363 Modesto Torré

ART DIRECTOR / DIRECTEUR ARTISTIQUE:

359 Heide Winds
360, 361 Dick de Moei
362 Jackie Young
363 Al Grossman

AGENCY / AGENTUR / AGENCE – STUDIO:

359 Linie-Grafik
362 Fifty Fingers Inc.
363 W. Minor Design

PUBLISHER / VERLEGER / EDITEUR:

359 Gruner & Jahr AG & Co.
360, 361 De Geillustreerde Pers NV
362 Financial Post Magazine
363 McCall Publishing Co.

361

363

365

366

ARTIST / KÜNSTLER / ARTISTE:

364, 365 Marshal Arisman
366, 367 George Tooker

ART DIRECTOR / DIRECTEUR ARTISTIQUE:

364–367 Frank DeVino

PUBLISHER / VERLEGER / EDITEUR:

364–367 Omni Publications International Ltd.

364, 365 Illustration in actual size and double spread from *Omni* magazine, for a novel about Hewitson, the man who built the thanatascope, a complicated cage-like contraption with sensors, mirrors and cameras within a Faraday cage, which closes upon the event of Death stepping into the cage. (USA)
366, 367 Introductory double spread and illustration from another fictional novel that appeared in *Omni*. Here, bureaucracy is taken to extremes: the President is watching his employees with cameras and gives notes for work executed in an extremely complicated way. (USA)

364, 365 Illustration in Originalgrösse und Doppelseite aus der Zeitschrift *Omni* zu einem Fiction-Roman über Hewitson, der das Thanataskop baute, ein komplizierter Käfig mit Sensoren, Spiegeln und Cameras, der sich in einem Faraday-Käfig befindet und zuschnappt, wenn der Tod sich darin befindet. (USA)
366, 367 Einleitende Doppelseite und Illustration aus einem anderen Fiction-Roman in *Omni*. Hier wird der Bürokratismus ad absurdum geführt, indem der oberste Boss seinen Angestellten, die er durch Cameras überwacht, Punkte verteilt, je komplizierter diese eine Sache anpacken oder ausführen. (USA)

364, 365 Illustration en grandeur nature et page double du magazine *Omni* introduisant un roman sur Hewitson, l'inventeur du thanatascope, une sorte de cage extrêmement compliquée, munie de senseurs, de miroirs et de caméras; toutes ses installations se trouvent dans une cage de Faraday qui se ferme aussitôt que la Mort s'y trouve. (USA)
366, 367 Première page d'un roman et illustration publiées dans le magazine *Omni*. Ici la bureaucratie est menée à outrance en ce que le PDG surveille ses employés par des caméras et donne des points à ceux qui trouvent la façon la plus compliquée pour exécuter un travail. En tons clairs. (USA)

Magazine Illustrations
Zeitschriften-Illustrationen
Illustrations de périodiques

367

what good is it to predict tomorrow's disasters if nobody believes you until it's too late?

BAD DREAMS IN THE FUTURE TENSE

article By WALTER L. LOWE

ON A THREE BLANKET NIGHT in January 1972, a middle-aged woman in New York had a dream about George Wallace. It is not clear whether that woman was fond of Wallace or disliked him, or thought about him at all. What is important is that in her dream, she saw him walk onto a stage in a brown suit, surrounded by an enormous crowd. Suddenly, she sensed danger and heard her own voice say, "George Wallace will be shot." On May 15, 1972, Wallace could have used that information.

But then, what would he have done with it?

What would *any* of us do with such information, coming, as it does, from beyond left field—from out of the ball park, so to speak? I asked a New York cabdriver what he would do with such

ILLUSTRATION BY KINUKO Y. CRAFT

368

369

368, 369 From an article that appeared in *Playboy* magazine. It deals with the question of whether one should predict catastrophes, even if no one believes them at the moment. Through the perforated eye-holes one can see the eyes on the next double spread (Fig. 369). (USA)
370, 371 A fanatical player and winner tempts his fate by combatting the balls with bound hands and feet in a giant pin-ball machine. (USA)

368, 369 Aus einem Artikel, der unter dem Titel «Böse Träume im Futurum» im *Playboy* erschien. Es geht darum, ob man Katastrophen voraussagen soll, auch wenn niemand daran glaubt. Durch die ausgestanzten Augenhöhlen sieht man die Augen auf der übernächsten Seite (Abb. 369). (USA)
370, 371 Ein fanatischer Spieler und Gewinner fordert sein Schicksal heraus, indem er in einem riesen Flipperkasten mit gebundenen Händen und Füssen auf einem Roller gegen die Bälle kämpft. (USA)

368, 369 D'un article du *Playboy,* intitulé «Des rêves chimériques au future»: est-ce qu'il est opportun de prédire les catastrophes bien que personne n'y croie. A travers les orbites découpées à l'emporte-pièce on voit les yeux à la double page suivante (fig. 369). (USA)
370, 371 Un joueur fanatique qui gagne toujours tente fortune en se rendant dans un immense billard électrique, où, avec les mains et pieds liés au moto, il doit renvoyer les billes avec son corps. (USA)

ARTIST / KÜNSTLER / ARTISTE:

368, 369 Kinuko Craft
370, 371 Di-Maccio

DESIGNER / GESTALTER / MAQUETTISTE:

368, 369 Bob Post

ART DIRECTOR / DIRECTEUR ARTISTIQUE:

368, 369 Tom Staebler
370, 371 Frank DeVino

PUBLISHER / VERLEGER / EDITEUR:

368, 369 Playboy Enterprises, Inc.
370, 371 Omni Publications International Ltd.

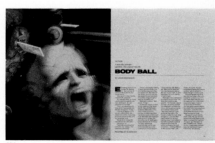

370

372

373

372, 373 Illustration in actual size and introductory double spread for another work of fiction published in *Omni,* about two rich beauties who are out to catch a sailor and who then suddenly find themselves snared in their own trap. (USA)
374 Full-page illustration for the work "The Big Book of Biological Agriculture". (AUT)
375 Full-page illustration in dark shades from an article entitled *Supergene* that appeared in *Omni* magazine. Richard Cutler discusses here the few important genes located on a single chromosome that could reveal the secret to aging and to life extension. (USA)

372, 373 Illustration (Originalgrösse) und einleitende Doppelseite eines weiteren Fiction-Romans aus *Omni.* Es geht um zwei sehr reiche Schönheiten, die in einem mondänen Ferienort auf Männerfang gehen und sich plötzlich in ihrer eigenen Falle finden. (USA)
374 Ganzseitige Illustration für das Werk *Das grosse Buch vom biologischen Landbau.* (AUT)
375 Ganzseitige Illustration in dunklen Farbtönen zu einem Artikel in der Zeitschrift *Omni,* der unter dem Titel «Supergene» erschien. Richard Cutler, ein bekannter Gerontologe, diskutiert hier in der Altersforschung erzielte Resultate. (USA)

374

PUBLISHER / VERLEGER / EDITEUR:

372, 373, 375 Omni Publications International Ltd.
374 Orag-Verlag

372, 373 Illustration (grandeur nature) et première page d'un autre roman paru dans le magazine *Omni*. Ici on raconte l'histoire de deux beautés très riches à la chasse aux hommes dans une station balnéaire mondaine où elles se trouvent prise dans leur propre piège. (USA)
374 Illustration d'un ouvrage intitulé «Le grand livre de l'agriculture biologique». (AUT)
375 Illustration pleine page en tons foncés accompagnant un article du magazine *Omni* qui a paru sous le titre «Supergènes». Richard Cutler, un gérontologue bien connu, discute ici les résultats obtenus dans l'étude de la vieillesse et des phénomènes du vieillissement. (USA)

Magazine Illustrations

375

Magazine Illustrations
Zeitschriften-Illustrationen
Illustrations de périodiques

ARTIST / KÜNSTLER / ARTISTE:

376 Jacqui Morgan
377 Pat Nagel
378 Joann Daley
379 Erhard Göttlicher
380 Fred-Jürgen Rogner

DESIGNER / GESTALTER / MAQUETTISTE:

377 Bruce Hansen
378 Bob Post

ART DIRECTOR / DIRECTEUR ARTISTIQUE:

376, 379, 380 Rainer Wörtmann
377, 378 Tom Staebler

PUBLISHER / VERLEGER / ÉDITEUR:

376, 379, 380 Heinrich Bauer Verlag
377, 378 Playboy Enterprises, Inc.

376

376 Double-spread illustration from the German edition of *Playboy*, for a story about Truman Capote. Blue sofa, beige and lilac dress, white suit. (GER)
377 *The tomorrow show* is the title of this article from *Playboy*. Five famous designers—here Bert Pulitzer and Calvin Klein—focus on "look-ahead looks" for the eighties. Olive-green, beige and brown. (USA)
378 Introductory double spread for an article about David Duke, one of the leaders of the Ku Klux Klan, and on its terror that is again widespread today. In full colour. (USA)
379 Double spread from a report in the German edition of *Playboy* about grants for German artists enabling them to undertake studies at the Villa Massimo in Rome. (GER)
380 This double spread from the German edition of *Playboy* introduces a report on sex clubs in Munich. Full-colour illustration. (GER)

Die Katzen sind aus dem Park verschwunden. Seitdem der Hund der Direktion, ein Labrador, groß ist, jagt er jede, die sich blicken läßt, über die Mauer zurück. Nur noch auf der Mauerkrone ist für sie Platz zum Sonnen da, auf der Südseite. Dort haben sie, jenseits der Straße, bei der alten Gräfin Ricotti ihren festen Futterplatz. Aber zu den Eisschränken der Stipendiaten führt kein Weg zurück. Kein Freitisch mehr. Keine Gelegenheit zum Familienanschluß. Das hat sein Gutes. Ich erinnere mich an ein Jahr der Katzenplage von biblischem Ausmaß. Sie hegten Junge in Wäschetruhen und leerstehenden Betten. Man konnte nachts kein Fenster offenhalten, ohne zu riskieren, plötzlich bei hoffnungslosen Steißlagen mit anfassen zu müssen. Abenteuerliche Kreuzungen sprangen herum, stummelbeinig, mit Bürzeln oder Knickschwänzen, kaninchenhaftes Kroppzeug, das einem den halben Finger abbiß, wenn man es fütterte. Als die Ausgaben für Dosenfutter in den knappen Etats durchschlugen, wurde Familienplanung unaufschiebbar. Aber wer nahm den jungen Müttern einen Teil der Brut, traute sich, sie gegen die Mauer zu werfen, im Brunnen zu ertränken, mit der Hacke zu erschlagen? Die Dichterin von Nummer zehn verwahrte sich gegen „KZ-Methoden". Blieb am Ende wie früher alle Schmutzarbeit am italienischen Gärtner hängen? „KZ-Methoden." Das kann passieren. Daß einer ganz gesund von Deutschland wegfährt, und plötzlich, nach zwei, drei Monaten Villa Massimo, fängt er an, „so merkwürdig zu reden". Noch niemand ist hier verrückt geworden. Aber überliefert ist, daß ein kleiner Vogel, mit „einer volksliedhaften Tonfolge, immer ein Taktdutzend, das sich unendlich

IHR DA DRAUSSEN, WIR DA DRINNEN

wer ein stipendium für die villa massimo bekommt, sollte sich so schnell wie möglich eine freundin suchen. denn einsamkeit stinkt
bericht von HERMANN PETER PIWITT

ILLUSTRATION: ERHARD GÖTTLICHER

167

379

377

378

376 Doppelseitige Illustration aus der deutschsprachigen Ausgabe des *Playboy* zu einer Geschichte über Truman Capote. Blaues Sofa, beiges und lila Kleid, weisser Anzug. (GER)
377 Doppelseite aus dem *Playboy*. Fünf bekannte Modeschöpfer – hier Bert Pulitzer und Calvin Klein – bringen einen Ausblick auf die 80er Jahre. Olivegrün, resp. Beige und Braun. (USA)
378 Einleitende Doppelseite zu einem Artikel über David Duke, einer der führenden Köpfe des Ku Klux Klans und den Terror, den er heute wieder vermehrt verbreitet. Mehrfarbig. (USA)
379 Doppelseite zu einem Bericht in der deutschsprachigen Ausgabe des *Playboy* über Förderstipendien für deutsche Künstler, die ihnen einen Studienaufenthalt in der Villa Massimo in Rom ermöglichen. (GER)
380 Diese Doppelseite aus der deutschsprachigen Ausgabe des *Playboy* leitet eine Reportage über Sexklubs in München ein. Mehrfarbige Illustration. (GER)

376 Illustration sur page double extraite de l'édition allemande du *Playboy*. Elle accompagne un récit sur Truman Capote. Canapé bleu, robes en beige et en lilas, complet blanc. (GER)
377 Page double du *Playboy*. Cinq créateurs de mode – ici Bert Pulitzer et Calvin Klein – donnent leur avis sur les tendances des années 80. Vert olive, resp. beige et brun. (USA)
378 Première page double d'un article sur David Duke, l'un des chefs de fil du Ku Klux Klan, et le terreur qui ravage de plus en plus violemment. En polychromie. (USA)
379 Page double d'un rapport publié dans l'édition allemande du *Playboy*: il est question des bourses offertes aux artistes et écrivains allemands et leur séjour à la Villa Massimo à Rome. (GER)
380 Cette page double extraite de l'édition allemande du *Playboy* introduit un reportage sur les sex clubs de Munich. Illustration en polychromie. (GER)

An Sexklubs
herrscht in München
kein Mangel. Und
auch am
einfühlsamen Service
fehlt's nicht
Reportage von
WOLFGANG FRANK

BÖRSE DER HEISSEN TRIEBE

Die drei Typen an der Bar gaben keinen Ton von sich. Saßen da wie Hinkelsteine und fixierten ihr Bier. Den Bartender mußten wir zweimal rufen, bevor er uns den Edelzwicker brachte. In der „Zenzi-Alm" im nördlichen Vorfeld Münchens war wohl nicht viel los. Als wir kamen, war mir eine Blondine aufgefallen, gleich rechts vom Eingang. Sie war die einzige Frau in dem Laden. Jemand hatte sich neben sie gesetzt, und sie lehnte sich an ihn;

380

381

382

ARTIST / KÜNSTLER / ARTISTE:

381 Kinuko Craft
382 Brad Holland
383 Fred-Jürgen Rogner
384 Thomas Ingham

DESIGNER / GESTALTER / MAQUETTISTE:

381, 384 Len Willis
382 Kerig Pope

ART DIRECTOR / DIRECTEUR ARTISTIQUE:

381 Arthur Paul
382, 384 Tom Staebler
383 Rainer Wörtmann

PUBLISHER / VERLEGER / EDITEUR:

381, 382, 384 Playboy Enterprises, Inc.
383 Heinrich Bauer Verlag

Magazine Illustrations

383

381 Illustration from an article that appeared in *Playboy* about twelve solicited magistrates. (USA)
382 Full-colour illustration from *Playboy* for a series of poems by Shel Silverstein about Uncle Don who used to read the funny stories on the radio on Sundays. (USA)
383 Double spread from a *Playboy* report about flying in formation, here in particular about the stuntflying squadron of the Royal Air Force, called the Red Arrows, and the daring acrobatics they perform. Illustration mainly in red and blue. (GER)
384 From a report in *Playboy* about William Harvey, the CIA's top agent. In actual size. (USA)

381 Illustration zu einem im *Playboy* erschienenen Artikel über zwölf angehende Laienrichter. (USA)
382 Farbillustration aus *Playboy* zu einer Serie von Gedichten von Shel Silverstein über Uncle Don, der jeweils am Sonntag im Radio eine witzige Unterhaltungssendung leitete. Das Gedicht zu dieser Illustration dreht sich um Figuren aus bekannten Comics, die auf dem Hutrand erscheinen. (USA)
383 Doppelseite zu einer *Playboy*-Reportage über den Formationsflug, hier im besonderen über die Kunstflugstaffel Red Arrows der Royal Air Force, die den Leuten in ihren roten Düsen-Trainern förmlich um die Nase sausen. Vorwiegend in Rot und Blau gehaltene Illustration. (GER)
384 Zu einem Bericht in *Playboy* über den Topspion der CIA, William Harvey. In Originalgrösse. (USA)

381 Illustration figurant dans un article du *Playboy* sur douze jurés futurs. (USA)
382 Illustration du *Playboy* accompagnant une série de poèmes de Shel Silverstein consacrés à Uncle Don, producteur d'une émission amusante diffusée à la radio. Dans le poème face à l'illustration il est question de personnages de fameuses bandes déssinées qu'on voit sur le bord du chapeau. (USA)
383 Page double initiale d'un reportage du *Playboy* sur le vol en formation, ici en particulier sur l'escadron Red Arrows de la Royal Air Force; les figures de voltige aérienne de leurs avions à réaction rouges sont aussi audacieuses que les spectateurs les poursuivent bouche bée. (GER)
384 D'un rapport du *Playboy* sur William Harvey, espion de première classe de la CIA. (USA)

385 Illustration in actual size from the magazine *Club* for an article entitled *Pictures of Innocence* on art hoaxes, fakes and forgeries. (GBR)
386 This illustration introduces a story in the German *Playboy* about an unsolved criminal case. The story is entitled "Do you know this man?" (GER)
387 Full-page illustration for a story that appeared in the German edition of *Playboy*. (GER)

385 Illustration (Originalgrösse) zu einem Artikel mit dem Titel «Bilder der Unschuld». Es geht hier um Fälscher und Sammler, die aus der Leichtgläubigkeit weniger versierter Kunstsammler mit Fälschungen Profit schlugen. (GBR)
386 Diese Illustration leitet im deutschen *Playboy* eine Geschichte über einen ungeklärten Kriminalfall mit dem Titel *Kennen Sie diesen Mann?* ein. (GER)
387 Ganzseitige Illustration, die eine in der deutschsprachigen Ausgabe des *Playboy* erschienene Erzählung mit dem Titel *Wie dem Tod die Tränen kamen* einleitet. (GER)

385 Illustration (grandeur nature) introduisant un article du magazine *Club*, intitulé «Images de l'innocence». Il traite de supercherie, de trucage et de falsification dans le commerce d'objets d'art et comment les collectionneurs versés profitent de la crédulité des autres. (GBR)
386 Cette illustration introduit un récit au sujet d'un cadavre non identifié qui a paru dans l'édition allemande du *Playboy* sous le titre «Connaissez-vous cet homme?». (GER)
387 Illustration pleine page introduisant un récit intitulée «Comment la mort se mettait à pleurer» qui a paru dans l'édition allemande du *Playboy*. (GER)

ARTIST / KÜNSTLER / ARTISTE:

385 James Marsh
386 Kinuko Craft
387 Gottfried Helnwein

DESIGNER / GESTALTER / MAQUETTISTE:

385 James Marsh
386, 387 George Guther

ART DIRECTOR / DIRECTEUR ARTISTIQUE:

385 Roger Watt
386, 387 Rainer Wörtmann

PUBLISHER / VERLEGER / EDITEUR:

385 Paul Raymond Publications
386, 387 Heinrich Bauer Verlag

Magazine Illustrations
Zeitschriften-Illustrationen
Illustrations de périodiques

386

387

388

ARTIST / KÜNSTLER / ARTISTE:

388, 389 David Frampton
390 Béat Brüsch
391 Terry Allen
392 Jan Sawka

DESIGNER / GESTALTER / MAQUETTISTE:

388, 389, 391, 392 Catherine Aldrich
390 Béat Brüsch

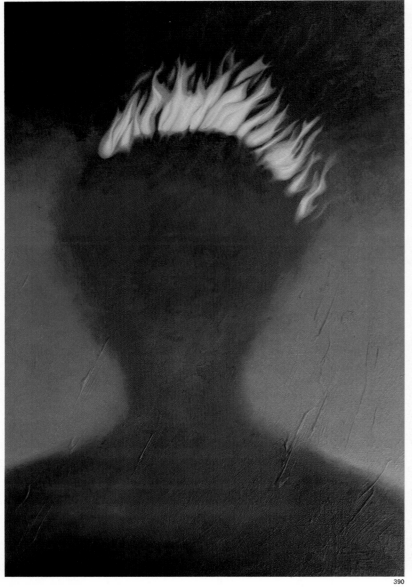

390

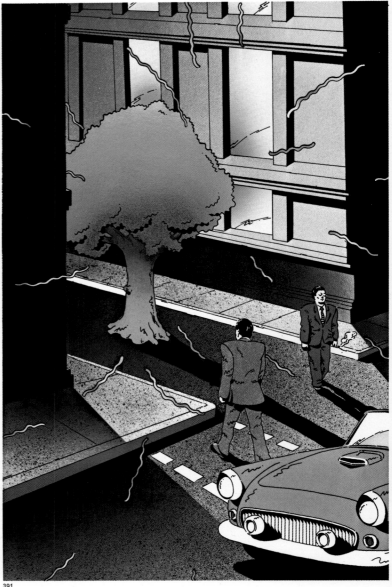

391

150

389

388, 389 Illustration and double spread from an article about special planting methods in the weekly magazine of the *Boston Globe*. In black and white. (USA)
390 Full-page illustration from the *Tages-Anzeiger-Magazin* for a short story entitled *Gli Gli*. (SWI)
391 Illustration from the garden section of the *Boston Globe Magazine* for an article about planting trees on city streets to improve the urban atmosphere. (USA)
392 This illustration introduces an article in the *Boston Globe Magazine* about Californian wines. (USA)

388, 389 Illustration und Doppelseite aus dem Wochen-Magazin des *Boston Globe*. Unter dem Titel «Die Franzosen fanden einen Weg» werden neue Anbaumethoden für Gemüse diskutiert. Schwarzweiss. (USA)
390 Ganzseitige Illustration aus dem *Tages-Anzeiger Magazin* zu einer Kurzgeschichte mit dem Titel *Gli Gli*. (SWI)
391 Illustration aus der Rubrik «Garten» des *Boston Globe Magazine*, hier über das Pflanzen von Bäumen entlang der Fahrbahn, das in den Städten forciert werden sollte. (USA)
392 Diese Illustration leitet einen Artikel über den Weinbau in Kalifornien ein, der nach französischem Muster mit Winzern und Weingrosshändlern reorganisiert werden soll. (USA)

388, 389 Illustration et page double du supplément illustré du *Boston Globe*. Sous le titre «Les Français ont trouvé un chemin» on discute de nouvelles méthodes pour la culture maraîchère. En noir et blanc. (USA)
390 Illustration pleine page du *Tages-Anzeiger Magazin* accompagnant une nouvelle intitulée *Gli Gli*. (SWI)
391 Illustration de la rubrique «Jardin» du magazine du *Boston Globe* où l'on lance un appel de planter davantage d'arbres dans les rues de la ville. (USA)
392 Cette illustration introduit un article sur la viticulture en Californie qui sera réorganisée d'après le modèle français du négociant-éleveur. (USA)

ART DIRECTOR / DIRECTEUR ARTISTIQUE:

388, 389, 391, 392 Ronn Campisi
390 Albert Kaelin

AGENCY / AGENTUR / AGENCE – STUDIO:

390 Béat Brüsch

PUBLISHER / VERLEGER / EDITEUR:

388, 389, 391, 392 The Boston Globe
390 Tages-Anzeiger AG

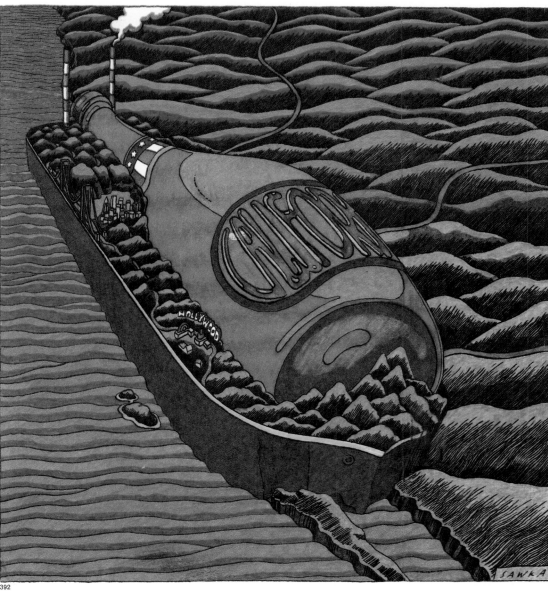

392

393

394

ARTIST / KÜNSTLER / ARTISTE:

393, 394 Mel Williges
395 Patrick Blackwell
396, 397 Jan Sawka

DESIGNER / GESTALTER / MAQUETTISTE:

393–395 Ronn Campisi
396, 397 Catherine Aldrich

ART DIRECTOR / DIRECTEUR ARTISTIQUE:

393–397 Ronn Campisi

PUBLISHER / VERLEGER / EDITEUR:

393–397 The Boston Globe

395

393, 394 Full-page illustration and double spread from the colour supplement of the *Boston Globe* for a preview of a book entitled *Children's Secrets* written by a psychiatry professor. In full colour. (USA)
395 *Healing in Court.* Illustration from the *Boston Globe Magazine* introducing an investigation on psychiatric court clinics whose clientele is the urban poor. They discuss whether the judicial system should punish and correct or whether it should rather follow the attitude "no justice without mercy". (USA)
396, 397 *Notes from the Underground.* From an article on root vegetables. (USA)

393, 394 Ganzseitige Illustration und Doppelseite aus dem Magazin des *Boston Globe* zu einem Vorabdruck aus dem Werk eines Psychiatrie-Professors über Geheimnisse und geheime Wünsche der Kinder. Mehrfarbig. (USA)
395 Illustration zu einer Untersuchung über psychiatrische Gefängniskliniken, in welchen vorwiegend Kinder und Jugendliche aus unterprivilegierten Bevölkerungsschichten einsitzen, und die Handhabung der Rechtssprechung, wobei die einen dem Grundsatz folgen, die Delinquenten zu «bestrafen und zu bessern», die anderen eher dazu tendieren, zu begnadigen und die sozialen Missstände zu bekämpfen. (USA)
396, 397 In diesem Artikel mit Rezepten geht es um Knollengewächse. (USA)

393, 394 Illustration pleine page et page double extraites du magazine illustré du *Boston Globe*. Elles accompagnent un extrait de l'ouvrage d'un professeur en psychiatrie sur les secrets des enfants. En polychromie. (USA)
395 Illustration extraite d'une enquête sur les cliniques psychiatriques des prisons où sont détenus surtout des jeunes de couches sociales inférieures et l'application de la jurisdiction qui signifie pour les uns «punir les délinquants et les corriger», pour les autres plutôt de supprimer la peine et de lutter contre le malaise social. En polychromie. (USA)
396, 397 Cet article avec des recettes est consacré aux tubercules. (USA)

396

397

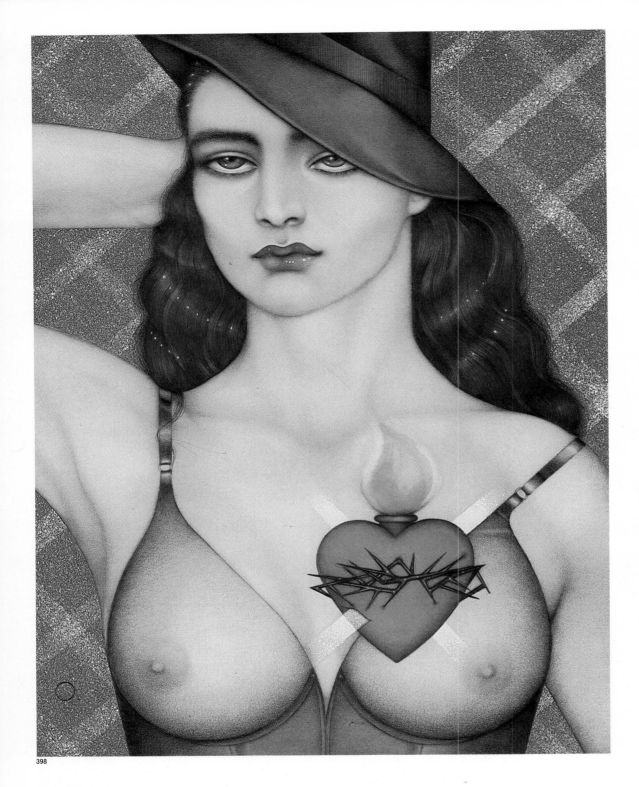

398

399

398 Full-page illustration for a novel by Sean O'Faolain that appeared in *Playboy*. (USA)
399–401 Double spread and full-page illustrations for an excerpt from a new novel about an outlaw and a princess finding true love, published in *Playboy* mgagzine. (USA)
402, 403 Illustration with a half-page overlay in *Playboy* on how to beat the bookies at their own game. In dark blue shades. (USA)
404 Illustration from an excerpt of *My Uncle Oswald* that appeared in *Playboy*. Thanks to a pill, he became a much desired young man. (USA)

398 Ganzseitige Illustration aus *Playboy* zu einem Roman von Sean O'Faolain über eine verführerische, schwarzhaarige, irische Schönheit. (USA)
399–401 Doppelseite und Illustrationen zu einem Auszug aus einem neuen Roman über eine romantische Liebe zwischen einem Verbrecher und einer Prinzessin. In Rot und hellen Beigetönen. (USA)
402, 403 Illustration mit halbseitigem Aufleger: Tips für Dummköpfe, wie Buchmacher bei den eigenen Rugby-Spielen geschlagen werden können. (USA)
404 Illustration zu einem Auszug aus einem Roman über Onkel Oswald, der dank einer Pille zu einem vielbegehrten jungen Mann wurde. (USA)

398 Illustration pleine page accompagnant un roman de Sean O'Faolain sur une Irlandaise séduisante aux cheveux noirs. De *Playboy*. (USA)
399–401 Page double et illustrations de l'extrait d'un nouveau roman sur un amour romantique entre un hors-la-loi et une princesse. (USA)
402, 403 Illustration avec demi page intercalée: on y donne quelques conseils permettant même aux imbeciles de battre les bookmakers dans leurs propres jeux de Rugby. (USA)
404 Illustration initiale de l'extrait d'un roman sur l'Oncle Oswald, devenu un jeune homme ardemment désiré grâce à une pillule. (USA)

ARTIST / KÜNSTLER / ARTISTE:

398–401, 404 Mel Odom
402, 403 Kunio Hagio

DESIGNER / GESTALTER / MAQUETTISTE:

398–401, 404 Kerig Pope
402, 403 Len Willis

ART DIRECTOR / DIRECTEUR ARTISTIQUE:

398–401, 404 Tom Staebler
402, 403 Arthur Paul/Tom Staebler

PUBLISHER / VERLEGER / EDITEUR:

398–404 Playboy Enterprises, Inc.

Magazine Illustrations
Zeitschriften-Illustrationen
Illustrations de périodiques

402

400

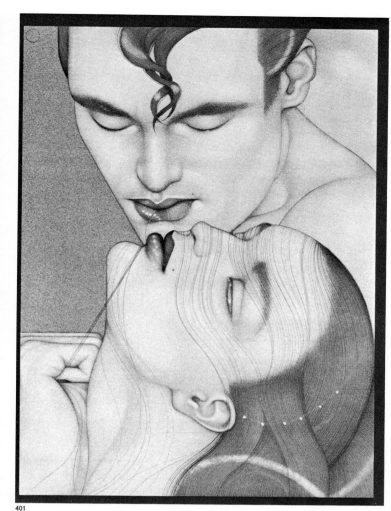

401

403

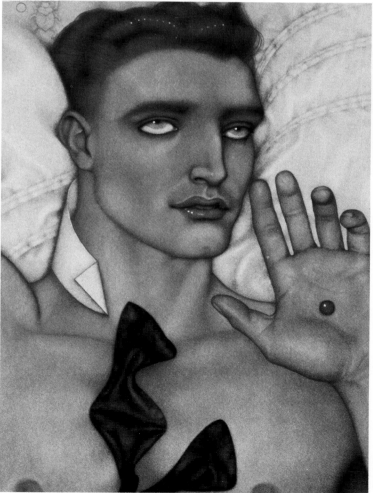

404

405 Full-page illustration from the magazine *Civiltà delle Macchine* for an article about religious behaviour and its meaning for the modern person and new aspects of the mutual influence of religion and culture. (ITA)
406 Spread from a publication aimed at children called *Stone and Steel*, here for a chapter on engineering. Illustration mainly in blue with white and pink. (USA)
407 Full-page illustration from *Penthouse* magazine for a humorous feature entitled *Dumb is good*, on the mind which is a terrible thing to waste, especially on thinking. (USA)
408, 409 Full-colour illustration for the third part of a satire series called *Weeds*, a parody of *Roots*, about an American politician's corrupted family tree. From *Penthouse*. (USA)

405 Ganzseitige Illustration aus der Zeitschrift *Civiltà delle Macchine* zu einem Artikel über das religiöse Verhalten und seine Bedeutung für den modernen Menschen und neue Aspekte der gegenseitigen Beeinflussung von Religion und Kultur. (ITA)
406 Seite aus einer für Kinder bestimmten Publikation mit dem Titel «Stein und Stahl», in welcher die verschiedenen technischen Möglichkeiten dieser Materialien diskutiert werden. Vorwiegend in Blau gehaltene Illustration mit Weiss und Rosa. (USA)
407 Ganzseitige Illustration aus der Zeitschrift *Penthouse* zu einem humorvollen Exkurs über den Geist, den man ja nicht vergeuden sollte, schon gar nicht mit Denken. (USA)
408, 409 Mehrfarbige Illustration zur dritten Folge einer Satire mit dem Titel «Unkraut», eine Parodie auf «Roots», in welcher es um den verfälschten Stammbaum eines weissen amerikanischen Politikers geht. Aus der Zeitschrift *Penthouse*. (USA)

405 Illustration pleine page figurant dans un article du magazine *Civiltà delle Macchine* sur l'attitude religieuse et sa signification pour l'homme moderne et de nouveaux aspects de l'influence mutuelle de la religion et de la culture. (ITA)
406 Page extraite d'une publication destinée aux enfants. Dans ce chapitre intitulé «Pierre et acier» un discute les diverses possibilités techniques qu'offrent ces matériaux. Prédominance de bleu avec du blanc et du rose. (USA)
407 Illustration pleine page du magazine *Penthouse* introduisant un récit humoristique sur l'esprit qu'on doit jamais gaspiller surtout pas en pensant. (USA)
408, 409 Illustration polychrome extraite de la troisième suite d'une satire intitulée *Weeds* (mauvaise herbe); c'est une parodie sur le livre *Roots* (racines), mais ici il est question d'un arbre généalogique falsifié d'un homme politique blanc. (USA)

406

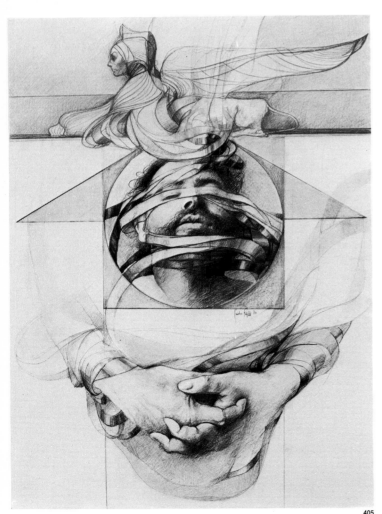

405

407

408

409

ARTIST / KÜNSTLER / ARTISTE:

405 Guido Razzi
406 Guy Billout
407 Fred-Jürgen Rogner
408, 409 James Endicott

DESIGNER / GESTALTER / MAQUETTISTE:

406 Carl Barile

ART DIRECTOR / DIRECTEUR ARTISTIQUE:

406 Ellen Roberts
407–409 Joe Brooks

PUBLISHER / VERLEGER / EDITEUR:

405 IRI Istituto per la Ricostruzione Industriale
406 Prentice-Hall
407–409 Penthouse International Ltd.

410

ARTIST / KÜNSTLER / ARTISTE:

410 Cathy Hull
411 Eduard Prüssen
412 Bob Newman
413, 414 Gary Viskupic
415 Adelchi Galloni

DESIGNER / GESTALTER / MAQUETTISTE:

411 Eduard Prüssen
413, 414 Lee Hill

ART DIRECTOR / DIRECTEUR ARTISTIQUE:

410 Bob Clive
412–414 Miriam Smith
415 Adelchi Galloni

PUBLISHER / VERLEGER / EDITEUR:

410 The News
411 Curt Visel
412–414 Newsday Inc.
415 Arnoldo Mondadori

411

Magazine Illustrations
Zeitschriften-Illustrationen
Illustrations de périodiques

410 Illustration on one and a half page from the *Sunday News Magazine*, for an article on Italian pasta recipes cooked with sea-food. On a light blue ground. (USA)
411 Woodcut as a supplement to the magazine *Illustration 63*, illustrating a fable by Aesop on a raven and a fox. Black on beige paper. (GER)
412–414 Illustration from *Newsday* magazine for two articles written by a psychologist about extramarital relations and making peace with your former husband or wife. (USA)
415 Introductory double spread for a pre-printing of a new novel by Irwin Shaw in a magazine published by *Mondadori*. In blue, green, yellow and pink. (ITA)

415

410 Eineinhalbseitige Illustration aus einem Sonntagsmagazin zu einem Artikel über italienische Teigwarenrezepte mit Meeresfrüchten. Auf hellblauem Grund. (USA)
411 Holzschnitt aus einer Beilage der Zeitschrift *Illustration 63* zur Fabel *Vom Raben und dem Fuchs* von Aesop. Schwarz auf beigem Papier. (GER)
412–414 Illustrationen aus der Zeitschrift *Newsday*. Die zwei Artikel eines Psychologen drehen sich um Ehebruch und um friedliches Auskommen mit dem Ex-Ehepartner. (USA)
415 Einleitende Doppelseite zu einem Vorabdruck eines neuen Romans von Irwin Shaw, der an seinen Roman *Aller Reichtum dieser Welt* anschliesst. In Blau, Grün, Gelb und Rosa. (ITA)

410 Illustration initiale d'un article paru dans un magazine de dimanche. Dans cet article on trouve des recettes italiennes pour des pâtes avec des fruits de mer. (USA)
411 Gravure sur bois d'un encart du magazine *Illustration 63* pour la fable *Du corbeau et du renard* d'Esope. Noir sur papier beige. (GER)
412–414 Illustrations tirées du magazine *Newsday*. Les deux articles d'un psychologue portent sur l'adultère et les bonnes relations entretenues avec l'ex-conjoint. (USA)
415 Première page double de l'extrait d'un nouveau roman d'Irwin Shaw, paru dans une publication des éditions *Mondadori*. L'illustration est en bleu, vert, jaune et rose. (ITA)

412

414

413

416

ARTIST / KÜNSTLER / ARTISTE:

416 Walter Grieder
417 Charles Waller
418 Patrick Redmond
419 Miro Malish

DESIGNER / GESTALTER / MAQUETTISTE:

419 Ursula Kaiser

ART DIRECTOR / DIRECTEUR ARTISTIQUE:

416 Hans-Peter Platz/Gérard Wirtz
417 Charles Waller
418 Patrick Redmond
419 Georges Haroutiun

AGENCY / AGENTUR / AGENCE – STUDIO:

418 Barbara & Patrick Redmond Design, Inc.

PUBLISHER / VERLEGER / EDITEUR:

416 Basler Zeitung
417 The Boston Globe
418 Minneapolis Star
419 Comac Communications

416 "Conveyer-belt communication." Illustration from Walter Grieder's Sketchbook, a column that appears regularly in the *Basler Magazin,* the Sunday supplement of the *Basler Zeitung.* (SWI)
417 Cover of a Sunday supplement for New England that appeared in the *Boston Globe* about *A subtle peril in the air* brought on by asbestos products. In full colour. (USA)
418 Page from the *Minneapolis Star* for an article on Maine food and specialities. (USA)
419 Illustration from *Homemaker's Magazine* for a report on how to rediscover pleasure. (USA)

416 *Rolltreppen-Kommunikation.* Illustration aus Walter Grieders Skizzenbuch, einer Rubrik, die regelmässig im *Basler Magazin,* der Sonntagsbeilage der *Basler-Zeitung* erscheint. (SWI)
417 Titelseite der für Neu England bestimmten Beilage des *Boston Globe,* hier geht es um die Gefährdung der Bevölkerung durch Asbestprodukte. Mehrfarbig. (USA)
418 Seite aus dem *Minneapolis Star* zu einem Artikel über Nahrungsmittel aus dem Staat Maine. (USA)
419 Illustration zu einem Bericht über die Wiederentdeckung des Lustprinzips. (USA)

416 Illustration en grandeur nature extraite d'une rubrique régulière du supplément week-end de la *Basler Zeitung.* Le sujet: communication sur l'escalier roulant. (SWI)
417 Première page du supplément illustré du *Boston Globe* consacré à la Nouvelle-Angleterre. Il est question des produits d'amiante et de la menace qu'ils représentent pour la population. (USA)
418 Page d'un article sur les produits alimentaires provenant du Maine. (USA)
419 Illustration extraite d'un rapport sur la redécouverte du sentiment de plaisir. (USA)

Newspaper Illustrations

160

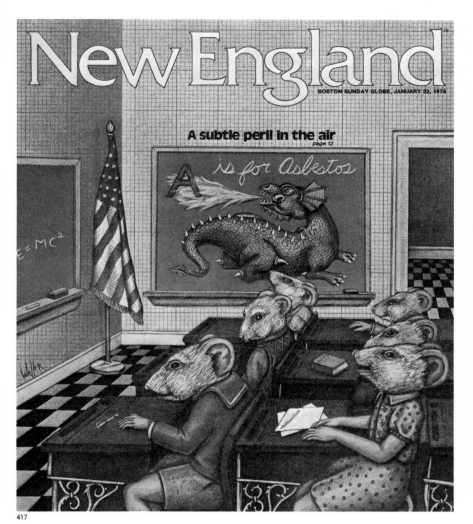

417

418

419

420

Newspaper Illustrations
Zeitungs-Illustrationen
Illustrations de journaux

420–426 Full-colour illustrations that appeared in a regular feature in the *Basler Magazin,* the week-end colour supplement of the *Basler Zeitung.* Fig. 420: "How was it with Darwin?"—this illustration is an allusion to the searching curiosity of man, who is eager not to leave things al they are, but to reveal every secret, even if it means ruining nature; Fig. 421: "The romantic aspect of time"—the past always seems more romantic than it actually was; Fig. 422: the proverb "To make an elephant out of a molehill" is illustrated here; Fig. 423: "Disclosures"—all kinds of weird machines, even for food and eating, are being developed due to advanced techniques; Fig. 424: "The applicant"—invariably she will be swamped by the immense machinery of bureaucracy; Fig. 425: this illustration deals with surgery, and Fig. 426 is another illustration for the "Disclosures" series. All illustrations are in full colour. (SWI)

420–426 Mehrfarbige Illustrationen, die regelmässig im *Basler-Magazin,* der Wochenendbeilage der *Basler Zeitung* erscheinen. Abb. 420: *Wie war das mit Darwin?* – es geht hier um die forschende Neugier des Menschen, die nichts auf sich beruhen lässt und jedes Geheimnis, selbst um den Preis der Zerstörung der Natur, lüften will. Abb. 421: *L'aspect romantique du temps* – die Vergangenheit erscheint immer viel romantischer als sie in Wirklichkeit war. Abb. 422: hier wird das Sprichwort «Aus einer Mücke einen Elefanten machen» illustriert. Abb. 423: *Enthüllungen* – mit der fortschreitenden Technik werden auch Spaghetti-Hack-und Fressmaschinen erfunden. Abb. 424: *Die Gesuchstellerin* – sie wird unweigerlich von der riesigen Maschinerie der Bürokratie überrollt. Abb. 425: *Chirurgie.* Abb. 426: *Enthüllungen.* Alle Illustrationen sind mehrfarbig. (SWI)

420–426 Illustrations polychromes, publiées dans une rubrique régulière du *Basler Magazin,* supplément de la fin de semaine de la *Basler Zeitung.* Fig. 420: «Comment est-ce déjà avec Darwin?» – la curiosité scrutatrice de l'homme ne se contente pas jusqu'à ce qu'elle a pénétré au fond de la matière, même au prix de la destruction de la nature; fig. 421: *L'aspect romantique du temps* – le passé a toujours l'air d'avoir été plus romantique que le présent; fig. 422: on illustre ici un proverbe allemand disant que la même histoire passée d'une personne à l'autre devient de plus en plus dramatique; fig. 423: «Découvertes» – avec le développement technique on inventera bientôt des machines à hâcher les spaghetti; fig. 424: «La requérante» sera dépassée par l'immense machinerie de la bureaucratie; fig. 425: «Chirurgie»; fig. 426: «Découvertes». Toutes les illustrations sont en polychromie. (SWI)

424

421

422

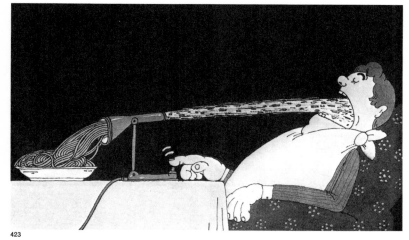

423

ARTIST / KÜNSTLER / ARTISTE:

420 Hans-Georg Rauch
421 Walter Grieder
422 Mario Grasso
423, 426 Hanspeter Wyss
424, 425 Hans Arnold

ART DIRECTOR / DIRECTEUR ARTISTIQUE:

420–426 Hans-Peter Platz/Gérard Wirtz

PUBLISHER / VERLEGER / EDITEUR:

420–426 Basler Zeitung

425

426

427

ARTIST / KÜNSTLER / ARTISTE:

427–432 Jean Claude Suarès
433 Robert Neubecker
434 Sandra Abdalla

428

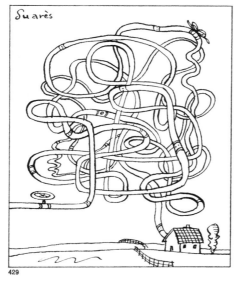

429

430

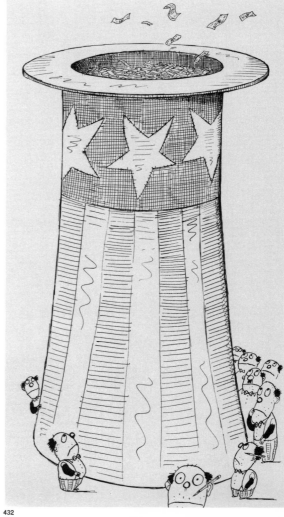

432

DESIGNER / GESTALTER / MAQUETTISTE:

434 Anélio Barreto

ART DIRECTOR / DIRECTEUR ARTISTIQUE:

427, 429–432 Jerelle Kraus
428 George Delmerico
433 John MacLeod

AGENCY / AGENTUR / AGENCE – STUDIO:

433 Inx Inc.

PUBLISHER / VERLEGER / EDITEUR:

427, 429–432 The New York Times
428 Village Voice
433 Inx Inc.
434 Jornal da Tarde

164

431

427, 429–432 Cartoons from the *New York Times*. Fig. 427: *Republicans, keep the speed limit at 55*—urging the new Administration not to abandon the 55 mi/h limit to save gas; Fig. 429: letter to the Editor on *The Folly of Decontrolling Natural Gas;* Fig. 430: letter to the Editor complaining that neither major political party's candidate is worthy of a vote; Fig. 431: *Produce Electric Cars*—the end of combustion engines; Fig. 432: *Make US Public Grants Competitive* – public grants should be harder to receive to squeeze out waste in programs. (USA)
428 From the *Village Voice:* note on the first female judge who also became the first to be removed from the bench because she was posing in her judicial robes for advertising. (USA)
433 Homeheating entails high costs and pollutes the environment (cloud as Dollar symbol). (USA)
434 Cover of a newspaper supplement with suggestions for Christmas gifts. (BRA)

427, 429–432 Aus der *New York Times*. Abb. 427: die neue Administration wird aufgefordert, als Energiesparmassnahme die Geschwindigkeitsbeschränkung beizubehalten; Abb. 429: Leserbrief zur unüberlegten Aufhebung der Preisbindung für Erdgas; Abb. 430: der Leserbriefschreiber meint, dass keiner der Präsidentschaftskandidaten einer Stimme wert waren; Abb. 431: Artikel über Elektro-Fahrzeuge; Abb. 432: Beschränkung der Staatsgelder zur Straffung der Programme. (USA)
428 Notiz über die erste Richterin, die auch die erste war, die ihres Amtes enthoben wurde, weil sie sich für Werbezwecke in ihrer Richterrobe photographieren liess. (USA)
433 Privathäuser einzeln zu heizen ist kostenintensiv und belastet die Umwelt, was durch die Wolke in der Form eines Dollarzeichens symbolisiert wird. (USA)
434 Titelblatt der Geschenkartikel-Beilage einer Abendzeitung. (BRA)

427, 429–432 Caricatures du *New York Times*. Fig. 427: la nouvelle Administration est exhortée de ne pas supprimer la limitation de vitesse pour économiser l'énergie; fig. 429: lettre à l'éditeur sur la folie de débloquer les prix du gaz naturel; fig. 430: l'auteur de la lettre est d'avis qu'aucun candidat à la présidence a mérité un vote; fig. 431: sur la fabrication d'électromoteurs; fig. 432: sur la restriction d'emprunts d'Etat en faveur de programmes plus efficaces et moins coûteux. (USA)
428 Caricature d'une note sur le premier juge féminin; elle était aussi la première à être relevée de ses fonctions car elle s'était fait photographier dans sa robe de juge pour la publicité. (USA)
433 Dans cet article il est question du chauffage individuel qui est plus coûteux et augmente la pollution de l'atmosphère, ce qu'illustre le nuage en forme du symbole du dollar. (USA)
434 Couverture du supplément d'un quotidien présentant des cadeaux de Noël. (BRA)

433

434

435, 436, 438 From the "Viewpoint" column in *The Miami Herald,* here for articles about the coming crisis in American-Israeli relations and the hard stand Israel takes on the Palestinian question, about the Cuban refugees and why the United States should welcome them and about Ramsey Clark's private diplomacy in the Iranian hostage crisis. (USA)
437 Illustration for a story in the Christmas edition of the *Kölnische Rundschau.* (GER)
439 For an article in the *Boston Globe* on public gardens and city planning. (USA)
440 From the *New York Times* about the dispute over teaching-physicians' salaries. (USA)

435, 436, 438 Aus der Rubrik «Blickpunkt» der Zeitung *The Miami Herald,* hier zu Artikeln über die harte Linie, die Israel in der Palästina-Frage einschlägt und die verstärkte Abhängigkeit von den USA, über den Exodus von Kubanern nach Florida und über die privaten Verhandlungen Ramsey Clarks über die Freilassung der US-Geiseln im Iran. (USA)
437 Illustration aus der Weihnachtsausgabe der *Kölnischen Rundschau* zu einer Geschichte mit dem Titel *Ein schwarzes Lamm zu Weihnachten.* (GER)
439 Zu einem Artikel über Parkanlagen und Stadtplanung aus der *New York Times.* (USA)
440 Über Lohnerhöhungen für den medizinischen Lehrkörper. Aus der *New York Times.* (USA)

435, 436, 438 Extraits de la rubrique «point de vue» du quotidien *Miami Herald,* ici accompagnant des articles sur la position intransigeante de l'Israël à l'égard de la solution du problème palestinien et sa dépendence des E.-U., sur l'exode des Cubains vers la Floride et sur les négociations privées de Ramsey Clark sur la libération des ôtages américains en Iran. (USA)
437 Illustration introduisant un récit intitulé «Un agneau noir pour Noël» qui a paru dans le numéro de Noël du quotidien *Kölnische Rundschau.* (GER)
439 D'un article sur les parcs et les problèmes urbanistes. De *Boston Globe.* (USA)
440 Article sur l'augmentation des salaires du corps enseignant en médecine. (USA)

435

436

437

440

438

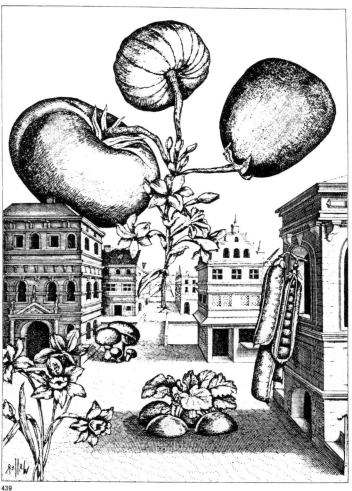

439

ARTIST / KÜNSTLER / ARTISTE:

435, 436, 438 Kent Barton
437 Eduard Prüssen
439, 440 Charles Waller

ART DIRECTOR / DIRECTEUR ARTISTIQUE:

435, 436, 438 Kent Barton
439 Charles Waller/Ronn Campisi
440 John Cayea

PUBLISHER / VERLEGER / EDITEUR:

435, 436, 438 The Miami Herald
437 Kölnische Rundschau
439 The Boston Globe
440 The New York Times

167

Newspaper Illustrations
Zeitungs-Illustrationen
Illustrations de journaux

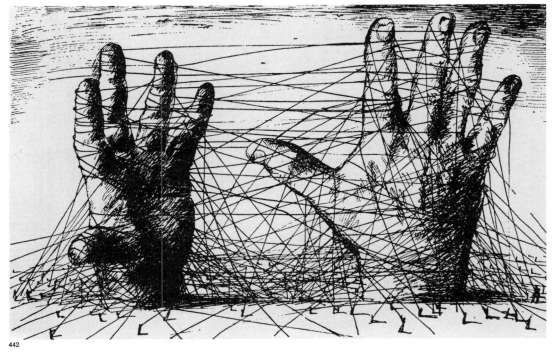
441

441 After the release of the hostages, the *Los Angeles Times* asks what the U.S. should do immediately afterwards. (USA)
442 *America's bounds.* The author is of the opinion that America has been turned into a monstrous abstraction without any hold on the real place. Illustration from the *New York Times.* (USA)
443 Cover of the *Washington Post's* literary supplement. (USA)
444 Looking back to the Fifties when many film and TV people were attacked by McCarthyism. From the *New York Times.* (USA)
445 The author of this article analyses the new box-office sensations of the 80's and states that the villain of films in this decade will be the impersonal bureaucrat. From the *Boston Globe.* (USA)
446 Two articles in the *Los Angeles Times* ask whether or not there should be greater governmental control over oil. (USA)

441 Zu einem Artikel über die amerikanische Politik in der Golfregion nach der Freilassung der Geiseln. (USA)
442 «Amerikas Grenzen.» Der Autor meint, Amerika sei ein monströses abstraktes Gebilde, das den natürlichen Gegebenheiten keine Rechnung trage. Illustration aus der *New York Times.* (USA)
443 Titelseite der Literatur-Beilage der *Washington Post.* (USA)
444 Rückblick auf die Ära des McCarthyismus, als viele Namen bei Film und TV «von der Leinwand verschwanden». (USA)
445 Der Autor analysiert die neuen Kassenschlager-Filme und meint, dass der «Bösewicht» im Film der 80er Jahre der unpersönliche Bürokrat sein wird. Aus dem *Boston Globe.* (USA)
446 In zwei Artikeln wird das Für und Wider verstärkter Staatskontrolle auf dem Ölsektor behandelt. *Los Angeles Times.* (USA)

441 Extrait d'un article sur la politique américaine dans la région du Golfe après la libération des ôtages. (USA)
442 «Les bornes des E.-U.» D'après l'auteur, le continent a été transformé en une abstraction monstrueuse qui ne tient absolument plus compte des données réelles. (USA)
443 Première page du supplément littéraire d'un quotidien. (USA)
444 Vue rétrospective sur les années 50: par le McCarthyisme, de grands noms avait disparu de l'écran du cinéma et de la TV. (USA)
445 L'auteur analyse les nouveaux films à succès et croit que le méchant dans le film des années 80 sera représenté par le bureaucrate impersonnel. Du feuilleton du *Boston Globe.* (USA)
446 Dans deux article on discute le pro et le contre d'un fort contrôle de l'Etat dans le domaine du pétrole. (USA)

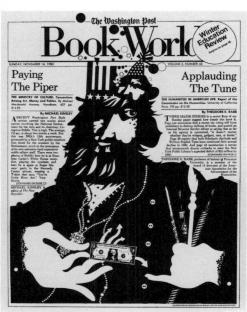

ARTIST / KÜNSTLER / ARTISTE:

441 Nancy Ohanian
442 Eugene Mihaesco
443 Michael David Brown
444 Brad Holland
445 Patrick Blackwell
446 Robert Pryor

ART DIRECTOR / DIRECTEUR ARTISTIQUE:

441 Tim Rutten
442, 444 Jerelle Kraus
443 Francis Tanabe
445 Terry Koppel

443
444

168

WHY THE HOLLYWOOD BAD GUY STICKS TO BUSINESS

Is the impersonal, bureaucratic figure the villain for the '80s?

Continued from the cover

he carries an innocent-looking attache case. In fact, he looks more like an insurance man than a hit man. He may not look like his dastardly ancestors but he's just as nasty.

The '80s may be the decade of movies with the bureaucratic bad guy. He's a classic buck passer who keeps the hero rushing from office to office, from corporate head to district attorneys, from Broadway investors to southern textile mills and never gets his hands dirty. He can afford to be above the scruffy street fighting of his lineage because he's well-educated and articulate. He uses verbal gobbledegook to fend off assaults and spends more time in board meetings than in local saloons.

The corporate villain, according to Hollywood insiders, will be with us for some time to come.

"People identify with the underdog who is up against it," says Jennings Lang, vice president of Universal Pictures, who confirms that several projects under consideration will feature bureaucratic villains who are just following orders. "The movies change with the times and people are too sophisticated to accept Jack Palance (the villain in "Shane") gunning for Alan Ladd. The world isn't like that anymore."

In such commercially successful movies as "Norma Rae," "Kramer vs. Kramer," "All That Jazz," "Apocalypse Now," "The China Syndrome" and "Hide in Plain Sight," the heroes and heroines of these films were up against the bureaucratic, impersonal villainy of the man in the three-piece suit.

Michael Blowen is a Globe correspondent.

"We live in an increasingly impersonal society," says George Englund, an independent producer at First Artists and Paul Newman's partner. "The forces that control our lives are becoming increasingly more difficult to understand. The individuality of the one-on-one confrontation in the old westerns doesn't apply anymore. That's why Paul's movie ("The Sting") was such a hit. They didn't just rip off one man, they conned the establishment."

From Norma Rae's battle with the institutionalized management of the textile industry to Tom Hackland's struggle against the US government in "Hide in Plain Sight," each hero and heroine has to first grapple with the indecipherable rules and regulations before they can meet the enemy. I'm sure that they'd prefer walking into the middle of Dodge City at High Noon and stand toe to toe against the fastest gun in the West rather than confront the endless red tape that hogties them.

Norma Rae would have done well in a gun fight. She's rough, tough and delicately macho. She represents the powerless against the powerful. She is willing to put her job on the line for what she believes in. She is willing to stand up on a textile loom and scream for unionization, for protection against occupational hazards and for her own self-respect. She is a traditional heroine confronting the "new" enemy. Who is she fighting?

She's not fighting the management that she sees every day. She's not fighting the men in their short sleeve shirts with blue collars. She's not fighting her friends and neighbors. She's fighting against an invisible

Continued on Page 12

445

AGENCY / AGENTUR / AGENCE – STUDIO:

443 Michael David Brown, Inc.
445 T. Koppel Graphics

PUBLISHER / VERLEGER / EDITEUR:

441, 446 Los Angeles Times
442, 444 The New York Times
443 Washington Post
445 The Boston Globe

446

448

447

449

Newspaper Illustrations
Zeitungs-Illustrationen
Illustrations de journaux

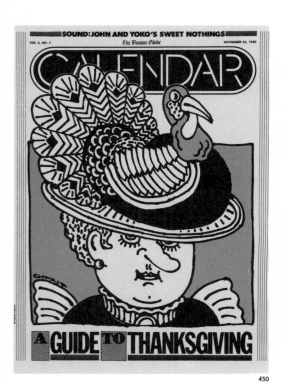
450

451

452

453

454

ARTIST / KÜNSTLER / ARTISTE:

447, 448 Renee Klein
449, 452 Patrick Blackwell
450 Seymour Chwast
451, 455 Jan Sawka
453 Arnie Sawyer
454 Mark Fisher

DESIGNER / GESTALTER / MAQUETTISTE:

447–455 Terry Koppel

ART DIRECTOR / DIRECTEUR ARTISTIQUE:

447–455 Terry Koppel

AGENCY / AGENTUR / AGENCE – STUDIO:

447–455 T. Koppel Graphics

PUBLISHER / VERLEGER / EDITEUR:

447–455 The Boston Globe

447–455 From the weekly supplement of the *Boston Globe*. Figs. 447, 448: a guide to area nightspots where the music swings and dancing isn't Disco; Fig. 449: a look ahead to the Artweek in which 500 artists open their studios to the public; Figs. 450–452: covers of the weekly Calender, here for Thanksgiving, visits to Boston's hidden gardens, Victorian houses and artists' lofts, and entertainment favorites as polled by readers; Fig. 453: analysis of Hollywood horror films—are they an escape from reality or a mirror of reality?; Fig. 454: a guide to courses for youngsters in music, painting, photography, dancing and creative writing; Fig. 455: *The Haunt is on:* on Halloween (eve of All Saints' Day) children wear grotesque masks and tour their neighbourhoods from house to house where they are given sweets and chocolate. (USA)

447–455 Aus der wöchentlichen Beilage der Tageszeitung *The Boston Globe*. Abb. 447, 448: Führer über Tanzlokale, wo die Musik noch swingt; Abb. 449: Vorschau auf eine Kunstwoche, während welcher 500 Künstler dem Publikum ihre Ateliers öffnen; Abb. 450–452: Titelblätter des Veranstaltungskalenders, hier zum Thanksgiving (Erntedanktag), zu einem Führer über versteckte Gärten, Häuser aus der viktorianischen Zeit und Künstlerateliers und zu einer Umfrage über kulturelle Veranstaltungen und Unterhaltungssendungen; Abb. 453: Analyse des Horrorfilms: ist er eine Flucht aus der Realität oder ein Spiegel der Realität? Abb. 454: Führer über Musik-, Mal-, Tanz- und Schreibkurse für Jugendliche; Abb. 455: an Halloween (Vorabend von Allerheiligen) ziehen Kinder mit scheusslichen Kürbismasken von Haus zu Haus für Bonbons und Schokolade. (USA)

447–455 Extraits du supplément hebdomadaire du quotidien *Boston Globe*. Figs. 447, 448: guide des dancings où la musique swingue encore; fig. 449: programme d'une semaine culturelle, pendant laquelle 500 artistes ouvrent leurs ateliers au public; figs. 450–452: couvertures du programme des manifestations, ici pour le jour de l'action de grâces, un guide sur les jardins cachés, les maisons victoriennes et les ateliers d'artistes, et un sondage d'opinion sur les manifestations culturelles et des emissions légères; fig. 453: analyse du film d'épouvante: est-ce une fuite de la réalité ou un miroir de la réalité? fig. 454: guide des cours de musique, de dessin, de dance etc. pour la jeunesse; fig. 455: le jour du Halloween (veille de Toussaint) les gosses mettent des masques horribles faites de courges et vont de porte à porte demander des bonbons. (USA)

455

ARTIST / KÜNSTLER / ARTISTE:

456 Cathy Hull
457, 460 Jan Sawka
458, 459, 461 Eugene Mihaesco

Newspaper Illustrations
Zeitungs-Illustrationen
Illustrations de journaux

456

457

458

461

459

460

ART DIRECTOR / DIRECTEUR ARTISTIQUE:

456 Nancy Kent
458 Steven Heller
459 Nicki Kalish
460 Pam Vassil
461 Jerelle Kraus

PUBLISHER / VERLEGER / EDITEUR:

456–461 The New York Times

456–461 Illustrations from various issues of the *New York Times*. Fig. 456: *A few cold facts about ice cream,* a historical account of this great favourite, which seems to have been invented by the Chinese; Fig. 457: an article on the Op-Ed page dealing with the Seventies; Fig. 458: title page of the literary supplement, here for works from the Third World; Fig. 459: *It's Time to Think About Early Planting* is the title of this article giving advice on the planting of vegetables; Fig. 460: for an ironical story on the Op-Ed page about an unsuccessful attempt to launch a popular play based on the Marxist economic system; Fig. 461: *A danger To Children*—for a report on pollution and how children are the ones who suffer most from it, directly or indirectly. (USA)

456–461 Illustrationen aus der *New York Times*. Abb. 456: «Einige kalte Fakten über Speiseeis» – in diesem historischen Abriss über die Herkunft des Speiseeises erfährt man, dass es von den Chinesen, mit ihrem 5000jährigen kulinarischen Vorsprung auf die westlichen Zivilisationen, «erfunden» wurde; Abb. 457: zu einem auf der Op-Ed-Seite (gegenüber dem Leitartikel) erschienenen Artikel über die 70er Jahre; Abb. 458: Titelblatt der Literatur-Beilage, hier über Werke aus der Dritten Welt; Abb. 459: zu einem Ratgeber über Anbauzeit und -methoden von Gemüsen; Abb. 460: zu einer ironischen Geschichte auf der Op-Ed-Seite über einen erfolglosen Versuch, ein volkstümliches Spiel zu lancieren, das auf dem marxistischen Wirtschaftssystem basiert; Abb. 461: zu einem Bericht, der darüber aufklärt, dass vor allem Kinder Opfer der zunehmenden Umweltverschmutzung sind und bleibende Schäden davontragen. (USA)

456–461 Illustrations extraites du *New York Times*. Fig. 456: «Quelques faits froids concernant la glace» – dans ce récit historique sur la provenance de la glace on apprend qu'elle a été «inventée» par les Chinois, qui ont une avance culinaire de 5000 ans sur les civilisations occidentales; fig. 457: pour un article en page Op-Ed (face à l'Editorial) sur les années 70; Fig. 458: première page du supplément littéraire qui est consacré entièrement à la littérature provenant du Tiers Monde; fig. 459: article sur la période et les méthodes de la culture maraîchère; fig. 460: pour un récit satirique en page Op-Ed sur l'inutilité des efforts promotionnels en faveur d'un nouveau jeu populaire à base d'économie marxiste; fig. 461: dans ce rapport il est question de la pollution de l'environnement dont les enfants sont les plus touchés et dont les effets nuisibles à longue durée ne sont pas encore connus. (USA)

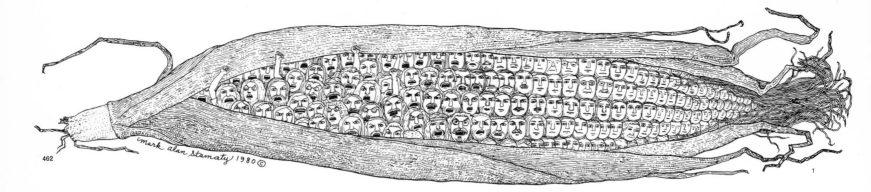

462

Newspaper Illustrations

ARTIST / KÜNSTLER / ARTISTE:

462 Mark Alan Stamaty
463, 464 Eugene Mihaesco
465 Brad Holland
466 Frances Jetter

ART DIRECTOR / DIRECTEUR ARTISTIQUE:

463, 465, 466 Jerelle Kraus

PUBLISHER / VERLEGER / EDITEUR:

462–466 The New York Times

462–466 Further illustrations from the *New York Times*. Fig. 462: for a report on the Op-Ed page about elections in Iowa, a state where the planting of maize plays a great role in the economy; Fig. 463: an article entitled *Authorizing Abuse* about the controlling of citizens by state authorities; Fig. 464: calculations made by the reporter on the food, money and energy aspects of transporting lettuce thousands of miles from coast to coast; Fig. 465: the Iranian Revolution exposes the shortcomings in the CIA's intelligence system which incorrectly analysed the situation; Fig. 466: this article reports on how the latest coup attempts from Korea to Latin American countries have been initiated by youth movements. (USA)

462–466 Weitere Illustrationen aus der *New York Times*. Abb. 462: zu einem Bericht auf der Op-Ed-Seite zum Thema «Wahlen in Iowa»; im Staat Iowa wird sehr viel Mais angepflanzt. Abb. 463: zu einem Artikel über den autorisierten Missbrauch der Überwachung von Bürgern durch staatliche Organe. Abb. 464: der Autor stellt Berechnungen darüber an, wie im Gemüsebau Energie und Geld gespart werden können, wenn Gemüse nicht über Tausende von Meilen von der einen Küste zur andern transportiert würden. Abb. 465: am Beispiel der iranischen Revolution wird gezeigt, weshalb es mit der Nachrichtenbeschaffung durch CIA-Agenten haperte und weshalb die Situation durch Analytiker total falsch eingeschätzt wurde; Abb. 466: der Artikel zeigt, dass die letzten Umsturzversuche von Korea bis Mittelamerika vorwiegend durch junge Leute initiiert wurden. (USA)

462–466 D'autres illustrations du *New York Times*. Fig. 462: pour un rapport paru en page Op-Ed au sujet des élections en Iowa; dans l'Iowa on plante beaucoup de maïs. Fig. 463: pour un article sur l'abus autorisé de la surveillance des citoyens par des organes d'Etat. Fig. 464: l'auteur calcule combien d'énergie et d'argent pourraient être économisés dans la culture maraîchère si les légumes n'étaient plus transportés d'une côte à l'autre. Fig. 465: la révolution islamique en Iran expose pourquoi le service de renseignements du CIA ne fonctionnait pas et pourquoi les analystes avaient totalement méconnu la situation. Fig. 466: l'auteur prouve que les coups d'État de la Corée à l'Amérique centrale ont été initiés par des mouvement de jeunes gens. (USA)

463

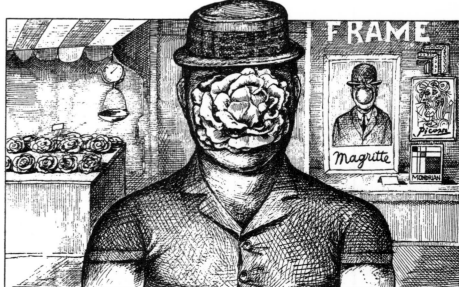

464

465

466

467

ARTIST / KÜNSTLER / ARTISTE:

467–469 Miran
470–472 Frances Jetter

DESIGNER / GESTALTER / MAQUETTISTE:

467–469 Oswaldo Miranda

468

469

Newspaper Illustrations
Zeitungs-Illustrationen
Illustrations de journaux

ART DIRECTOR / DIRECTEUR ARTISTIQUE:

467–469 Oswaldo Miranda
470, 472 Jerelle Kraus
471 John MacLeod

AGENCY / AGENTUR / AGENCE – STUDIO:

467–469 Miran Estudio
471 Inx Inc.

PUBLISHER / VERLEGER / EDITEUR:

467–469 City News
470, 472 The New York Times
471 Inx Inc.

467 Introductory double spread for an article entitled "Prison Cell No. 7". (BRA)
468 First double spread of a satire on the tango, here for Uruguayan and Chilean rhythms. (BRA)
469 Introductory double spread in the *City News* newspaper for the first part of a series of a novel entitled *Don Ricco Castilho* by Eduardo Neto. (BRA)
470 Illustration from the *New York Times* for an article on caring for the old and the lack of sufficient beds in nursing homes and hospitals. (USA)
471 Illustration of an article dealing with the separation of Church and State. (USA)
472 For an article on the evaluation of arms sales and their political consequences. (USA)

467 Einleitende Doppelseite zu einem Artikel mit dem Titel «Gefängniszelle Nr. 7». (BRA)
468 Erste Doppelseite zu einer Satire über den Tango, hier zu Rhythmen aus Uruguay und Chile. (BRA)
469 Einleitende Doppelseite aus der Zeitung *City News* zur ersten Folge eines Romans mit dem Titel *Don Ricco Castilho* von Eduardo Neto. (BRA)
470 Illustration aus der *New York Times* zu einem Artikel über Altersfürsorge und den Mangel an Betten in Pflegeheimen und Krankenhäusern. (USA)
471 Illustration zu einem Artikel über die Trennung von Kirche und Staat. (USA)
472 Zu einem Artikel über Waffenverkäufe und politische Probleme, die daraus resultieren. (USA)

467 Double page initiale d'un article intitulé «Cellule de prison no 7». (BRA)
468 Première page d'une satire sur le tango, ici sur les rythmes de l'Uruguay et le Chili. (BRA)
469 Page double du journal *City News* introduisant la première suite d'un roman intitulé *Don Ricco Castilho* d'Eduardo Neto. (BRA)
470 Illustration extraite du *New York Times* pour un article sur l'aide aux personnes âgées et le manque de lits dans des maisons de retraite et des hôpitaux. (USA)
471 Illustration accompagnant un article sur la séparation de l'Eglise et de l'Etat. (USA)
472 Pour un article sur l'exportation d'armes et les problèmes politiques en résultant. (USA)

470

471

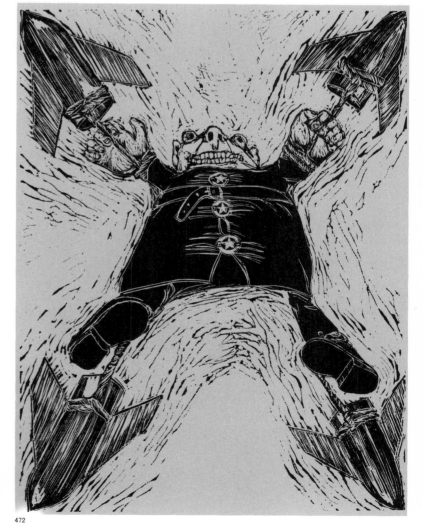

472

473

474

ARTIST / KÜNSTLER / ARTISTE:

473, 474, 476 Rubem Campos Grilo
475 Tim

PUBLISHER / VERLEGER / EDITEUR:

473, 474, 476 Folha de São Paulo
475 Weltwoche Verlag

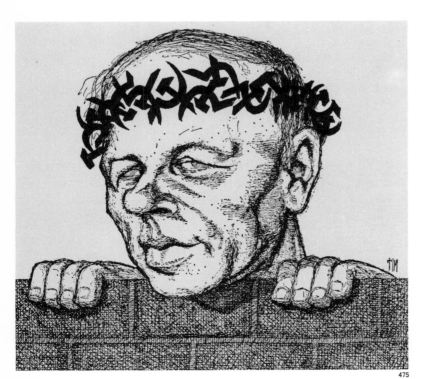

475

473 This woodcut was used as an illustration for an article on the Federative Republic of Brazil. Black and white with orange and yellow. (BRA)
474 Woodcut from the feuilleton of the *Folha de São Paulo* newspaper for an interview with politicians, union leaders and professors on the question of union autonomy. (BRA)
475 Illustration from *Die Weltwoche* for an article on Andrei Sakharov's exile, entitled "Heart and Soul of Resistance". (SWI)
476 Woodcut from the feuilleton of the *Folha de São Paulo* newspaper for an interview with Marcio Moreira Alves on the immunity and inviolability of members of parliament. (BRA)

473 Dieser Holzschnitt wurde als Illustration zu einem Artikel über die Föderative Republik Brasilien verwendet. Schwarzweiss mit Orange und Gelb. (BRA)
474 Holzschnitt aus dem Feuilleton der Zeitung *Folha de São Paulo* zu einem Interview mit Politikern, Gewerkschaftsführern und Professoren über die Frage der gewerkschaftlichen Autonomie. (BRA)
475 Illustration aus der Wochenzeitung *Die Weltwoche* zu einem Artikel über Andrej Sacharows Verbannung mit dem Titel *Herz und Geist des Widerstands*. (SWI)
476 Holzschnitt aus dem Feuilleton der Zeitung *Folha de São Paulo* zu einem Interview mit Marcio Moreira Alves, über die Immunität und Unverletzlichkeit von Abgeordneten. (BRA)

473 Cette gravure sur bois illustre un article consacré à la République Fédérale du Brésil. En noir et blanc avec jaune et orange. (BRA)
474 Gravure sur bois extraite du feuilleton du journal *Folha de São Paulo;* elle accompagne une interview avec des hommes politiques, des représentants des syndicats et des professeurs ès science politique sur l'autonomie syndicale. (BRA)
475 Illustration de l'hebdomadaire *Die Weltwoche* extraite d'un article sur la relégation d'Andreï Sakharov, défenseur des droits de l'homme. (SWI)
476 Gravure sur bois du feuilleton du quotidien *Folha de São Paulo* figurant dans une interview avec Marcio Moreira Alves sur l'immunité et l'inviolabilité parlementaires. (BRA)

**Newspaper Illustrations
Zeitungs-Illustrationen
Illustrations de journaux**

477

Magazine Illustrations
Zeitschriften-Illustrationen
Illustrations de périodiques

477 Illustration from the Russian edition of *America* magazine, published by the U.S. International Communication Agency. The article deals with American principles: equality and dynamics. (USR)
478 Spread from *Extra* magazine with various linocuts about a New York porno area. (USA)
479 Linocut from *Prime Time* magazine for an article on sex therapy. This periodical is primarily aimed at the elder generation. (USA)
480 Illustration from *Scouting* magazine. (USA)

477 Illustration aus der russischen Ausgabe der Zeitschrift *America*, die von der U.S. International Communication Agency herausgegeben wird. Der Artikel behandelt einen amerikanischen Grundsatz: Gleichheit und Dynamik. (USR)
478 Seite aus der Zeitschrift *Extra* mit verschiedenen Linolschnitten über ein Newyorker Pornoviertel. (USA)
479 Linolschnitt aus der Zeitschrift *Prime Time*, die sich vor allem an die ältere Generation richtet. Im Artikel geht es um Sex-Therapie. (USA)
480 Illustration aus der Zeitschrift *Scouting* zu einem Bericht über eine Gruppe von Leuten, die die Kinderfernseh-Programme überwachen. (USA)

477 Illustration de l'édition russe du magazine *America*, publié par l'U.S. International Communication Agency. L'article porte sur un principe américain: l'égalité et le dynamisme. (USR)
478 Page extraite du journal *Extra*. Linogravures sur un quartier porno de New York. (USA)
479 Illustration d'un article sur la thérapie sexuelle publié dans *Prime Time*, un magazine s'adressant à des gens d'un certain âge. Linogravure en noir-blanc. (USA)
480 Illustration pour le magazine *Scouting*: un groupe de contrôle de la TV pour enfants. (USA)

ARTIST / KÜNSTLER:

477 Brad Holland
478–480 Randall Enos

ART DIRECTOR:

477 Dorothy Fall
478 Herb Lubalin
479 Judy Fendelman
480 Joseph Conolly

PUBLISHER / VERLEGER:

477 US International
    Communication Agency
478 Avant-Garde Media, Inc.
479 Prime Time Communications
480 Scouting Magazine

478

479

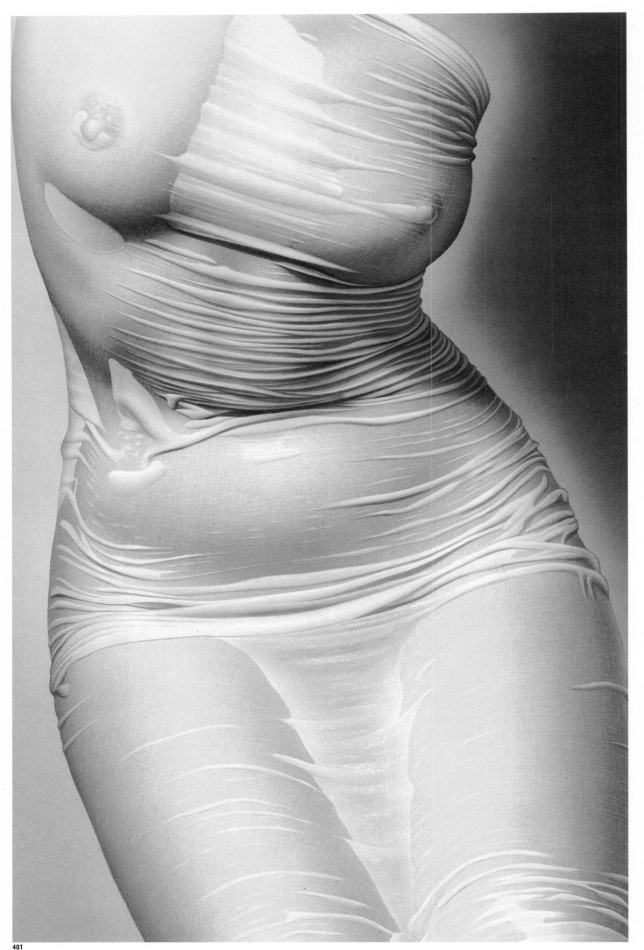

481

481 From an article in *Illustration* magazine devoted entirely to the super-realism of Yosuke Onishi. The artist draws the illustration according to a photograph, applies various mask screens (wet fabric, shadow, etc.) and then completes the illustration with a paintbrush, scraper and airbrush. (JPN)
482 For an article in *Wharton Magazine* about the shaping of cities and their corresponding land-use controls and zoning ordinance regulations. (USA)
483 Cover illustration from *Venture*, a magazine for entrepreneurs, here referring to an article entitled *Information, please.* (USA)
484 From *Nursing* magazine for an article dealing with battered wives. (USA)
485 Illustration introducing an article in *Science* magazine entitled *Images of the Night*, dealing with the physiological roots of dreaming. (USA)

ARTIST / KÜNSTLER / ARTISTE:

481 Yosuke Ohnishi
482 Ed Soyka
483 Geoffrey Moss
484 Bea Weidner
485 Ron Miller

DESIGNER / GESTALTER / MAQUETTISTE:

482 Mitch Shostak
484 Bea Weidner
485 Rodney Williams/Mary Challinor

ART DIRECTOR / DIRECTEUR ARTISTIQUE:

481 Yosuke Ohnishi
482 Mitch Shostak
483 Barrie Davidson
484 Jake Smith

PUBLISHER / VERLEGER / EDITEUR:

481 Genkosha Publishing Co.
482 The Wharton Magazine
483 Venture Magazine
484 Intermed Communications, Inc.
485 A.A.A.S.

Trade Magazines

482

484

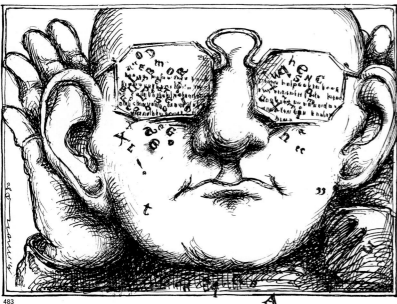

483

481 Zu einem Artikel aus *Illustration* über den Super-Realismus von Yosuke Onishi. Er überträgt die Illustration nach einem Photo, legt verschiedene Masken an (nasses Gewebe, Schatten etc.) und arbeitet dann mit Pinsel, Schaber und Spritzpistole die Illustration aus. (JPN)
482 Zu einem Artikel über New Yorks Bauzonen-Plan und die Bebauungs-Reglemente. (USA)
483 Umschlagillustration einer Unternehmerzeitschrift zum Thema «Mehr Information». (USA)
484 Aus einer Zeitschrift für Krankenpflegepersonal: Artikel über geschlagene Frauen. (USA)
485 Illustration zu einem Artikel über die physiologischen Hintergründe des Träumens. (USA)

481 Extrait d'un article d'*Illustration* sur l'hyper-réalisme de Yosuke Onishi. Il fait ses illustrations d'après une photo, puis il met des masques (tissu mouillé, ombres etc.) et commence à l'exécuter en détail avec le pinceau, le couteau à racler et l'aérographe. (JPN)
482 D'un article sur la réglementation et la planification de la construction à New York. (USA)
483 Illustration de couverture d'un magazine pour entrepreneurs: plus d'information s.v.p. (USA)
484 Extrait d'un magazine destiné aux gardes malades: article sur les femmes battues. (USA)
485 Illustration introduisant un article sur le processus physiologique des rêves. (USA)

485

487

486

488

ARTIST / KÜNSTLER / ARTISTE:

486 Juan José Balzi
487–489 Francisco Graells (Pancho)
490 Carol Wald
491 Bob Susuki
492 Frances Jetter

DESIGNER / GESTALTER / MAQUETTISTE:

490 Frank Rothman
491 Stephen Costello

ART DIRECTOR / DIRECTEUR ARTISTIQUE:

486 Juan José Balzi
490 Frank Rothman
491 Stephen Costello
492 Sheila Wolf

AGENCY / AGENTUR / AGENCE – STUDIO:

486 Estudio Balzi

PUBLISHER / VERLEGER / EDITEUR:

486 Argos Vergara S. A.
487–489 El Nacional
490 Hearst Corp.
491 Comac Communications
492 Harper's Magazine, Inc.

490

A CONSUMING PASSION

For many people compulsive eating is no joke — it's a slow form of suicide.
By Bill Gladstone

The history of man has been called the chronicle of his quest for food. In every age and in every land people have starved and the 20th century is no exception. Obesity has been conceived of as a defence against the dreaded fate of starvation.
— Hilde Bruch, MD, in *Eating Disorders: Obesity, Anorexia Nervosa, and the Person Within*

What would happen if your body suddenly lost its ability to burn calories, and every morsel of food you swallowed turned into fat?

Within a week, it would strike you that you had begun to balloon outward at an astounding rate. Assuming you are an adult man of average weight, you would suddenly find you were gaining almost one pound

491

486 Illustration form a publication entitled "The Witty". Black and white and red. (SPA)
487–489 Three cartoons from the daily newspaper *El Nacional* based on topical themes, here international personalities Alexander Solzhenitsyn, Henry Miller, Masayoshi Ohira. (VEN)
490 From *Science Digest* magazine dealing with healing by means of hypnosis. (USA)
491 From an article about compulsive eating as a slow form of suicide. (USA)
492 Illustration for a short story entitled *Good morning to you, Lieutenant* that appeared in *Harper's Magazine,* about a former Vietnam soldier and his nightmares. (USA)

486 Photomontage aus einer Publikation, die unter dem Titel «Der Geistreiche» erschien. Es geht hier um Werbeleute, die sich als Hähne aufspielen und singen bis sie ärgern. (SPA)
487–489 Drei Karikaturen aus der Tageszeitung *El Nacional,* die zu aktuellen internationalen Geschehnissen erschienen – Alexander Solschenizyn, Henry Miller, Masayoshi Ohira. (VEN)
490 Aus einer populär-wissenschaftlichen Zeitschrift: Heilung durch Hypnose. (USA)
491 Zu einem Artikel über den Essensdrang, der einem langsamen Selbstmord gleichkommt. (USA)
492 Illustration zu einer Kurzgeschichte mit dem Titel «Guten Morgen, Leutnant». Es ist die Geschichte eines ehemaligen Vietnam-Kämpfers und seiner Alpträume. (USA)

486 Photomontage d'une publication intitulée «L'esprit pétillant». Ici on parle des coqs de la publicité. (SPA)
487–489 Trois caricatures du quotidien *El Nacional* illustrant des événements d'actualité internationale – Aleksandre Soljenitsyne, Henry Miller, Masayoshi Ohira. (VEN)
490 D'un magazine scientifique vulgarisé pour un article sur la guérison par hypnose. (USA)
491 Dans cet article il est question de l'impulsion à manger ce qui est une forme lente du suicide. (USA)
492 Illustration en regard de la page initiale d'un récit intitulé «Bonjour, Lieutnant». On y raconte l'histoire d'un ancien combattant de la guerre au Viêt-Nam et de ses cauchemars. (USA)

Trade Magazines

489

492

493

GETTING
THE TEETH INTO
TRAUMA

493, 494 Illustration and double spread from an article in *Emergency Medicine* about jaw fractures. In black and white. (USA

495 For an article in *Emergency Medicine* on test methods for physical strain. Red heart, green title, yellow borders. (USA)

496 Photo-montage as cover of an art magazine. (FRA)

497 *Audible Woes.* An article in *Emergency Medicine* dealing with the problems of hoarseness. (USA)

498 Illustration from *Photography* magazine. (AUS)

499 Illustration mainly in brown for an article in *Chief Executive* magazine advising against choosing your successor. (USA)

500 Cover of a magazine for gourmets and wine connoisseurs. Spaghetti in a red tomato sauce. (AUS)

501 Cover of *Technology Review* for an article entitled *When computers play the human role.* (USA)

502 Cover of a scientific magazine. (POL)

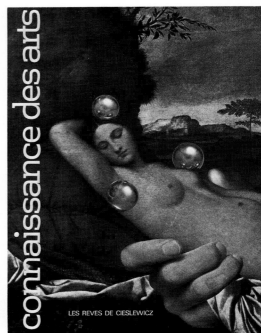

connaissance des arts

LES REVES DE CIESLEWICZ

496

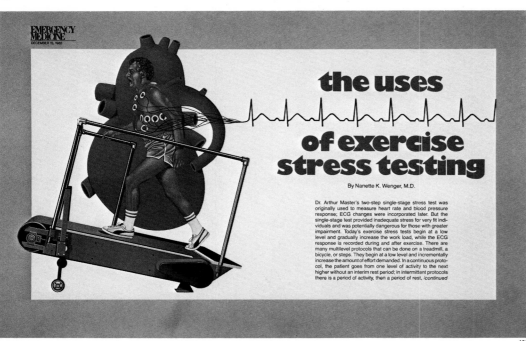

EMERGENCY MEDICINE
DECEMBER 15, 1980

the uses
of exercise
stress testing

By Nanette K. Wenger, M.D.

Dr. Arthur Master's two-step single-stage stress test was originally used to measure heart rate and blood pressure response; ECG changes were incorporated later. But the single-stage test provided inadequate stress for very fit individuals and was potentially dangerous for those with greater impairment. Today's exercise stress tests begin at a low level and gradually increase the work load, while the ECG response is recorded during and after exercise. There are many multilevel protocols that can be done on a treadmill, a bicycle, or steps. They begin at a low level and incrementally increase the amount of effort demanded. In a continuous protocol, the patient goes from one level of activity to the next higher without an interim rest period; in intermittent protocols there is a period of activity, then a period of rest, *continued*

495

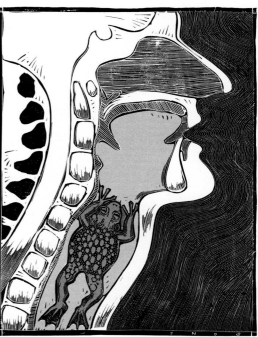

497

ARTIST / KÜNSTLER / ARTISTE:

493, 494, 497 Randall Enos
495 Allen Welkis
496 Roman Cieslewicz
498 Flett Henderson & Arnold
499 Phillipe Weisbecker
500 Waldemar Swierzy
501 Geoffrey Moss
502 Mieczyslaw Wasilewski

502

493, 494 Illustration und Doppelseite aus einem Artikel über die Behandlung von Kieferfrakturen. Schwarzweiss. (USA)
495 Zu einem Artikel über Testmethoden bei körperlicher Anstrengung. Rotes Herz, grüner Titel, senfgelber Rahmen. (USA)
496 Photomontage als Titelblatt einer Kunstzeitschrift. (FRA)
497 «Hörbare Leiden», dies ist der Titel eines Artikels über Heiserkeit in einer medizinischen Fachzeitschrift. (USA)
498 Schwarzweiss-Illustration aus einer Photozeitschrift. (AUS)
499 Vorwiegend in Braun gehaltene Illustration zu einem Artikel, der davon abrät, seinen eigenen Nachfolger auszuwählen. (USA)
500 Titelblatt einer Zeitschrift für Feinschmecker und Weinliebhaber. Spaghettis in roter Tomatensauce. (AUS)
501 Titelblatt einer technischen Fachzeitschrift, hier zum Thema «Wenn Computer die Rolle des Menschen übernehmen». (USA)
502 Titelblatt einer wissenschaftlichen Zeitschrift. (POL)

493, 494 Illustration et page double initiale d'un article sur le traitement de fractures des maxillaires. En noir et blanc. (USA)
495 Illustration introduisant un article sur l'excès de dépense physique et les méthodes de contrôle. En polychromie. (USA)
496 Photomontage en couverture d'un magazine d'art. (FRA)
497 «Affections audibles», c'est le titre d'un article d'un périodique médicale sur la raucité. (USA)
498 Illustration noir-blanc extraite d'un magazine de photo. (AUS)
499 Dans cet article on déconseille de choisir son propre successeur. Illustration en tons bruns prédominants. (USA)
500 Couverture d'un magazine s'adressant aux gourmets et connaisseurs en vins. Spaghetti avec sauce aux tomates. (AUS)
501 Couverture d'un périodique technique se référant à un article intitulé «Quand les ordinateurs jouent le rôle de l'homme». (USA)
502 Couverture d'une revue scientifique. (POL)

498

499

Trade Magazines

500

501

DESIGNER / GESTALTER / MAQUETTISTE:

493, 494 Barbara Spina
495 James T. Walsh
496 Roman Cieslewicz
497 Diane Greene
498 Flett Henderson & Arnold
500 Ken Cato
502 Mieczyslaw Wasilewski

ART DIRECTOR / DIRECTEUR ARTISTIQUE:

493–495, 497 Tom Lennon
496 Gilles Néret
498 Flett Henderson & Arnold
499 Rostislav Eismont
500 Ken Cato
501 Nancy C. Pokross
502 Mieczyslaw Wasilewski

AGENCY / AGENTUR / AGENCE – STUDIO:

498 Flett Henderson & Arnold
500 Cato Hibberd Design Pty Ltd
501 MIT Design Services

PUBLISHER / VERLEGER / EDITEUR:

493–495, 497 Fischer Medical Publications
496 Connaissance des Arts
498 Professional Photography Magazine
499 Chief Executive Magazine, Inc.
500 Lawrence Publishing Company
501 Massachusetts Institute of Technology
502 Krajowe Wydawnictwo Czasopism

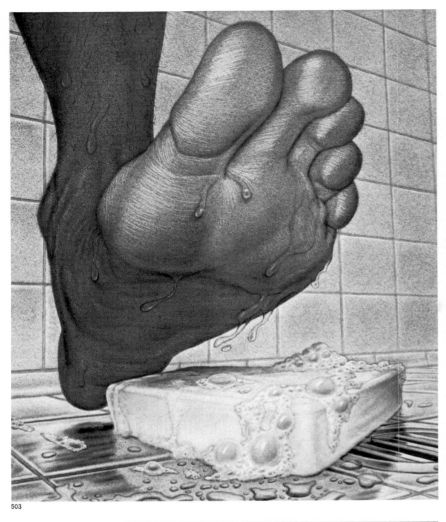

503

505

504

506

507

508

ARTIST / KÜNSTLER / ARTISTE:

503 Ed Soyka
504 Robin Harris
505 Burkey Belser
506 Alan Cober
507 Gerry Daly
508 Jack Pardue
509 Lonnie Sue Johnson

DESIGNER / GESTALTER:

503 Eichinger, Inc.
505 Burkey Belser
506 Herb Lubalin
507, 509 John DeCesare

ART DIRECTOR

503 Bob Eichinger
504 Roland Schenk/Peter Derschka
505 Michelle Brace
506 Herb Lubalin
507, 509 Tina Adamek
508 Jesse R. Nichols

AGENCY / AGENTUR / AGENCE:

503 Eichinger, Inc.
505 Burkey Belser
506 Lubalin Peckolick Assoc. Inc.

PUBLISHER / VERLEGER / EDITEUR:

503 A. T. and T.-Long Lines
504 Management Today/
    Manager Magazin
505 Audiovisual Instruction
506 International Typeface Corp.
507, 509 McGraw Hill Publications Co.
508 US Department of Health,
    Education & Welfare

509

503 Full-page illustration for an article about calculated risk. In full colour. (USA)
504 Black-and-white illustration entitled "The drive for Precision", from *Manager Magazin*. (GER)
505 Cover of *Audiovisual Instruction* magazine. Full-colour illustration. (USA)
506 Illustration from the magazine *U&lc* of the International Typeface Corp., for an article dealing with skull and crossbones. In black and white. (USA)
507, 509 Illustrations from *Emergency Medicine* magazine for articles on rehabilitation after myocardial infarction, and persistent hoarseness. (USA)
508 From *Consumer* magazine for an article about watching the food given to animals. (USA)

503 Ganzseitige Illustration zu einem Artikel über kalkulierbare Risiken. Mehrfarbig. (USA)
504 Schwarzweiss-Illustration zum Thema Manager und Beruf aus einem Artikel mit dem Titel *Zwang zur Präzision, der im Manager Magazin* erschien. (GER)
505 Titelblatt einer Zeitschrift über audiovisuelles Lernen, eine Art von Lernen also, die im Kampf gegen den Analphabetismus zukunftsweisend ist. Mehrfarbige Illustration. (USA)
506 Illustration aus der Zeitschrift *U&lc* der International Typeface Corp., zu einem Artikel über Schädel und Knochen. In Schwarzweiss. (USA)
507, 509 Illustrationen aus einer medizinischen Fachzeitschrift, hier zu Artikeln über die Wiedereingliederung nach einem Herzinfarkt und chronische Heiserkeit. (USA)
508 Aus einer Konsumentenzeitschrift: vermehrte Kontrolle der Tiernahrung. (USA)

503 Illustration pleine page accompagnant un article sur les risques à prévoir. (USA)
504 Illustration noir-blanc au sujet du manager et de la profession, extraite d'un article intitulé «Contraint à la perfection» qui a paru dans le magazine *Manager*. (GER)
505 Couverture d'un magazine consacré à l'enseignement audiovisuel, une méthode d'enseignement prometteuse dans la lutte contre l'analphabétisme. Illustration polychrome. (USA)
506 Illustration figurant dans le magazine *U&lc* de l'International Typeface Corp., ici pour un article consacré au crâne et aux os. En noir et blanc. (USA)
507, 509 Illustrations d'un périodique médical pour deux articles où il est question de la réhabilitation après l'infarctus du myocarde et de la raucité chronique. (USA)
508 D'un magazine destiné au consommateur: contrôle sévère des aliments pour animaux. (USA)

510

511

512

513

Trade Magazines

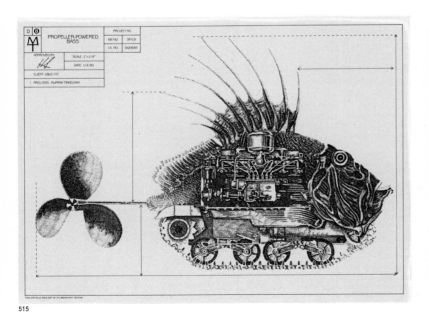

515

516

ARTIST / KÜNSTLER / ARTISTE:

510 Alan Cober
511 Stephen Alcorn
512 Hans-Joachim Burgert
513 Tom Carnase
514 Jim Spanfeller
515 Murray Tinkelman
516, 517 Stan Brod

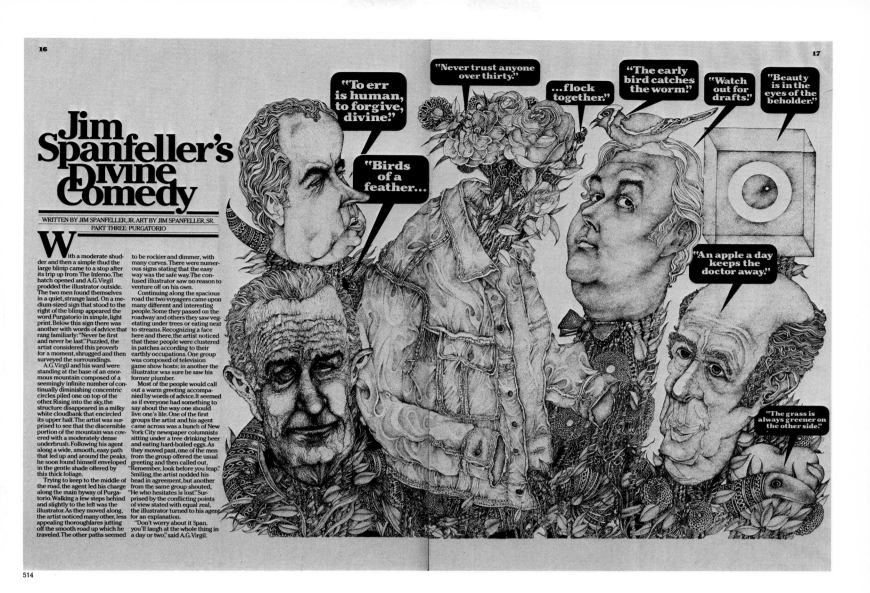

Jim Spanfeller's Divine Comedy

WRITTEN BY JIM SPANFELLER, JR. ART BY JIM SPANFELLER, SR.
PART THREE: PURGATORIO

With a moderate shudder and then a simple thud the large blimp came to a stop after its trip up from The Inferno. The hatch opened and A.G. Virgil prodded the illustrator outside. The two men found themselves in a quiet, strange land. On a medium-sized sign that stood to the right of the blimp appeared the word Purgatorio in simple, light print. Below this sign there was another with words of advice that rang familiarly: "Never be first and never be last." Puzzled, the artist considered this proverb for a moment, shrugged and then surveyed the surroundings.

A.G. Virgil and his ward were standing at the base of an enormous mountain composed of a seemingly infinite number of continually diminishing concentric circles piled one on top of the other. Rising into the sky, the structure disappeared in a milky white cloudbank that encircled its upper half. The artist was surprised to see that the discernible portion of the mountain was covered with a moderately dense underbrush. Following his agent along a wide, smooth, easy path that led up and around the peaks, he soon found himself enveloped in the gentle shade offered by this thick foliage.

Trying to keep to the middle of the road, the agent led his charge along the main byway of Purgatorio. Walking a few steps behind and slightly to the left was the illustrator. As they moved along, the artist noticed many other, less appealing thoroughfares jutting off the smooth road up which he traveled. The other paths seemed to be rockier and dimmer, with many curves. There were numerous signs stating that the easy way was the safe way. The confused illustrator saw no reason to venture off on his own.

Continuing along the spacious road the two voyagers came upon many different and interesting people. Some they passed on the roadway and others they saw vegetating under trees or eating next to streams. Recognizing a face here and there, the artist noticed that these people were clustered in patches according to their earthly occupations. One group was composed of television game show hosts; in another the illustrator was sure he saw his former plumber.

Most of the people would call out a warm greeting accompanied by words of advice. It seemed as if everyone had something to say about the way one should live one's life. One of the first groups the artist and his agent came across was a bunch of New York City newspaper columnists sitting under a tree drinking beer and eating hard-boiled eggs. As they moved past, one of the men from the group offered the usual greeting and then called out, "Remember, look before you leap." Smiling, the artist nodded his head in agreement, but another from the same group shouted, "He who hesitates is lost." Surprised by the conflicting points of view stated with equal zeal, the illustrator turned to his agent for an explanation.

"Don't worry about it Span, you'll laugh at the whole thing in a day or two," said A.G. Virgil.

514

517

DESIGNER / GESTALTER / MAQUETTISTE:
510–517 Herb Lubalin

ART DIRECTOR / DIRECTEUR ARTISTIQUE:
510–517 Herb Lubalin

AGENCY / AGENTUR / AGENCE – STUDIO:
510–517 Lubalin Peckolick Assoc. Inc.

PUBLISHER / VERLEGER / EDITEUR:
510–517 International Typeface Corp.

510–517 Double spreads, full-page illustrations and cover illustration from various editions of the trade magazine *U&lc* of the International Typeface Corp. Fig. 510: another illustration from the skull and crossbone article (see Fig. 506); Fig. 511: from an article entitled *Stephen Alcorn's Ritratti degli Artisti più celebri*, here El Greco, Rubens, Rembrandt and Goya; Fig. 512: introductory double spread from an article about Professor Hans Joachim Burgert's prodigious little handpress; Fig. 513: double spread with New Year's greetings; Fig. 514: for Jim Spanfeller's *Divine Comedy;* Fig. 515: the diesel-driven guppy; Figs. 516, 517: cover illustration. (USA)

510–517 Doppelseiten, ganzseitige Illustrationen und Umschlagillustration verschiedener Ausgaben der Fachzeitschrift *U&lc* der International Typeface Corp. Abb. 510: weitere Illustration aus einem Artikel über Schädel und Knochen (s. Abb. 506); Abb. 511: aus einem Artikel mit dem Titel *Stephen Alcorn's Ritratti degli Artisti più celebri,* hier El Greco, Rubens, Rembrandt und Goya; Abb. 512: einleitende Doppelseite zu einem Artikel über Hans-Joachim Burgerts Schriftbilder; Abb. 513: Doppelseite mit Neujahrsglückwunsch; Abb. 514: zu Jim Spanfeller's *Göttlicher Komödie,* 3. Teil: Das Fegefeuer; Abb. 515: der Diesel-Guppy; Abb. 516, 517: Umschlagillustration. (USA)

510–517 Pages doubles, illustrations pleines pages et illustration de couverture de divers numéros du magazine professionnel *U&lc* de l'International Typeface Corp. Fig. 510: une autre illustration extraite d'un article consacré au crâne et aux os (v. Fig. 506); fig. 511: extrait d'un article intitulé *Stephen Alcorn's Ritratti degli Artisti più celebri* – ici El Greco, Rubens, Rembrandt et Goya; fig. 512: première page double d'un article sur Hans-Joachim Burgert et sa presse à bras; fig. 513: page double portant des vœux de Nouvel An; fig. 514: *Comédie Divine* de Jim Spanfeller, 3e suite: le purgatoire; fig. 514: guppy à propulsion diesel; figs. 516, 517: illustrations de couverture. (USA)

Trade Magazines

518

519

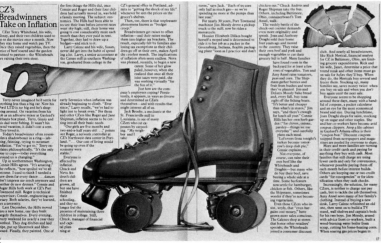

521

522

518, 519 Two covers from the *Esso* house organ dealing with the subjects of energy saving on the part of oil refineries and the search for new oil sources. Full-colour illustrations. (FRA)
520 From the *Crown Zellerbach* house organ, about fighting inflation. (USA)
521 From a business-manager magazine: how do managers cope with restructuring? (USA)
522 Cover of the *Citroën* house organ illustrating a quotation on spring by Jacques Prévert. (FRA)
523 Cover of a chemical company's house organ. Mostly in shades of blue and lilac. (JPN)
524 From the house organ of *Burroughs & Man.* On a yellow ground. (JPN)
525 From an article on patriotism that appeared in the house organ of HNG Corp. Red lettering. (USA)
526 From the *Shell News* house organ with an article on voluntary work. (USA)

518, 519 Zwei Umschläge der Hauszeitschrift von *Esso*, hier zu den Themen: Energieeinsparungen bei der Ölraffinierung und Suche nach neuen Ölvorkommen. Mehrfarbige Illustrationen. (FRA)
520 «Wie *Crown-Zellerbachs* Brotverdiener mit der Inflation fertig werden.» Hauszeitschrift. (USA)
521 Aus einer Manager-Zeitschrift: wie überlebt der Manager Umstrukturierungen? (USA)
522 Hauszeitschrift von *Citroën.* Zu einem Zitat über den Frühling von Jacques Prévert. (FRA)
523 Umschlag der Hauszeitschrift eines Chemiekonzerns. Vorwiegend in Blau- und Lilatönen. (JPN)
524 Hauszeitschrift eines Unternehmens für technische Ausrüstungen. Auf gelbem Grund. (JPN)
525 «Erhebe Dich für Amerika.» Zu einem Artikel über Patriotismus. Rote Schrift. (USA)
526 Zu einem Programm für Freiwilligenarbeit von *Shell*-Angestellten und -Pensionierten. (USA)

518, 519 Deux couvertures du journal d'entreprise d'*Esso France*, ici se référant à un article intitulé *Energie, Economies, Raffineries* et à la découverte de nouveaux gisements. (FRA)
520 «Comment les gagne-pain de *Crown Zellerbach* s'arrangent avec l'inflation.» (USA)
521 D'un magazine pour managers: le manager, comment fait-il face aux changements? (USA)
522 Du magazine d'entreprise de *Citroën*: citation de Jacques Prévert sur le printemps. (FRA)
523 Couverture du journal d'entreprise d'une fabrique de produits chimiques. (JPN)
524 Journal d'entreprise d'une société d'équipements techniques. Sur fond jaune. (JPN)
525 «Lève toi pour l'Amérique!» Illustration accompagnant un article sur le patriotisme. (USA)
526 On présente un nouveau programme d'aide bénévole des employés et retraités de *Shell*. (USA)

520

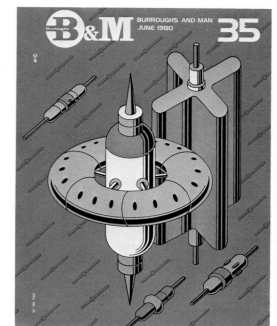

35

524

525

ARTIST / KÜNSTLER / ARTISTE:

518 Michel Palix
519 Chantal Floury
520 Renate Schwartz
521 John Hyatt
522 Joseph Staebell
523 Yoji Kuri
524 Yukio Kanise
525 Jerry Jeanmard
526 Tom Evans

DESIGNER / GESTALTER:

518, 519 Any Dubois
521 Sidjakov & Berman Assoc.
525 Steven Sessions

ART DIRECTOR:

518, 519 Jacques Tribondeau
520 Jacques Wolgensinger
521 Nicolas Sidjakov/Mike Mabry
524 Yukio Kanise
525 Steven Sessions
526 James Groff

AGENCY / AGENTUR / AGENCE:

521 Sidjakov & Berman Assoc.
525 Baxter & Korge, Inc.

PUBLISHER / VERLEGER / EDITEUR:

518, 519 Esso France
520 Citroën S.A.
521 Crown Zellerbach
522 Southwestern Bell
523 Nippon Upjohn Ltd.
524 Burroughs and Man
525 HNG Corp.
526 Shell Oil Company

523

**House Organs
Hauszeitschriften
Journaux d'entreprise**

526

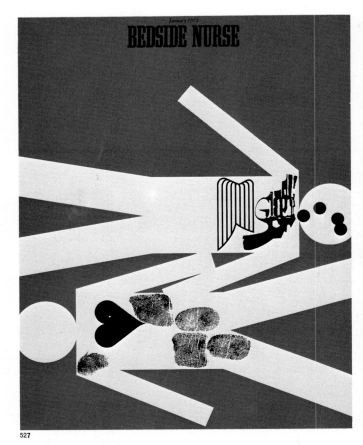

527

528

529

530

House Organs
Hauszeitschriften
Journaux d'entreprise

527 Cover of *Bedside Nurse* magazine. On a blue ground. (USA)
528, 529 From the *Unilever* house organ. Fig. 528: about the "visiting firemen" from the head office coming to see the branch offices; Fig. 529: cover—for an article on China after Mao's death and its gradual opening of its doors to the West. Both illustrations are in full colour. (USA)
530 Original linocut as cover of a special issue by Eduard Prüssen of Daniel Wilhelm Triller's fable *Der Affe, ein seltsamer Buchdrucker, und ein Eremit*. (GER)
531, 532 Double spreads of *Home Cooking*, the Kikkoman Corp. house organ. Strong colours. (JPN)
533 Double spread from the *Donkey-Post*, of which forty copies were printed as a house organ for Eduard Prüssen's friends. Shown here is a tank, added to the usual roundabout in fairs. (GER)
534 Illustration from the house organ *Electric Company Magazine*. (USA)

527 Umschlag der Hauszeitschrift einer Krankenpflegerinnen-Organisation. Blauer Grund. (USA)
528, 529 Aus der Hauszeitschrift von *Unilever*. Abb. 528: über Blitzbesuche von Leuten der Geschäftsleitung bei Niederlassungen; Abb. 529: Titelblatt – zu einem Artikel über China seit Maos Tod und seine Öffnung gegenüber dem Westen. Beide Illustrationen sind mehrfarbig. (USA)
530 Original-Linolschnitt als Titelblatt eines Sonderdrucks von Eduard Prüssen zu Daniel Wilhelm Trillers Fabel *Der Affe, ein seltsamer Buchdrucker, und ein Eremit*. (GER)
531, 532 Doppelseiten aus der Hauszeitschrift eines Soja-Saucen-Fabrikanten. Kräftige Farben. (JPN)
533 Doppelseite aus der *Donkey-Post*, der in 40 Exemplaren erscheinenden Hauszeitschrift für Freunde von Eduard Prüssen, hier zu einer Erweiterung des Karussells durch einen Panzerwagen. (GER)
534 Illustration aus der Zeitschrift *Electric Company Magazine*. (USA)

ART DIRECTOR:

528, 529 Tony Stanford/Kate Lackie
531, 532 Tadashi Ohashi
534 Ron Barret

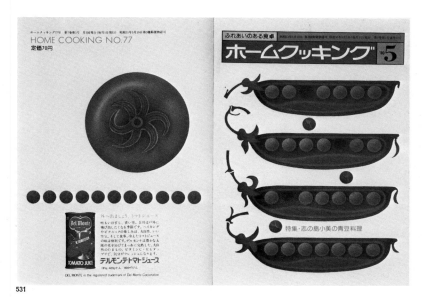

531

532

Ein Karussell drehte inmitten der üblichen Pferde, Feuerwehrautos, Motorräder auch einen Panzerwagen im Kreis herum.

533

527 Couverture du journal d'une organisation d'infirmières. Fond bleu. (USA)
528, 529 Extraits de la revue d'entreprise d'*Unilever*. Fig. 528: sur les visites éclair de gens du siège central dans les succursales; fig. 529: couverture se référant à un article sur la Chine depuis la mort de Mao et son ouverture vis-à-vis les pays occidentaux. (USA)
530 Linogravure originale en guise de couverture d'une édition spéciale d'Eduard Prüssen consacrée à une fable de Daniel Wilhelm Triller (Le singe, un imprimeur étrange et un ermite). (GER)
531, 532 Pages doubles du journal d'entreprise d'un fabricant de sauces soja. (JPN)
533 Page double extraite de *Donkey-Post*, une revue à tirage limité qu'Eduard Prüssen distribue à ses amis – ici la modernisation du carrousel par un char. (GER)
534 Dessin tiré de *The Electric Company Magazine*. (USA)

AGENCY / AGENTUR:

528, 529 Unilever Ltd./Information Workshop

PUBLISHER / VERLEGER / EDITEUR:

527 Bedside Nurse
528, 529 Unilever Ltd.
530 Curt Visel
531, 532 Kikkoman Corp.
533 Donkey-Press
534 Electric Company

534

536

537

ARTIST / KÜNSTLER / ARTISTE:

535 Richard Mantel
536, 537 Barbara Sandler
538 Seymour Chwast

DESIGNER / GESTALTER / MAQUETTISTE:

535–538 Richard Mantel

ART DIRECTOR / DIRECTEUR ARTISTIQUE:

535–538 Seymour Chwast

**House Organs
Hauszeitschriften
Journaux d'entreprise**

535–538 Full-page illustrations and a double spread from various editions of the house organ *Push Pin Graphic*. Fig. 535: illustration in actual size from the *Not quite human* edition; Figs. 536, 537: full-page illustrations for an edition devoted to calamities—here the bursting of the dam at Johnstown, Pa., and the sinking of the *Titanic*; Fig. 538: for an edition about new crime favourites. (USA)

535–538 Ganzseitige Illustrationen und Doppelseite aus verschiedenen Ausgaben der Hauszeitschrift *Push Pin Graphic*. Abb. 535: Illustration in Originalgrösse aus einer Ausgabe, die dem Thema «nicht ganz menschlich» gewidmet war. Abb. 536, 537: ganzseitige Illustrationen zu einer Ausgabe zum Thema «Kalamitäten» – hier zum Dammbruch in Johnstown, Pennsylvania, und zum Untergang der *Titanic*. Abb. 538: zu einer Ausgabe über neue Krimi-Favoriten – hier ein Suchbild, auf welchem die Mordwaffe gefunden werden sollte und ein Kurz-Krimi. (USA)

535–538 Illustrations pleines pages et page double de divers numéros du journal d'entreprise *Push Pin Graphic*. Fig. 535: illustration (grandeur originale) d'un numéro consacré au sujet «pas tout à fait humain». Figs. 536, 537: illustrations en vert pour un numéro consacré aux catastrophes, ici la rupture du barrage de Johnstown (Pa., USA) et le naufrage du *Titanic*. Fig. 538: extrait d'un numéro sur les nouveaux favoris criminels – ici une illustration où l'on doit trouver l'arme du meurtrier et un roman policier. (USA)

AGENCY / AGENTUR / AGENCE – STUDIO:

535–538 Push Pin Studios, Inc.

PUBLISHER / VERLEGER / EDITEUR:

535–538 Push Pin Graphic, Inc.

538

539

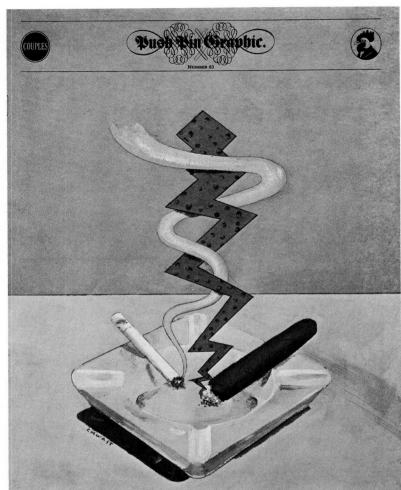

540

541

House Organs
Hauszeitschriften
Journaux d'entreprise

ARTIST / KÜNSTLER / ARTISTE:

539, 541 Emanuel Schongut
540, 542, 543 Seymour Chwast
544, 545 William Gass

DESIGNER / GESTALTER / MAQUETTISTE:

539–545 Richard Mantel

ART DIRECTOR / DIRECTEUR ARTISTIQUE:

539–545 Seymour Chwast

AGENCY / AGENTUR / AGENCE – STUDIO:

539–545 Push Pin Studios, Inc.

PUBLISHER / VERLEGER / EDITEUR:

539–545 Push Pin Graphic, Inc.

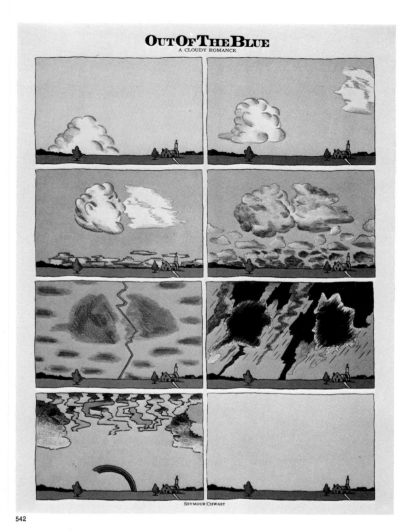

542

543

539–545 Further illustrations, cover illustrations and double spreads from the house organ of the *Push Pin Studios* (see Figs. 535–538). Figs. 539, 540: illustration entitled *Leda and the Swan* and cover illustration of an edition devoted to the subject of couples; Fig. 541: cover illustration of an edition on happiness, raspberry-red ground; Fig. 542: illustration from the *All blue* issue entitled *Out of the blue—a cloudy romance*; Fig. 543: *Guess who's coming to dinner*, all available Italian pastas are portrayed here; Figs. 544, 545: from the *All blue* issue with a series of five double spreads designed in the collage technique to illustrate different expressions with blue (blue blood, blue nose, etc.). (USA)

539–545 Weitere Illustrationen, Titelbilder und Doppelseiten aus der Hauszeitschrift der *Push Pin Studios* (s. Abb. 535–538). Abb. 539, 540: Illustration zum Thema *Leda und der Schwan* und Umschlagillustration einer Ausgabe, die dem Thema Paare gewidmet war. Abb. 541: Titelbild einer Ausgabe über Glück, himbeerroter Grund. Abb. 542: Illustration mit dem Titel «Aus heiter hellem Himmel – eine wolkige Romanze» aus der Ausgabe «Alles in Blau». Abb. 543: aus allen erhältlichen italienischen Teigwaren zusammengesetztes Portrait. Abb. 544, 545: aus der Ausgabe «Alles in Blau» – aus einer Serie von fünf Doppelseiten, auf welchen in Collage-Technik immer neue Illustrationen zu Ausdrücken mit Blau (blaues Blut, blaue Nase) dazukommen. (USA)

539–545 D'autres illustrations, couvertures et pages doubles du journal d'entreprise des *Push Pin Studios* (v. figs. 535–538). Figs. 539, 540: illustration intitulée *Léda et le cygne* et couverture d'un numéro consacré au sujet des couples. Fig. 541: couverture d'un numéro sur le bonheur; fond en rouge framboise. Fig. 542: illustration d'une romance nuageuse extraite d'un numéro paru sous le titre «Tout en bleu», Fig. 543: portrait composé de toutes sortes de pâtes italiennes. Figs. 544, 545: extraits du numéro «Tout en bleu» – en feuilletant cette suite de doubles pages (collages) on voit sur chacune d'elles des illustrations d'autres expressions avec bleu (sang bleu, Barbe-Bleue etc.). (USA)

544

545

546

547

ARTIST / KÜNSTLER / ARTISTE:

546, 547 John Martin
548 Yves Racheter
549, 550 Kjell Ivan Anderson
552 Marcus Hodel

DESIGNER / GESTALTER / MAQUETTISTE:

549, 550 Olle Engström
551 Edward C. Kensinger/Franklin Lakes

ART DIRECTOR / DIRECTEUR ARTISTIQUE:

546, 547 Andrew Smith
549, 550 Olle Engström
551 Edward C. Kensinger/Franklin Lakes
552 Jacques Hauser

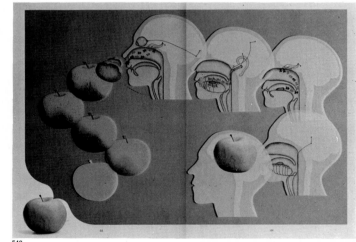

548

549

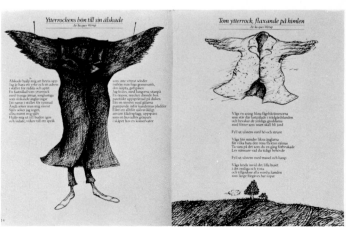

550

AGENCY / AGENTUR / AGENCE – STUDIO:

546, 547 Fifty Fingers, Inc.
548 Atelier graphique Nestlé
551 IBM Design
553 University of Tsukuba/Institute of Art and Design

PUBLISHER / VERLEGER / EDITEUR:

546, 547 Graduate Magazine
548 Nestlé S. A.
549, 550 Relationskonsult
551 IBM Corp.
552 F. Hoffmann-La Roche
553 University of Tsukuba

Utilizing the Opinion Survey for Effective People Management
IBM
551

552

546, 547 Illustration in actual size and complete cover of *Graduate,* the magazine of the University of Toronto alumni. (CAN)
548 For an article in a *Nestlé* brochure entitled *Sensory Evaluation or Sensory Measurement?* Grey shades, apples in red and yellow. (SWI)
549, 550 From the company publication of an advertising bureau, entitled "Of course you can fly!" Here to a still-life with the scarecrow and family and stories about a coat. (SWE)
551 Cover of the IBM company brochure. Grey shades. (USA)
552 From an article that appeared in *Hexagon,* the *Roche* house organ, about psychosomatic disorders. In black and white. (SWI)
553 From the magazine of the design faculty of a university. Japanese characters form a letter. (JPN)

546, 547 Illustration (Originalgrösse) und vollständiger Umschlag der Zeitschrift für ehemalige Studenten der Universität Toronto, hier zu einem Artikel über den Lehrkörper an den Universitäten. (CAN)
548 Aus einer Broschüre von *Nestlé* zum Thema der sensorischen Interaktion. Grautöne, Äpfel in Rot und Gelb. (SWI)
549, 550 Aus der Firmenpublikation eines Werbeberatungsbüros mit dem Titel «Sicher kannst du fliegen!» – hier zu Stilleben mit Popanz und Familie und zu Geschichten über den Mantel. (SWE)
551 Titelblatt der Firmenbroschüre der IBM. Grautöne. (USA)
552 Zu einem in der *Roche*-Hauszeitschrift *Hexagon* veröffentlichten Artikel über psychosomatische Störungen. Schwarzweiss. (SWI)
553 Aus der Zeitschrift des Fachbereichs Design einer Universität. Japanische Schriftzeichen bilden ein Schriftzeichen. (JPN)

546, 547 Illustration (grandeur originale) et couverture complète du magazine des anciens étudiants de l'Université de Toronto, ici se référant à un article sur le corps enseignant de l'université. (CAN)
548 D'une brochure publiée par *Nestlé* au sujet de l'interaction sensorielle. En tons gris, pommes en rouge et jaune. (SWI)
549, 550 D'une publication d'entreprise d'un bureau de publicité, intitulée «Sûr que tu sais voler!» – ici une nature morte avec épouvantail et famille et une illustration accompagnant un récit sur un manteau. (SWE)
551 Couverture d'une publication de prestige IBM. Tons gris. (USA)
552 Du journal d'entreprise *Hexagon* de *Roche* pour un article sur les troubles psychosomatiques. En noir et blanc. (SWI)
553 Extrait du magazine de la faculté d'arts graphiques d'une université. Des symboles japonais forment un autre symbole. (JPN)

Corporate Publications
Firmenpublikationen
Publications d'entreprise

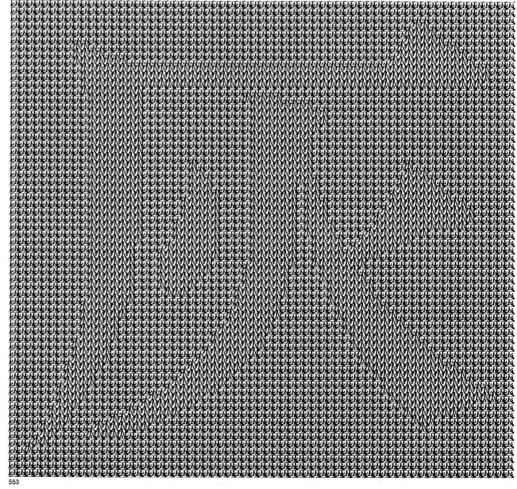

553

ARTIST / KÜNSTLER:

554 Jene Hands
555 Don Weller
556, 557 Studio Springmann
558 Bernard Blatch
559 Greg King
560 Don Oka/Koji Takei
562, 563 Alfred Lutz

DESIGNER / GESTALTER:

554 Sjoerd de Vries
555 Jerry Pavey
556, 557 Gerlinde Mader
558 Bernard Blatch
559 Stephen Miller
560 Koji Takei
561 Courtney Reeser/ Ed Kysar
562, 563 Alfred Lutz

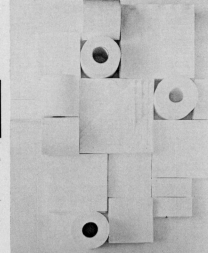

PAPIER FABRIK LAAKIRCHEN AG

556

LETRON GMBH & CO KG ASCHAFFENBURG

557

554

Farm Credit Banks Report to Investors 1979

555

The Sev. Dahl Group

558

559

560

ART DIRECTOR:

554 Sjoerd de Vries
555 Jerry Pavey
556, 557 Norfried &
    Gerlinde Mader
559 Stephen Miller
560, 561 Tom Ohmer
562, 563 Alfred Lutz

AGENCY / AGENTUR:

554 Gratama & de Vries
555 Farm Credit
    Administration
556, 557 Serviceplan
558 Anisdahl
    & Christenson A/S
559 The Richards Group
560, 561 Advertising
    Designers, Inc.

554 Full-page pencil drawing form the Bank Mees & Hope NV annual report and its financial institutions. (NLD)
555 Full-colour cover of the *Farm Credit Bank's* 1979 report to investors. (USA)
556, 557 Two double spreads from the annual report of the MD paper company. Full-colour illustrations. (GER)
558 Annual report on the 100th anniversary of The Sev. Dahl Group. Dark shades. (NOR)
559 Double spread from the 1980 annual report of the Triton Oil & Gas Corp. In bright colours. (USA)
560 Cover of the annual report of Everest and Jennings International, a multi-national. Light green on grey. (USA)
561 Cover of the Financial Federation, Inc. annual report. Red, black, white and blue on grey. (USA)
562, 563 From the annual report of the 101st business year of an insurance company. On silver. (GER)

554 Ganzseitige Bleistiftzeichnung aus dem Jahresbericht einer Grossbank und ihrer Finanzinstitute. (NLD)
555 Mehrfarbiger Umschlag des Geschäftsberichtes 1979 eines Instituts für Landwirtschaftskredite. (USA)
556, 557 Zwei Doppelseiten aus dem Jahresbericht der Papierfabriken MD. Mehrfarbige Illustrationen. (GER)
558 Dieser Jahresbericht wurde anlässlich des 100jährigen Jubiläums herausgegeben. Dunkle Farbtöne. (NOR)
559 Doppelseite aus dem Geschäftsbericht 1980 eines petrochemischen Konzerns. In bunten Farben. (USA)
560 Umschlag des Jahresberichts eines diversifizierten multinationalen Konzerns. Hellgrün auf Grau. (USA)
561 Geschäftsbericht einer Spar- und Darlehensholding. Rot, Schwarz, Weiss und Blau auf Grau. (USA)
562, 563 Aus dem Jahresbericht zum 101. Geschäftsjahr der *Schwäbisch Gmünder Ersatzkasse*. Auf Silber. (GER)

554 Dessin au crayon pleine page extrait du rapport annuel d'une banque et de ses sociétés de financement. (NLD)
555 Couverture polychrome du rapport annuel 1979 d'un crédit agricole. (USA)
556, 557 Pages doubles du rapport annuel d'une papeterie. Illustrations polychromes. (GER)
558 Rapport annuel publié à l'occasion du centenaire d'une société. Tons foncés. (NOR)
559 Page double du rapport de gestion d'une compagnie pétrolière et minière. En couleurs vives. (USA)
560 Couverture du rapport annuel d'une entreprise multinationale diversifiée. Vert pâle sur fond gris. (USA)
561 Couverture du rapport de gestion d'un holding d'épargne et de prêts. Rouge, noir, blanc, bleu et gris. (USA)
562, 563 Du rapport annuel pour le 101e année d'existence d'une caisse maladie. Sur fond argenté. (GER)

Corporate Publications
Firmenpublikationen
Publications d'entreprise

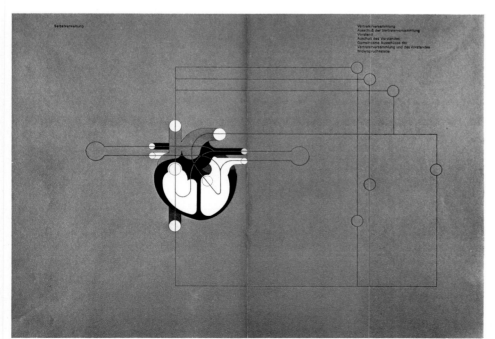

562

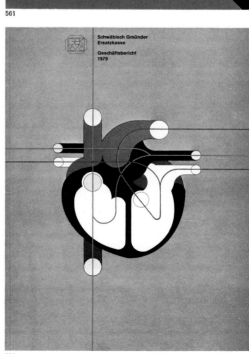

561

563

564

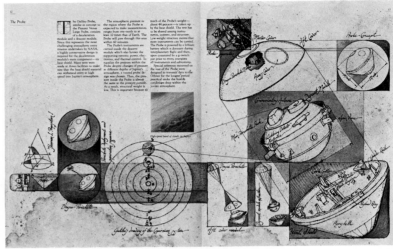

565

566

ARTIST / KÜNSTLER / ARTISTE:

564, 565 Jim Lamb
566 Bernd Keller
567 Haruo Miyauchi
568 Nancy Stahl
569 Norman Walker

DESIGNER / GESTALTER:

564, 565 Ken White
566 Bernd Keller
569 Jim Horne/Norman Walker
570, 571 Bob Paganucci

ART DIRECTOR:

564, 565 Ken White/John Kempton
566 Bernd Keller
567, 568 Alan J. Klawans
569 Jim Horne
570, 571 Bob Paganucci

AGENCY / AGENTUR:

564, 565 Ken White Design Office, Inc.
566 Cevey Keller
567, 568 Jonson Pedersen Hinrichs & Shakery
569 Current Concepts, Inc.
570, 571 Bob Paganucci

PUBLISHER / VERLEGER / EDITEUR:

564, 565 NASA
566 SESA-Deutschland GmbH
567, 568 Smith Kline & French Labs.
569 Sandoz, Inc.
570, 571 IBM

567

568

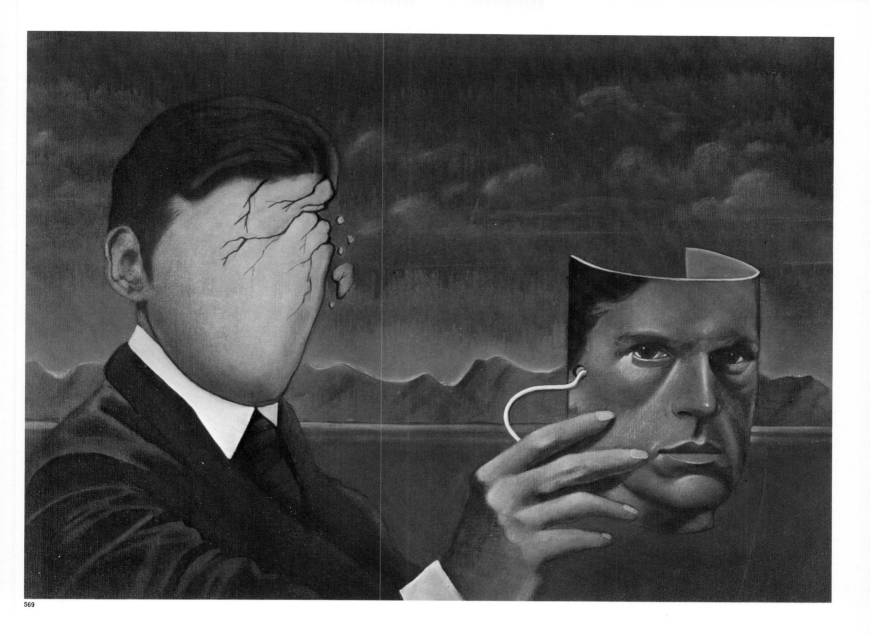

569

570

571

564, 565 Opened cover and double spread from a NASA publication entitled *Galileo to Jupiter—probing the Planet and mapping its Moons.* In beige shades. (USA)
566 Company publication issued by SESA, a software company. (GER)
567, 568 Brochures of a pharmaceutical manufacturer about the historical and socio-cultural background of coloured minority groups, and psychiatric treatment relating to these factors. (USA)
569 From *Depression,* a *Sandoz* publication sent regularly to medical practitioners. (USA)
570, 571 From an IBM publication on promotion possibilities. (USA)

564, 565 Geöffneter Umschlag und Doppelseite aus einer Prestigepublikation der NASA mit dem Titel «Von Galileo zu Jupiter – von der Raumsonde zur genauen Darstellung der Monde». Beigetöne. (USA)
566 Firmenpublikation der SESA, eines Softwarehauses: Lenksysteme für den Schienentransport. (GER)
567, 568 Broschüren einer Arzneimittelfabrik über die historischen und soziokulturellen Hintergründe

farbiger Minderheiten, die bei der psychiatrischen Behandlung berücksichtigt werden sollten. (USA)
569 Aus *Depression,* einer regelmässig an praktizierende Ärzte versandten *Sandoz*-Publikation. (USA)
570, 571 Aus einer IBM-Publikation über Aufstiegsmöglichkeiten in der Büromittel-Abteilung. (USA)

564, 565 Recto et verso de la couverture et page double extraite d'une publication de prestige de la NASA inititulée «De Galilée au Jupiter – de la sonde spatiale à la représentation de ses lunes». Tons beiges. (USA)
566 Publication d'une société travaillant dans le domaine du logiciel, ici en faveur des systèmes de guidage pour le transport ferroviaire. (GER)
567, 568 Petites brochures d'une société de produits pharmaceutiques sur les problèmes socio-culturels des minorités de couleur qui devraient etre pris en considération en psychiatrie. (USA)
569 D'une publication périodique que la société *Sandoz* expédie au corps médical nordaméricain. (USA)
570, 571 D'une publication IBM sur les possibilités d'avancement. (USA)

ARTIST / KÜNSTLER / ARTISTE:
572–580 Heinz Edelmann

DESIGNER / GESTALTER / MAQUETTISTE:
572–580 Heinz Edelmann

ART DIRECTOR / DIRECTEUR ARTISTIQUE:
572–580 Heinz Edelmann

PUBLISHER / VERLEGER / EDITEUR:
572–580 Klett-Cotta

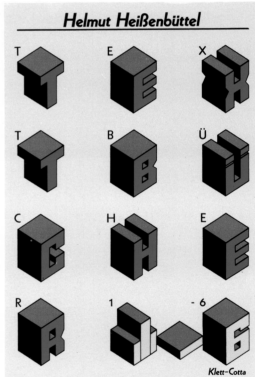

Pedro Salinas
Verteidigung des Briefes
Ein Essay / Klett-Cotta

573

Helmut Heißenbüttel

Klett-Cotta

577

Wilhelm Muster
Roman / Klett-Cotta
Der Tod kommt ohne Trommel

572

Book Covers
Buchumschläge
Couvertures de livres

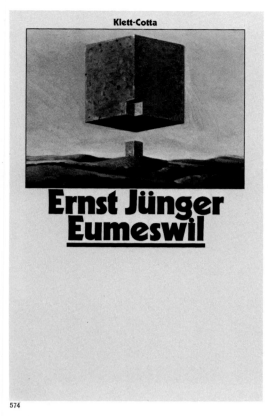

Ernst Jünger Eumeswil

574

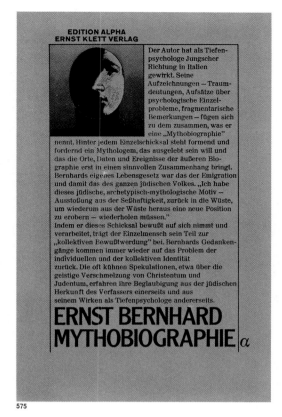

ERNST BERNHARD MYTHOBIOGRAPHIE α

575

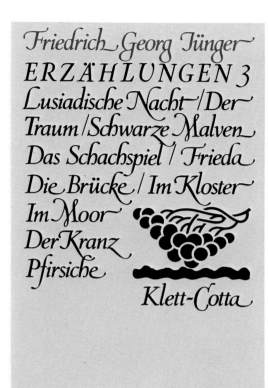

Friedrich Georg Jünger ERZÄHLUNGEN 3 *Lusiadische Nacht / Der Traum / Schwarze Malven Das Schachspiel / Frieda Die Brücke / Im Kloster Im Moor Der Kranz Pfirsiche* Klett-Cotta

576

JORGE CARRERA ANDRADE POEMAS GEDICHTE spanisch und deutsch Übertragung und Nachwort von Fritz Vogelgsang - Klett-Cotta -

578

MICHEL LEIRIS: DIE TREPPE

579

Robert S. Weiss Trennung vom Ehepartner

580

572–580 The *Klett-Cotta* publishing company has entrusted a single artist with the design of its books. Heinz Edelmann is in charge of covers, illustrations, typography and, above all, the scientific and literary programmes. Here we show some examples:
572 Cover of a novel entitled "Death Comes without a Drum".
573 Cover of a book of Pedro Salinas' essays, translated from the Spanish. Black on a cream-coloured background.
574 Full-colour cover of a novel by Ernst Jünger.
575 Cover of a work on mythobiography from a series of psychological books. Black on silver.
576 For the 3rd volume of Friedrich Georg Jünger's stories.
577 Cover for the textbooks 1–6 of lyric poetry.
578 Cover of a collection of poems in Spanish with the German translation. Black on green.
579 Opening page of a story in a literary magazine.
580 Cover of a book on the separation of married couples. Full-colour illustrations, black lettering on yellow.

572–580 Der Verlag *Klett-Cotta* hat Heinz Edelmann mit der Gestaltung der gesamten Buchproduktion beauftragt, sowohl des wissenschaftlichen und literarischen Universalprogramms wie auch der Buchreihen. Wir zeigen hier einige Beispiele:
572 Umschlag für einen ethnographisch-patriotischen Roman.
573 Umschlag eines aus dem Spanischen übersetzten Essays von Pedro Salinas. Schwarz auf cremefarbenem Hintergrund.
574 Mehrfarbiger Umschlag eines Romans von Ernst Jünger.
575 Umschlag eines Werkes über Mythobiographie aus einer Reihe von psychologischen Titeln. Schwarz auf Silber.
576 Für den 3. Band von Friedrich Georg Jüngers Erzählungen.
577 Umschlag für die *Textbücher 1–6* mit lyrischen Gedichten.
578 Umschlag eines Gedichtbandes in spanischer Sprache mit deutscher Übersetzung. Schwarz auf Grün.
579 Erste Seite einer Erzählung in einer literarischen Zeitschrift.
580 Umschlag eines Werkes aus dem Gebiet der Populärpsychologie. Farbige Illustrationen, schwarze Schrift auf Gelb.

572–580 Les Editions *Klett-Cotta* ont chargé Heinz Edelmann de la conception de leur production entière, de leur programme universel de publications littéraires et scientifiques ainsi que de leurs séries. Nous présentons ici quelques couvertures:
572 Couverture du roman «La Mort vient sans tambour».
573 Couverture d'un essai de «défense et illustration de la lettre» traduit de l'espagnol. Noir sur crème.
574 Couverture d'un roman d'Ernst Jünger.
575 Couverture d'un ouvrage de «mythobiographie» dans une collection de psychologie. Noir sur argent.
576 Couverture d'un recueil de récits de Friedrich Georg Jünger.
577 Couverture d'un recueil de chansons, «Manuels 1–6».
578 Couverture d'un recueil poétique espagnol, avec traduction allemande en regard. Noir sur fond vert.
579 Page initiale d'un récit publié dans une revue littéraire.
580 Couverture d'un ouvrage sur la séparation de corps. Le médaillon couleur symbolise la séparation de corps et de biens.

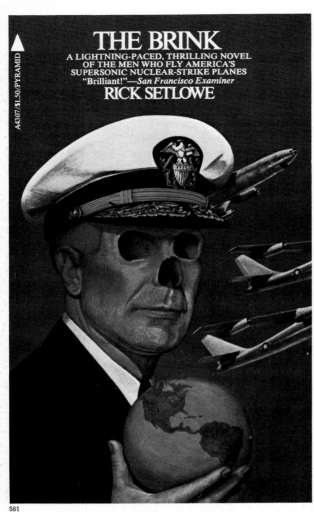

581

582

583

581 Cover of a paperback entitled *The Brink,* a lightning-paced, thrilling novel of the men who fly America's supersonic nuclear-strike planes. The illustration is in dark shades. (USA)
582–584 Dust jackets of a series of books published by *Chikuma Shobo* under the title *Meini Taisho Zushi.* Fig. 584 is in original size. (JPN)

581 Umschlag eines packenden Taschenbuchromans über die Männer, welche die mit Atomwaffen bestückten Überschalljäger Amerikas fliegen. Illustration in dunklen Farbtönen. (USA
582–584 Umschläge aus einer Buchreihe mit dem Titel *Meini Taisho Zushi.* Abb. 584 ist in Originalgrösse. (JPN)

581 Couverture d'un roman captivant publié dans une série de poche. Il traite des hommes qui pilotent les avions de chasse supersoniques munis de missiles nucléaires. En tons foncés. (USA
582–584 Couvertures d'une série d'ouvrages intitulée *Meini Taisho Zushi.* Fig. 584 en grandeur originale. (JPN)

ARTIST / KÜNSTLER / ARTISTE:

581 Richard Mantel
582–584 Tadanori Yokoo

DESIGNER / GESTALTER / MAQUETTISTE:

581 Richard Mantel
582–584 Tadanori Yokoo

ART DIRECTOR / DIRECTEUR ARTISTIQUE:

581 Harris Lewine
582–584 Tadanori Yokoo

AGENCY / AGENTUR / AGENCE – STUDIO:

581 Push Pin Studios, Inc.

PUBLISHER / VERLEGER / EDITEUR:

581 Harcourt Brace Jovanovich
582–584 Chikuma Shobo Ltd.

明治大正図誌 1

東京（二）

585

586

585 Cover of a Shakespeare comedy published in a complete pocket-edition by *Methuen*. (USA)
586 Dust jacket evoking an old manuscript for *The Life and times of Chaucer* published by *Alfred Knopf*. (USA)
587 Cover of Zabra's book of recipes for gourmets, by *Push Pin Studios*. (USA)
588 Cover in dark shades of a novel issued by *Richard Marek Publishers*. (USA)
589 Dust jacket of a novel issued by *Alfred Kopf* publishers. (USA)
590 Cover of Charlotte Chandler's biography published by *Sphere Books*, about Groucho Marx and his friends with the authoress's personal reminiscences and talks with personalities in the film business. Yellow ground. (USA)
591, 592 Covers of a quarterly. In brown as well as violet. (USA)

585 Umschlag von Shakespeares Lustspiel *Verlorene Liebesmüh,* das in einer Taschenbuch-Gesamtausgabe bei *Methuen* herauskam. (USA)
586 Alten Handschriften nachempfundener Schutzumschlag eines Werkes über das Leben und die Zeit des englischen Dichters Chaucer. (USA)
587 Umschlag von Zabras Rezeptbuch für Feinschmecker. (USA)
588 In dunklen Farbtönen gehaltener Umschlag für einen Roman. (USA)
589 Für einen Roman über Onkel Oswald und seine Entdeckung. (USA)
590 Umschlag von Charlotte Chandlers Biographie über Groucho Marx und seine Freunde mit persönlichen Erinnerungen der Autorin und Gesprächswiedergaben mit Persönlichkeiten aus dem Filmbusiness. Gelber Grund. (USA)
591, 592 Umschläge einer Vierteljahresschrift. In Braun, resp. Violett. (USA)

585 Couverture de la comédie *Peine d'amour perdue* de Shakespeare, un volume de l'œuvre complet paru dans une série de poche. (USA)
586 Jaquette d'un ouvrage sur la vie et l'époque du poète anglais Chaucer. La couverture évoque un vieux manuscrit. (USA)
587 Couverture d'un livre de recettes pour les gourmets. (USA)
588 Couverture pour un roman. Prédominance de tons foncés. (USA)
589 Jaquette d'un roman consacré à l'Oncle Oswald et ses découvertes. (USA)
590 Couverture d'une biographie de Charlotte Chandler sur Groucho Marx et ses amis avec des souvenances personnelles de l'auteur et des entretiens avec des personnages du cinéma. Fond jaune. (USA)
591, 592 Couverture d'une publication trimestrielle. Brun et violet. (USA)

Book Covers
Buchumschläge
Couvertures de livres

587

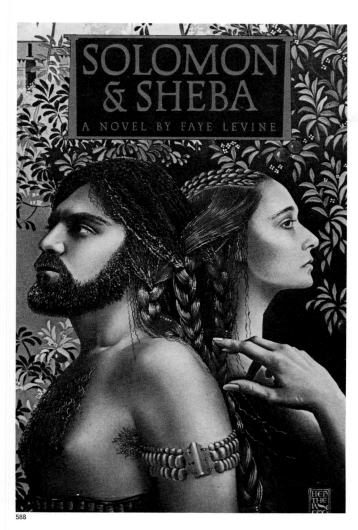

588

589

ARTIST / KÜNSTLER / ARTISTE:

585 David Inshaw
586 J. Wolf
587 Seymour Chwast
588 Heather Cooper
589 Fred Marcellino
590 Bob Norrington
591, 592 David Battle

DESIGNER / GESTALTER / MAQUETTISTE:

585 Adam Yeldham
586 Camilla Filancia
587 Seymour Chwast
588 Lynn Hollyn/Iris Bass
589 Fred Marcellino
590 Bob Norrington

ART DIRECTOR / DIRECTEUR ARTISTIQUE:

585 Adam Yeldham
586 Betty Anderson
587 Seymour Chwast
588 Lynn Hollyn
589 Lidia Ferrara
590 Liz Lazcynska
591, 592 David Battle

AGENCY / AGENTUR / AGENCE – STUDIO:

587 Push Pin Studios, Inc.

PUBLISHER / VERLEGER / EDITEUR:

585 Methuen & Co. Ltd.
586, 589 Alfred A. Knopf, Inc.
587 Hawthorn Books
588 Richard Marek Publishers
590 Sphere Books
591, 592 Antioch Review

590

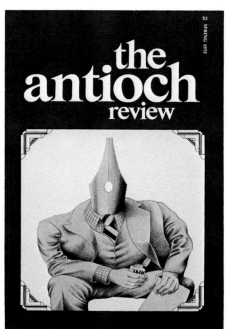

591

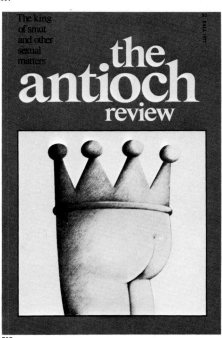

592

211

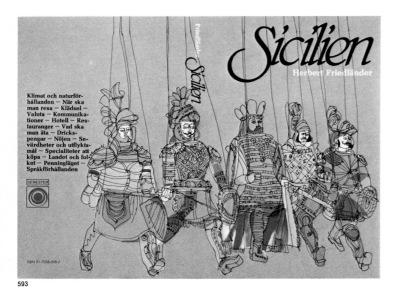

593

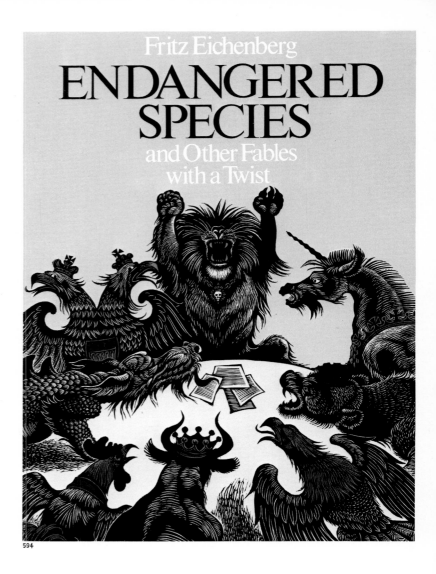

594

ARTIST / KÜNSTLER / ARTISTE:

593 Stellan Kristenson
594 Fritz Eichenberg
595 Richard Hess
596 Ronald Searle
597 Alain Gauthier

ART DIRECTOR / DIRECTEUR ARTISTIQUE:

593 Stellan Kristenson
595 Lidia Ferrara
597 François Ruy Vidal

PUBLISHER / VERLEGER / EDITEUR:

593 Generalstabens Litografiska Anstalt
594 Stemmer House
595 Alfred A. Knopf, Inc.
596 Rowohlt Verlag
597 Editions de l'Amitié / G. T. Rageot

596

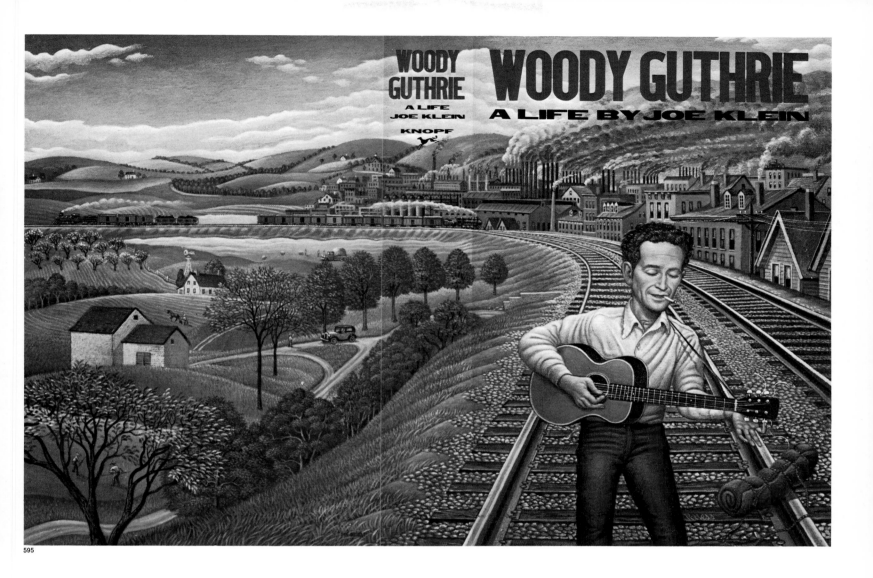

595

597

593 Opened cover of a *Semester Publications* pocket-book guide of Sicily. In full colour. (SWE)
594 Dust jacket of a book of fables about endangered animal species, published by *Stemmer House*. Animals in black, yellow and red on a blue ground. (USA)
595 Opened dust jacket of a Woody Guthrie biography. Full-colour illustration. (USA)
596 *The Cultivated*. This illustraton was originally a design draft for the curtain at the Royal Opera House, Covent Garden. It is shown in *Rowohlt's* book about Searle. (GER)
597 Cover in bright colours for a book of numerical rhymes for children and parents. (FRA)

593 Geöffneter Umschlag eines Taschenbuch-Reiseführers für Sizilien. Mehrfarbig. (SWE)
594 Schutzumschlag eines Fabelbuches über gefährdete Tierarten und andere eigentümliche Fabeln. Tiere in Schwarz, Gelb und Rot auf blauem Grund. (USA)
595 Geöffneter Schutzumschlag einer Biographie über Woody Guthrie, einer der Väter der Country-Musik. Mehrfarbige Illustration. (USA)
596 *Die Kultivierten*. Diese Illustration, ursprünglich als Entwurf für den Vorhang des Royal Opera House, Covent Garden, London entstanden, wird in *Rowohlts* Buch über Searle gezeigt. (GER)
597 Umschlag in bunten Farben eines Buches mit Abzählreimen für Kinder und Eltern. (FRA)

593 Recto et verso d'un guide touristique de la Sicile, paru dans une série de poche. (SWE)
594 Jaquette d'un recueil de fables d'espèces en péril et d'autres fables extraordinaires. Animaux en noir, jaune et rouge sur fond bleu. (USA)
595 Recto et verso de la jaquette d'une biographie de Woody Guthrie, représentant célèbre de la musique country. Illustration polychrome. (USA)
596 «Les gens cultivés». Projet de rideau pour l'Opéra royal de Covent Garden paru dans une publication de *Rowohlt* consacrée à Ronald Searle. (GER)
597 Couverture (couleurs vives) d'un livre de comptines et formulettes des *Editions de l'Amitié*. (FRA)

Book Covers
Buchumschläge
Couvertures de livres

598

599

FRIEDRICH DÜRRENMATT

Grieche sucht Griechin

600

598 Cover illustration of *The natural cat,* a comprehensive guide for cat-owners. (USA)
599 "Let's pretend to be teaching." Cover illustration in pink, brown and yellow. (ITA)
600 Full-colour dust jacket for a comedy in prose by Dürrenmatt. (GER)
601, 602 Recto and verso in actual size of a portfolio entitled "Seven Years of History in 350 covers from 1974–1980", containing the covers of *L'Espresso* magazine. (ITA)

598 Umschlagillustration eines umfassenden Führers für Katzenbesitzer. (USA)
599 «Tun als ob man lehren würde.» Umschlagillustration in Rosa, Braun und Gelb. (ITA)
600 Farbiger Schutzumschlag zu Dürrenmatts Prosakomödie *Grieche sucht Griechin.* (GER)
601, 602 Vorderseite und Rückseite (in Originalgrösse) eines Portfolios mit dem Titel «Sieben Jahre Geschichte auf 350 Umschlägen von 1974–1980», in welchem die Titelblätter des wöchentlich erscheinenden Nachrichtenmagazins *L'Espresso* enthalten sind. (ITA)

598 Illustration de couverture d'un guide pour ceux qui tiennent un chat. (USA)
599 «Faire feint d'enseigner.» Illustration en rose, brun et jaune. (ITA)
600 Jaquette polychrome de la comédie *Grec cherche Grecque* de Dürrenmatt. (GER)
601, 602 Recto et verso (grandeur originale) d'un portfolio intitulé «Sept ans d'histoire sur 350 couvertures de 1974 à 1980», dans lequel étaient recueillis les couvertures du magazine d'information hebdomadaire *L'Espresso.* (ITA)

601

ARTIST / KÜNSTLER:

598 Lowell Herreo
599 Giuseppe Rampazzo
600 Michael Mathias Prechtl
601, 602 Tullio Pericoli

DESIGNER / GESTALTER:

598 Lynn Hollyn
599 Giuseppe Rampazzo
600 Michael Mathias Prechtl

ART DIRECTOR:

598 Lynn Hollyn
599 Giuseppe Rampazzo
600 Andreas Zebrowski

PUBLISHER / VERLEGER:

598 Harbor Publishers
599 La Linea Editrice
600 Europäische Bildungs-
    gemeinschaft
601, 602 L'Espresso

602

603 Dust jacket of a science-fiction novel entitled "On the dark side of ... " (JPN)
604 Dust jacket of *Nana* by Emile Zola. Pink-coloured shoes on a brown floor. (GER)
605 Illustration on the opened dust jacket of *Their Gracious Pleasure*, the third volume of a series about the French Revolution published by *Knopf*. (USA)
606, 607 Illustration in actual size and complete dust jacket of a *Crown* publishers book entitled *Showdown Semester: Advice from a writing Professor*. (USA)

603 Umschlag eines Science-Fiction-Romans mit dem Titel «Auf der Schattenseite von ...» (JPN)
604 Schutzumschlag für Zolas berühmten Roman. Rosafarbene Schuhe auf braunem Boden. (GER)
605 Geöffneter Schutzumschlag des 3. Bandes eines Geschichtswerkes über die französische Revolution, hier über die Regierungszeit von Louis XVI. (USA)
606, 607 Illustration in Originalgrösse und vollständiger Schutzumschlag zu einem Werk mit dem Titel «Abschlusssemester: Ratschläge eines schreibenden Professors». (USA)

603 Jaquette d'un roman de science-fiction intitulé «Dans l'ombre de...». (JPN)
604 Jaquette du roman *Nana* d'Emile Zola. Chaussures roses sur fond brun. (GER)
605 Recto et verso de la jaquette du troisième volume d'une histoire de la Révolution Française, ici de l'époque de Louis XVI. (USA)
606, 607 Illustration (grandeur originale) et jaquette complète d'un ouvrage intitulé «Aux classes terminales: conseils d'un professeur écrivain». (USA)

ARTIST / KÜNSTLER / ARTISTE:

603 Tadami Yamada
604 Erhard Göttlicher
605 Wendell Minor
606, 607 Geoffrey Moss

DESIGNER / GESTALTER / MAQUETTISTE:

603 Tadami Yamada
605 Lidia Ferrara

ART DIRECTOR / DIRECTEUR ARTISTIQUE:

603 Yoshio Shishido/Yoshimi Sugiyama
605 Lidia Ferrara
606, 607 Jim Davis

AGENCY / AGENTUR / AGENCE – STUDIO:

605 Wendell Minor Design

PUBLISHER / VERLEGER / EDITEUR:

603 Kodansha Ltd.
604 Büchergilde Gutenberg
605 Alfred A. Knopf, Inc.
606, 607 Crown Publishers

603

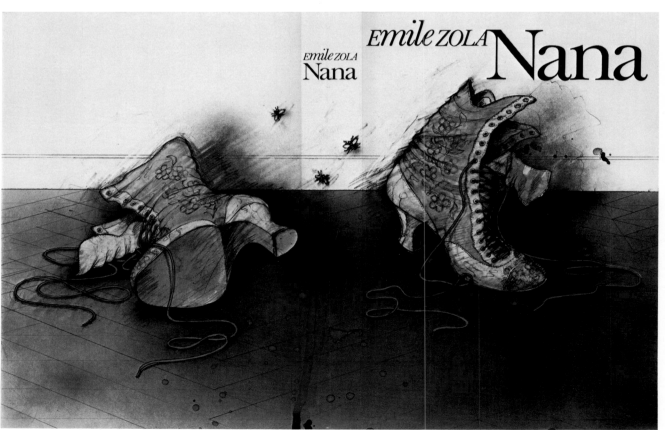

604

606

605

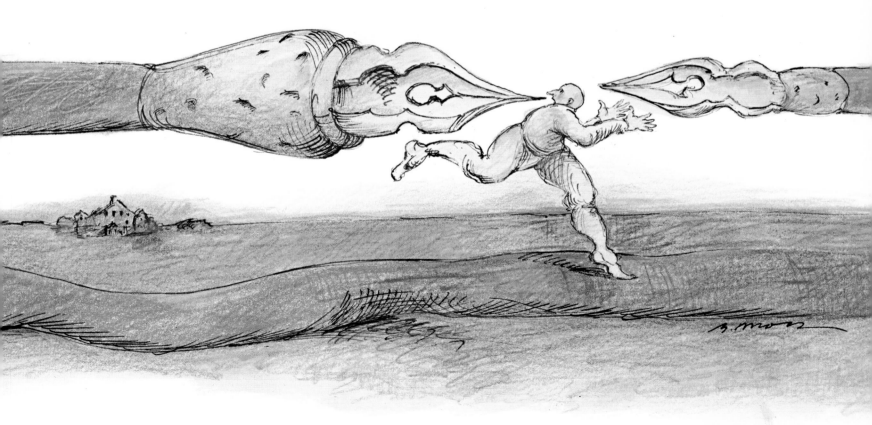

607

217

DANDELION CLOCKS

Stories of Childhood
Edited by Alfred Bradley
and Kay Jamieson

608

608 Cover in actual size of a pocket-book of children's stories that appeared in a *Penguin* series. (GBR)
609 Cover of a *Zindermans* pocket-book of twenty crossword puzzles that are difficult to crack. Black lettering on a light green background. (SWE)
610 Full-colour cover of a book for young people from the *Rotfuchs* series of pocket-books by *Rowohlt.* (GER)
611 Photo-montage of a pocket-book cover. Red ground. (FRA)
612 Pocket-book cover of Dürrenmatt's thriller *Der Richter und sein Henker* (The Pledge). Full-colour illustration. (NOR)
613 Full-colour dust jacket of a novel. (USA)
614 Pocket-book cover of a thriller. In full colour. (USA)
615 Dust jacket of a novel. Pink and light green. (USA)
616 Cover for a blank book. Red "O". (USA)

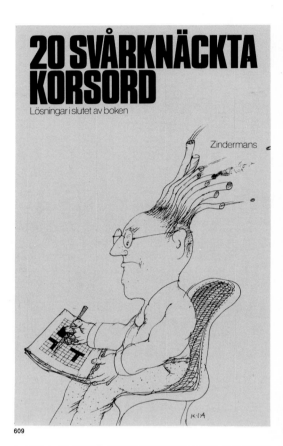

20 SVÅRKNÄCKTA KORSORD
Lösningar i slutet av boken

Zindermans

609

Far From Home
BY OUIDA SEBESTYEN

613

ARTIST / KÜNSTLER / ARTISTE:

608 James Marsh
609 Kjell Ivan Anderson
610 Dietrich Lange
611 Roman Cieslewicz
612 Bernard Blatch
613 Wendell Minor
614 Richard Mantel
615 Seymour Chwast

DESIGNER / GESTALTER / MAQUETTISTE:

608 James Marsh
609 Kjell Ivan Anderson
611 Roman Cieslewicz
612 Bernard Blatch
613 Wendell Minor
614 Richard Mantel
615 Seymour Chwast
616 Alan Peckolick / Tom Carnase

ART DIRECTOR / DIRECTEUR ARTISTIQUE:

608 David Pelham
610 Manfred Waller
611 François Maspero
613 Char Lappan
614, 615 Harris Lewine
616 Jim Davis

AGENCY / AGENTUR / AGENCE – STUDIO:

613 Wendell Minor Design
614, 615 Push Pin Studios, Inc.
616 Lubalin Peckolick Assoc. Inc.

PUBLISHER / VERLEGER / EDITEUR:

608 Penguin Books
609 Zindermans
610 Rowohlt Verlag
611 François Maspero
612 Gyldendal
613 Atlantic-Little, Brown
614, 615 Harcourt Brace Jovanovich
616 Crown Publishing

608 Umschlag (in Originalgrösse) eines Taschenbuches mit Kindergeschichten, das in einer *Penguin*-Reihe erschienen ist. (GBR)
609 Umschlag eines Taschenbuches mit 20 «schwer zu knackenden» Kreuzworträtseln. Schwarze Schrift auf Hellgrün. (SWE)
610 Mehrfarbiger Umschlag für ein Jugendbuch aus der Taschenbuch-Reihe *Rotfuchs* von *Rowohlt*. (GER)
611 Photomontage als Umschlag eines Taschenbuches über die Wiederherstellung der Ordnung. Roter Grund. (FRA)
612 Taschenbuchumschlag zu Dürrenmatts Kriminalroman *Der Richter und sein Henker*. Mehrfarbige Illustration. (NOR)
613 Mehrfarbiger Schutzumschlag für einen Roman. (USA)
614 Taschenbuchumschlag eines Kriminalromans. Mehrfarbig. (USA)
615 Schutzumschlag eines Romans. Rosa und Hellgrün. (USA)
616 Umschlag für einen Blindband. Rotes «O». (USA)

608 Couverture (grandeur originale) d'un livre de poche de contes d'enfants, paru dans une série de *Penguin*. (GBR)
609 Couverture d'un livre de poche avec 20 mots croisés difficiles à faire. Typographie noire sur fond vert pâle. (SWE)
610 Couverture polychrome d'un livre pour la jeunesse qui a paru dans la série de poche *Rotfuchs* (alezan) de *Rowohlt*. (GER)
611 Photomontage pour la couverture d'un livre de poche. (FRA)
612 Couverture du roman policier de Dürrenmatt *Le juge et son bourreau*, qui a paru dans une série de poche. (NOR)
613 Couverture polychrome d'un roman. (NOR)
614 Couverture d'un roman policier paru dans une série de poche. Illustration en polychromie. (USA)
615 Jaquette d'un roman. Rose et vert pâle. (USA)
616 Couverture d'un livre aux pages vierges. «O» rouge. (USA)

610

611

612

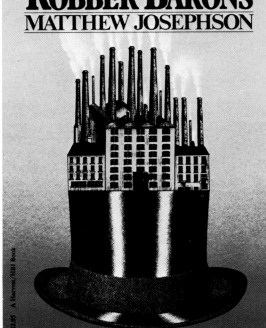

614

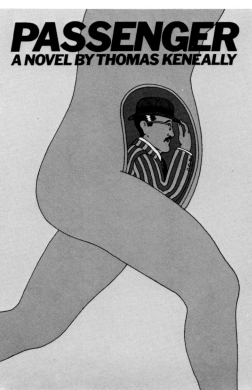

615

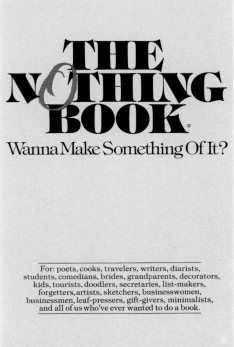

616

4

Calendars

Trademarks

Letterheads

Record Covers

Packaging

Kalender

Schutzmarken

Briefköpfe

Schallplattenhüllen

Packungen

Calendriers

Marques et emblèmes

En-têtes

Pochettes de disques

Emballages

617

618

Calendars/Kalender/Calendriers

619

620a

617, 618 Two illustrations from the horoscope calendar of the Polish sports pools association, here for Taurus and Cancer. (POL)
619 In 1979 the *Mitchell Press* issued a calendar sheet for each quarter portraying famous Australians of the same name, here Helen Porter Mitchell, a world-renowned opera singer. (AUS)
620, 620a "The Mustard King." Complete sheet and illustration in actual size from Binette Schroeder's birthday calendar, published by the *Nord-Süd* publishing company. (SWI)

617, 618 Zwei Illustrationen aus dem Horoskop-Kalender der polnischen Sport-Toto-Vereinigung, hier zu den Sternzeichen Stier und Krebs. (POL)
619 Die *Mitchell Press* gab 1979 für jedes Quartal ein Kalenderblatt heraus mit berühmten Australiern, die den selben Namen trugen: hier ein Porträt von Helen Porter Mitchell, die anfangs dieses Jahrhunderts unter dem Namen Nellie Melba als Opernsängerin auftrat. (AUS)
620, 620a *Der Senfkönig.* Vollständiges Blatt und Illustration in Originalgrösse aus Binette Schroeders immerwährendem Geburtstags-Kalender, der vom *Nord-Süd Verlag* herausgegeben wurde. (SWI)

617, 618 Deux illustrations d'un calendrier de l'association polonaise du sport-toto. Il est entièrement consacré aux signes du Zodiaque, ici on voit le taureau et le cancer. (POL)
619 En 1979, la *Mitchell Press* avait publié quatre feuilles trimestrielles présentant chacune un personnages portant le même nom: ici on voit le portrait d'Helen Porter Mitchell, fameuse cantatrice d'opéra au début de ce siècle, connue sous le nom de Nellie Melba. (AUS)
620, 620a «Le roi moutarde.» Feuille complète et illustration d'un calendrier perpétuel que Binette Schroeder a réalisé pour les éditions *Nord-Süd*. (SWI)

ARTIST / KÜNSTLER / ARTISTE:

617, 618 J. Rafal Olbinski
619 Maire Smith
620, 620a Binette Schroeder

DESIGNER / GESTALTER / MAQUETTISTE:

617, 618 J. Rafal Olbinski
619 Barrie Tucker
620, 620a Binette Schroeder/
Nord-Süd Verlag

ART DIRECTOR / DIRECTEUR ARTISTIQUE:

617, 618 Maciej Raducki
619 Barrie Tucker

621

Calendars
Kalender
Calendriers

621–624 Full-page illustrations from an agenda sent to doctors by the *Wyeth* laboratories, on the twelve labours of Hercules—here the birds of the Stymphalian Marshes, the lion of Nemea, the golden apples of the Hesperides and the hydra of Lerna. (BEL)
625, 626 Illustration in actual size from a calendar issued by *Tundra Books,* here for the game of fox and geese from the book *A Prairie Boy's Winter,* illustrated by the late William Kurelek. (CAN)

621–624 Ganzseitige Illustrationen aus einer Ärzte-Agenda der *Wyeth*-Laboratorien zu den zwölf Arbeiten des Herkules – hier die Vögel der Stymphälischen Sümpfe, der Nemeïsche Löwe, die goldenen Äpfel der Hesperiden und die Lernäische Schlange. (BEL)
625, 626 Illustration in Originalgrösse aus dem Kalender von *Tundra Books* mit Bildern aus verschiedenen Kinderbüchern des verstorbenen Malers William Kurelek. (CAN)

621–624 Illustrations pleines pages pour un agenda offert aux médecins par les Laboratoires *Wyeth* en Belgique. Il prend pour sujet les douze travaux d'Hercule – nous montrons ici les oiseaux du lac Stymphale, le lion de Némée, les pommes d'or du jardin d'Hespérides et l'hydre de Lerne. (BEL)
625, 626 Illustration (grandeur originale) et feuillet d'un calendrier des *Livres Toundra* avec des illustrations de livres d'enfant de feu William Kurelek, ici du livre *A Prairie Boy's Winter.* (CAN)

ARTIST / KÜNSTLER / ARTISTE:

621–624 Josse Goffin
625, 626 William Kurelek

DESIGNER / GESTALTER / MAQUETTISTE:

625, 626 Dan O'Leary

ART DIRECTOR / DIRECTEUR ARTISTIQUE:

621–624 Gilles Fiszman/Josse Goffin
625, 626 May Cutler

622

625

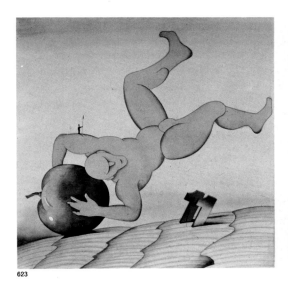
623

624

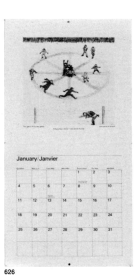
626

627

ARTIST / KÜNSTLER / ARTISTE:

627 Barbara Nessim
628 Shinta Cho
629 George Giusti
630 Kazuo Aoki
631 Ian Beck
632 Glynn Boyd Harte

DESIGNER / GESTALTER:

627–630 Mitsuo Katsui
631, 632 Trickett & Webb Ltd.

ART DIRECTOR:

627–630 Yasuhara Nakahara/
Mitsutoshi Hosaka/ Shinichiro Tora
631, 632 Lynn Trickett/Brian Webb/
Colin Sands

AGENCY / AGENTUR:

631, 632 The Jenni Stone Partnership

628

629

631

632

627–630 From the calendar of the *Hotel Barmen's Association*. Twelve well-known illustrators contributed one illustration each for a certain cocktail, whose mixture is also described. Here for Bronx, Lady 80 No. 1, Million-Dollar and Galaxy. (JPN)
631, 632 *Trickett & Webb* and illustrators of the artists' agency *Jenni Stone Partnership*, issued this limited-edition calendar in conjunction with the silkscreen printer *August Martin*. (GBR)

627–630 Aus dem Kalender der Vereinigung japanischer Barmen. Zwölf bekannte Illustratoren steuerten je eine Illustration zu einem Cocktail bei, dessen Rezept auf dem Kalendarstreifen gegeben wird, hier für die Cocktails Bronx, Lady 80 No. 1, Million-Dollar und Galaxy. (JPN)
631, 632 *Trickett & Webb*, die Illustratoren der Künstleragentur *Jenni Stone Partnership* und der Siebdrucker *August Martin* gaben gemeinsam diesen in beschränkter Auflage gedruckten Kalender heraus. Alle Illustrationen sind in bunten Farben. (GBR)

627–630 Illustrations figurant dans le calendrier de l'association japonaise des barmen. Douze illustrateurs de renom ont contribué chacun une illustration interprétant un cocktail, dont on trouve la recette sur une bande en-dessous de l'illustration: ici pour Bronx, Lady 80 No 1, Million-Dollar et Galaxy. (JPN)
631, 632 *Trickett & Webb*, les illustrateurs de l'agent *Jenni Stone Partnership* et l'imprimerie *August Martin* (sérigraphies) ont réalisé ensemble ce calendrier à tirage limité. (GBR)

630

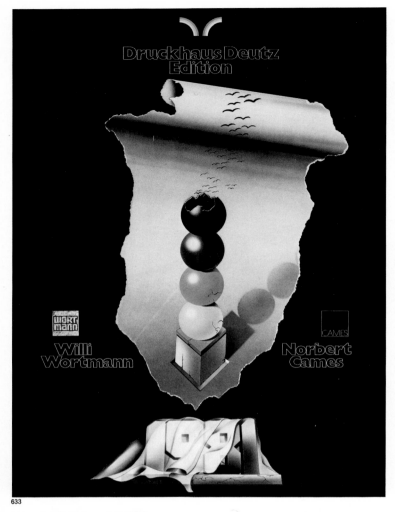

633

634

635

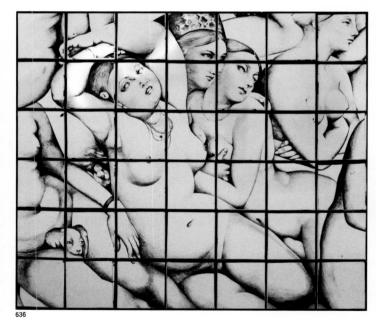

636

ARTIST / KÜNSTLER / ARTISTE:

633 Norbert Cames
634 Willi Wortmann

DESIGNER / GESTALTER / MAQUETTISTE:

633, 634 Franz Schumacher
635 Joseph Hutchcroft
636, 637 Uwe Loesch

ART DIRECTOR / DIRECTEUR ARTISTIQUE:

633, 634 Franz Schumacher
635 Joseph Hutchcroft
636, 637 Uwe Loesch

637

AGENCY / AGENTUR / AGENCE – STUDIO:

633, 634 Franz Schumacher
635 Container Corporation of America/
Communication Department
636, 637 Arbeitsgemeinschaft für visuelle Kommunikation

633, 634 Cover and illustration entitled "The Road to Sartan" from the calendar of the *Deutz* printers. The hyper-realistic illustrations were done by two artists. (GER)
635 Container Corp. of America's desk calendar. Three-part calendar in red, blue and green in a plexiglas cylinder. (USA)
636, 637 Perpetual calendar of a typesetting company. The cubes show an illustration evoking an Ingres with details of the illustration, numbers and days of the week on the sides. (GER)

633, 634 Titelblatt und Illustration mit dem Titel *Die Strasse nach Sartan* aus dem Kalender des *Druckhauses Deutz*. Die hyperrealistischen Illustrationen wurden von zwei Künstlern geschaffen. (GER)
635 Pultkalender eines Verpackungsherstellers. Dreiteiliges Kalendarium in Rot, Blau und Grün in Plexiglas-Zylinder. (USA)
636, 637 Immerwährender Kalender einer Schriftsetzerei. Die Würfel zeigen eine Ingres nachempfundene Illustration und Ausschnitte daraus, mit Ziffern und Wochentagen auf den Seitenflächen. (GER)

633, 634 Couverture et illustration intitulée «La route pour Sartan» figurant dans le calendrier d'une imprimerie. Les illustrations hyperréalistes ont été créées par deux artistes. (GER)
635 Calendrier d'un fabricant de conditionnements. Cylindre en plexiglas, trois calendriers individuels en rouge, bleu et vert. (USA)
636, 637 Calendrier perpétuel d'un atelier de composition. Les cubes montrent une illustration évoquant un Ingres, avec des détails agrandis, des chiffres et jours de semaine sur les côtés. (GER)

639

640

638 Symbol of the Danville Resources Company. (USA)
639 Quality-guarantee trademark of the Association of Suppliers of Silver-Plated Cutlery. Stylized fork, spoon and knife. (SWI)
640 Symbol of the Baltimore aquarium. In blue and white. (USA)
641 Symbol of a major bank that has over forty branches. (ARG)
642 Symbol of the international union of television archives. (ITA)
643 Sign of the Turin *Open Design* studio. (ITA)
644 Symbol of the Dallas Services for the Visually Impaired. (USA)
645 Trademark of *Diblo,* an industrial holding company. (MEX)
646 Symbol of a company that makes fittings for Buddhist altars. (JPN)
647 Symbol of the breakdown service *Reggiana Rimorchi* in Reggio Emilia. (ITA)
648 Symbol of the Marcona Shipping & Mining Co. (USA)
649 Symbol of the Jewish community centre *Camp Rafa-El.* (USA)
650 Symbol of the *Time Equities* real-estate company. (USA)
651 Sign of the Nichii Co., a chain of food stores. (JPN)
652 Trademark of the *Silver Diffusion* company in New York. (USA)
653 Symbol of *Century Partners,* a real estate partnership company. (USA)

638 Schriftzug der Firma *Danville Resources.* (USA)
639 Qualitäts-Garantie-Schutzmarke des Verbandes von Lieferanten versilberter Bestecke. Stilisierte Gabel, Löffel und Messer. (SWI)
640 Symbol des Baltimore Aquariums. In Blau und Weiss. (USA)
641 Symbol einer Grossbank mit über vierzig Niederlassungen. (ARG)
642 Symbol der internationalen Vereinigung der Fernseh-Archive. (ITA)
643 Marke des Turiner Ateliers für Produktgestaltung *Open Design.* (ITA)
644 Symbol einer Hilfsorganisation für Sehbehinderte in Dallas, Texas. (USA)
645 Schutzmarke der Firma *Diblo,* einer industriellen Holdinggesellschaft. (MEX)
646 Symbol einer Firma, die Ausstattungen für buddhistische Altare macht. (JPN)
647 Symbol des Abschleppdienstes *Reggiana Rimorchi* in Reggio Emilia. (ITA)
648 Symbol eines Bergbau- und Transportunternehmens. (USA)
649 Symbol des jüdischen Begegnungszentrums *Camp Rafa-El.* (USA)
650 Symbol der Immobiliengesellschaft *Time Equities.* (USA)
651 Marke der Nichii Co., einer Kette von Nahrungsmittelgeschäften. (JPN)
652 Schutzmarke der Firma *Silver Diffusion* in New York. (USA)
653 Symbol einer kalifornischen Immobiliengesellschaft. (USA)

638 Logo de la société *Danville Resources.* (USA)
639 Garantie de qualité de l'Association de Fournisseurs de Couverts argentés. (SWI)
640 Symbole pour l'Aquarium de Baltimore. En bleu et blanc. (USA)
641 Symbole d'une grande banque avec quarante succursales. (ARG)
642 Symbole de la Fédération internationale des Archives de Télévision. (ITA)
643 Logo d'un atelier d'esthétique industrielle à Turin. (ITA)
644 Organisation d'assistance aux handicapés de vue. (USA)
645 Marque de fabrique de *Diblo,* un holding industriel. (MEX)
646 D'une fabrique de décors pour les autels buddhistes. (JPN)
647 Logo du service de dépannage *Reggiana Rimorchi* de Reggio Emilia. (ITA)
648 Symbole d'une société de transport et d'exploitation minière. (USA)
649 Symbole du centre juif de communication *Camp Rafa-El.* (USA)
650 Logo de la société immobilière *Time Equities.* (USA)
651 Marque d'une chaîne de magasins alimentaires. (JPN)
652 Marque de fabrique de la société *Silver Diffusion,* New York. (USA)
653 Symbole d'une société immobilière californienne. (USA)

644

645

649

650

638

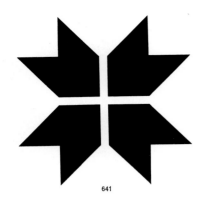

641

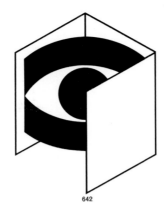

642

643

646

647

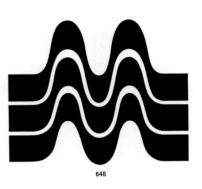

648

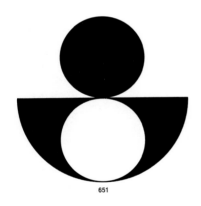

651

652

653

654

655

656

Trademarks
Schutzmarken
Marques et emblèmes

654 Symbol identifying all publications of the US Department of Housing and Urban Development. (USA)
655 Symbol of a prize for skiers sponsored by the cigarette manufacturers *Benson & Hedges*. (USA)
656 Symbol of the *Allegheny Group,* a management consulting firm. (USA)
657 Trademark of the Morse Shoe Co., used also for decorative effects. (USA)
658 Signet of the Radio-Station KCBQ. (USA)
659 Symbol of *The Anchorage* shopping/hotel complex at San Francisco's Fisherman's Wharf. (USA)
660 Symbol of the town of San Antonio, Texas. (USA)
661 Trademark of the *Ellis Container* company that manufactures packaging materials. (USA)
662 Symbol of the French banking group *Société Générale.* (FRA)
663 Logo of the *Communication Workers of America.* (USA)
664 Signet of the Ismalia Central Housing Board of India, an institution for improvement in housing. (IND)
665 Symbol of the public-relations company *Edward Brown.* (USA)
666 Trademark of the business-machines manufacturer *Pitney Bowes.* (USA)
667 Trademark of the Horizon Lighting Co., a manufacturer of lighting equipment. (USA)

654 Symbol auf allen Veröffentlichungen des Ministeriums für Wohnbau- und Städteplanung. (USA)
655 Rotes Symbol für einen vom Zigarettenhersteller *Benson & Hedges* gestifteten Preis für Skifahrer. (USA)
656 Symbol der *Allegheny Group,* einer Management-Beratungsfirma, die Modelle ausarbeitet, wonach
der Geschäftsgang vorausgesagt und die entsprechenden Entscheidungen gefällt werden können. (USA)
657 Schutzmarke eines der grössten Schuhfabrikanten der USA, die auch dekorative Zwecke erfüllt. (USA)
658 Signet der Radio-Station KCBQ. (USA)
659 Symbol des Einkaufszentrums *The Anchorage* auf einem Pier im Hafen von San Francisco. (USA)
660 Symbol der Stadt San Antonio in Texas. (USA)
661 Markenzeichen der Firma *Ellis Container,* die Verpackungsmaterial herstellt. (USA)
662 Symbol der französischen Bankengruppe *Société Générale.* (FRA)
663 Symbol der amerikanischen Medienschaffenden *(Communication Workers of America).* (USA)
664 Signet einer zentralen Beratungsstelle für die Verbesserung der Bau- und Wohnqualität in Indien. (IND)
665 Symbol der Public-Relations-Firma *Edward Brown.* (USA)
666 Markenzeichen der Büromaschinen-Fabrik *Pitney Bowes.* (USA)
667 Markenzeichen der Horizon Lighting Co., einer Firma, die Beleuchtungskörper herstellt. (USA)

654 Symbole d'identification pour toutes les publications du Ministère de logement et d'urbanisme. (USA)
655 Symbole d'un prix de compétition à skis parrainé par les cigarettes *Benson & Hedges*. (USA)
656 Logo de l'*Allegheny Group,* experts conseil, qui établissent des modèles afin que le management puisse
prendre les démarches appropriés pour améliorer les chiffres d'affaires. (USA)
657 Marque de fabrique d'un important fabricant de chaussures; elle sert aussi à des fins décoratives. (USA)
658 Logo de la station de radiodiffusion KCBQ. (USA)
659 Symbole du supermarché *The Anchorage* qui se trouve sur un ancien embarcadère à San Francisco. (USA)
660 Symbole de la ville San Antonio au Texas. (USA)
661 Marque de fabrique de la société *Ellis Container* qui fabrique du matériel d'emballage. (USA)
662 Logo pour la *Société Générale,* un groupe bancaire français. (FRA)
663 Logo de la confédération américaine des employés des mass media. (USA)
664 Symbole du bureau de consultation central pour l'amélioration des conditions de logement en Inde. (IND)
665 Logo de la société *Edward Brown,* spécialisée dans le domaine des relations publiques. (USA)
666 Marque de fabrique de *Pitney Bowes,* entreprise spécialisée dans la fabrication de machines à bureau. (USA)
667 Marque de fabrique de *Horizon Lighting,* fabricant d'appareils d'éclairage. (USA)

660

664

DESIGNER / GESTALTER / MAQUETTISTE:

654 Steve Korbet
655, 660 Tony DiSpigna
656 Craig Srebnik
657 Sidney Herman
658 Cody Newman
659 Robert Pease/Mario Zelaya
661 Gordon Tani/Scott A. Mednick
662 Alan Peckolick
663 Ivan Chermayeff
664 W. John Lees
665, 666 Robert A. Gale
667 Rudolph de Harak

ART DIRECTOR / DIRECTEUR ARTISTIQUE:

654, 664 W. John Lees
656 Craig Srebnik
657 Sidney Herman
658 Arthur Eisenberg/Ron Hudson
659 Robert Pease
661 Douglas Boyd
663 Ivan Chermayeff
665, 666 Robert A. Gale

AGENCY / AGENTUR / AGENCE – STUDIO:

654, 657, 664 Herman & Lees Associates
655, 660, 662 Lubalin Peckolick Assoc. Inc.
656 Srebnik Design
658 Eisenberg, Inc.
659 Robert Pease & Co
661 Douglas Boyd Design & Marketing
663 Chermayeff & Geismar Assoc.
665 Robert A. Gale, Inc.
666 Siegel & Gale
667 Rudolph de Harak & Associates Inc.

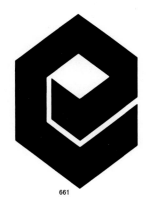

657

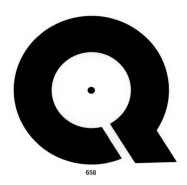

658

659

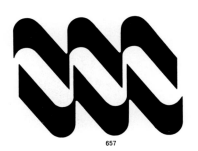

661

662

663

665

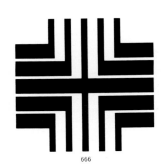

666

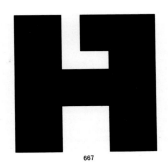

667

233

668

669

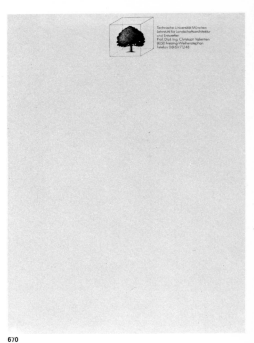

670

672

673

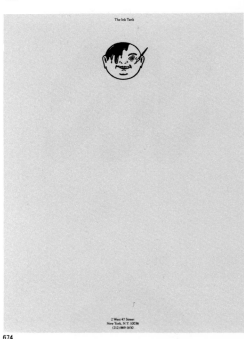

674

Letterheads
Briefköpfe
En-têtes

674a

668 For announcements in connection with the TV programme *The Search for Alexander the Great*, sponsored by *Mobil*. (USA)
669 Stationery of the graphic designer Judit Dànos. (HUN)
670 Stationery of the faculty of landscape architecture and design at the Munich technical university. (GER)
671 Stationery of the *Pfanzelt* studio (green cucumber), stuck to a grey sheet which serves as an envelope. (GER)
672 For Dot Baker. The name can be traced along the numbered dots with a pen or pencil. (USA)
673 Personal stationery of Mr. & Mrs. M. Berman. (GBR)
674, 674a Stationery and letterhead of *The Ink Tank*. (USA)
675 Business stationery of the photographer B. Schwortz. (USA)
676, 676a The star, which plays an important role in the Islam, was chosen as the symbol for the *Commercial Bank of Kuwait*. It is made up of the Arabic words for "Commercial" and "Bank". The Kufic style of calligraphy enables lettering to become a semi-abstract design. Calligrapher: Jamil Majid. (KUW)
677 Stationery of an advertising agency. Green, orange. (USA)
678 Stationery for the *Professional Typographic Services*. (USA)

668 Für Mitteilungen über die von *Mobil* finanzierte TV-Sendung «Auf den Spuren Alexanders des Grossen». (USA)
669 Briefbogen der Graphikerin Judit Dànos. (HUN)
670 Briefbogen der Fakultät für Landschaftsarchitektur und Entwerfen der Technischen Universität München. (GER)
671 Briefbogen des Ateliers *Pfanzelt* (grüne Gurke), an einen grauen Bogen geheftet, der als Briefumschlag dient. (GER)
672 Für Dot Baker. Namenszug kann den numerierten Punkten entlang nachgezeichnet werden: «Dot» = Punkt. (USA)
673 Persönliches Briefpapier des Ehepaars M. Berman. (GBR)
674, 674a Briefbogen und Briefkopf für *The Ink Tank*. (USA)
675 Geschäftspapier des Photographen B. Schwortz. (USA)
676, 676a Der Stern, der im Islam eine wichtige Rolle spielt, wurde als Symbol für die Handelsbank von Kuwait gewählt. Er setzt sich aus den arabischen Worten für «Handel» und «Bank» zusammen, die durch die gewählte kufische Schrift ein halbabstraktes Muster bilden. Schriftzeichner: Jamil Majid. (KUW)
677 Geschäftspapier einer Werbeagentur. Grün, Orange. (USA)
678 Briefbogen für *Professional Typographic Services*. (USA)

668 Pour des communications en rapport avec l'émission TV «Les vestiges d'Alexandre le Grand» financée par *Mobil*. (USA)
669 En-tête de la graphiste Judit Dànos. (HUN)
670 Lettre de la faculté de planification et d'architecture paysagiste de l'Université Technique de Munich. (GER)
671 Briefbogen de l'atelier *Pfanzelt* (concombre verte): lettre attachée à une feuille grise qui sert d'enveloppe. (GER)
672 En-tête de Dot Baker. En suivant les points numérotés avec un crayon le nom Dot apparaît. «Dot» signifie point. (USA)
673 Lettre personnelle de M. et Mme Berman. (GBR)
674, 674a Lettre et en-tête de la société *The Ink Tank*. (USA)
675 Papier à lettre du photographe Barry Schwortz. (USA)
676, 676a L'étoile, symbole essentiel dans la religion islamique, a été choisie comme signe de la Banque commerciale du Koweit. Elle est composée des deux mots arabes pour «commerce» et «banque» écrits en coufique, forme d'écriture rigide et angulaire qui est souvent utilisée en décoration épigraphique. (KUW)
677 En-tête d'une agence de publicité. En vert et orange. (USA)
678 En-tête des *Professional Typographic Services*. (USA)

671

676 a

DESIGNER / GESTALTER / MAQUETTISTE:

668 George Shakespear
669 Judit Dános
670 Dietmar Burger/Uwe Lohrer
671 Harry Pfanzelt
672 Dick Mitchell
673 Mervyn Kurlansky/Paul Vickers
674, 674a Seymour Chwast
675 Marty Neumeier
676, 676a Paul Anthony
677 Constance Kovar
678 Norm Bendell

ART DIRECTOR / DIRECTEUR ARTISTIQUE:

668 Ivan Chermayeff
669 Judit Dános
670 Uwe Lohrer
671 Harry Pfanzelt
672 Dick Mitchell
674, 674a Seymour Chwast
677 Constance Kovar
678 Norm Bendell

AGENCY / AGENTUR:

668 Chermayeff
     & Geismar Assoc.
670 Atelier Lohrer
671 Harry Pfanzelt
672 The Richards Group
673, 676, 676a Pentagram
674, 674a Push Pin Studios Inc.
675 Neumeier Design Team
677 Constance Kovar Ltd

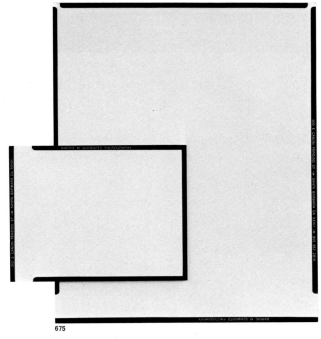

675

676

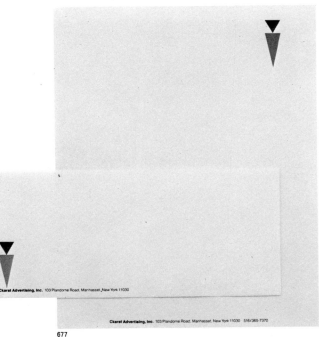

677

678

DESIGNER / GESTALTER / MAQUETTISTE:

679 Rudolph de Harak/Frank Benedict
680 Michael Gericke
681 Christian Westman
682 Sam Schmidt
683 Steff Geissbuhler
684 Jodi Luby
685 Alan Fletcher/Jennie Burns
686 Ivan Chermayeff/Alice Bissell (Photo)
687 Patrick Florville
688 Hans Goedicke

ART DIRECTOR / DIRECTEUR ARTISTIQUE:

680 Richard Foy
681 Christian Westman
683 Steff Geissbuhler
684 Eugene J.Grossman
686 Ivan Chermayeff
687 Patrick Florville
688 Hans Goedicke

AGENCY / AGENTUR / AGENCE – STUDIO:

679 Rudolph de Harak & Associates Inc.
680 Communication Arts, Inc.
681 Christian Westman
684 Anspach Grossman Portugal, Inc.
685 Pentagram
686 Chermayeff & Geismar Associates
687 Patrick Florville Graphic Design
688 KVH/GGK

679

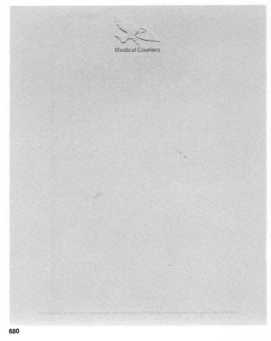

680

683

684

686

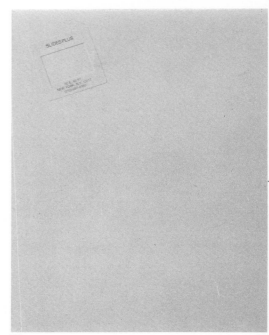

687

Letterheads
Briefköpfe
En-têtes

681

682

685

688

689

690

691

692

Record Covers
Schallplattenhüllen
Pochettes de disques

689 Full-cover sleeve of a rock record from *Ariola-Eurodisc*. (GER)
690 Sleeve of a pop record called *Something Magic,* issued by *Phonogram*. (GER)
691 Disco-music record issued by the *Karma* company. Landscape in rich green. (GER)
692 Record sleeve for a CBS production. Full-colour illustration. (USA)
693 Henri Dès sings for children. Full-colour sleeve for a record of children's songs. (SWI)
694 Record sleeve mainly in grey shades for rock music played by Ironhorse. (USA)
695 Black-and-white fingerprint as a cover illustration for the Chicago group. (USA)
696 Record sleeve for light-entertainment music, issued by *Ariola-Eurodisc*. (GER)

689 Mehrfarbige Hülle einer Rock-Platte von *Ariola-Eurodisc: Realität in weissen Westen*. (GER)
690 Hülle einer Pop-Platte mit dem Titel *Something Magic,* herausgegeben von *Phonogram*. (GER)
691 Von der Firma *Karma* herausgegebene Platte mit Disco-Musik. Landschaft in kräftigem Grün. (GER)
692 Schallplattenhülle für Camille Saint-Saëns *Karneval der Tiere*. Mehrfarbige Illustration. (USA)
693 Henri Dès singt für die Kinder. Mehrfarbige Hülle für eine Kinderlieder-Platte. (SWI)
694 Vorwiegend in Grautönen gehaltene Schallplattenhülle für Rock-Musik von Ironhorse. (USA)
695 Schwarzweisser Fingerabdruck als Umschlagillustration einer Platte der Gruppe Chicago. (USA)
696 Schallplattenhülle für Unterhaltungsmusik, herausgegeben von *Ariola-Eurodisc*. (GER)

689 Pochette polychrome d'un disque de musique rock publié par *Ariola-Eurodisc*. (GER)
690 Pochette pour un disque de musique pop, intitulé *Something Magic*. (GER)
691 Pour un disque de musique disco, publié par *Karma*. Paysage en couleurs vives. (GER)
692 Pochette pour le disque *Carneval des animaux* de Camille Saint-Saëns. En polychromie, (USA)
693 Pochette polychrome pour un disque d'Henry Dès, qui chante pour les enfants. (SWI)
694 Pochette de disque pour les enregistrements du groupe Ironhorse. Prédominance de tons gris. (USA)
695 Empreinte digitale en noir-blanc pour un enregistrement du groupe Chicago. (USA)
696 Pochette pour un disque de musique légère publié par *Ariola-Eurodisc*. (GER)

693

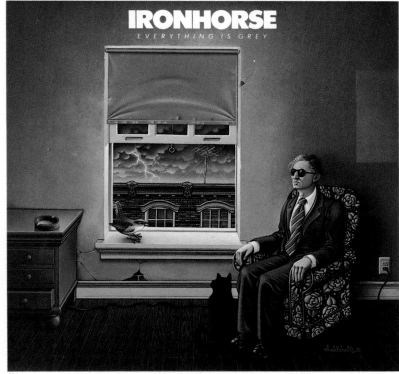

694

695

696

ARTIST / KÜNSTLER / ARTISTE:

689 Tom Vormstein
690 Bruce Meek
691 Dieter Ziegenfeuter
692 Edward Sorel
693 Etienne Delessert
694 Braldt Bralds
695 Gerard Huerta
696 Mouche Vormstein

DESIGNER / GESTALTER / MAQUETTISTE:

689, 696 Ariola Eurodisc/Studios
690 Bruce Meek
692 Henrietta Condak
693 Etienne Delessert
694 Bob Defrin
695 John Berg

ART DIRECTOR / DIRECTEUR ARTISTIQUE:

689, 696 Manfred Vormstein
691 Manfred Manke
692 Henrietta Condak
693 Etienne Delessert
694 Bob Defrin
695 John Berg

PUBLISHER / VERLEGER / EDITEUR:

689, 696 Ariola-Eurodisc
690 Phonogram GmbH
691 Karma Musikproduktion GmbH
692, 695 CBS Records
693 Mary-Josée
694 Atlantic Recording Corp.

ARTIST / KÜNSTLER / ARTISTE:

697, 697a Betty Swanwick
698, 700 Mark Hess
699 David Wilcox
701 Robert Giusti

DESIGNER / GESTALTER / MAQUETTISTE:

698, 701 Paula Scher
699 Paula Scher/Gene Greif
700 John Berg

ART DIRECTOR / DIRECTEUR ARTISTIQUE:

698, 699, 701 Paula Scher
700 John Berg/Paula Scher

AGENCY / AGENTUR / AGENCE – STUDIO:

698–701 CBS Records

PUBLISHER / VERLEGER / EDITEUR:

697, 697a Phonogram GmbH
698–701 CBS Records

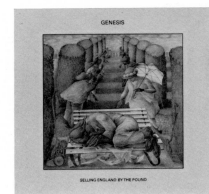

697a

697

240

698

699

700

701

697, 697a Illustration in actual size and complete sleeve for a recording by the Genesis rock group entitled *Selling England by the Pound,* issued by *Phonogram.* (GER)
698 Cover in sombre shades of a jazz-rock record of the Manhattan group, a CBS production. (USA)
699 Record sleeve for Googy and Tom Coppola's *Shine the Light of Love,* by CBS. In full colour. (USA)
700 CBS record sleeve for a recording by a jazz band entitled Chaser. In dark shades. (USA)
701 CBS record sleeve for *Rush Hour* by the David Chesky Big Band. Blue, yellow, lilac and green. (USA)

697, 697a Illustration (Originalgrösse) und vollständige Hülle für eine Aufnahme der Rockgruppe Genesis mit dem Titel *Selling England by the Pound,* herausgegeben von *Phonogram.* (GER)
698 In düstern Farben gehaltener Umschlag einer Jazz-Rock-Platte der Gruppe Manhattan. (USA)
699 Schallplattenhülle für die Aufnahmen einer Big Band mit religiösen Texten. Mehrfarbig. (USA)
700 Schallplattenhülle für Aufnahmen einer Jazz-Band mit dem Titel *Chaser.* Dunkle Farben. (USA)
701 Hülle für die Platte *Rush Hour* (Stossverkehr) der David Chesky Big Band. Illustration in kräftigem Blau, Gelb, Lila und Grün. (USA)

Record Covers
Schallplattenhüllen
Pochettes de disques

697, 697a Illustration (grandeur originale) et pochette complète pour un enregistrement du groupe rock Genesis, intitulé *Selling England by the Pound* (L'Angleterre est vendue livre par livre). (GER)
698 Couverture d'un disque de musique jazz-rock du groupe Manhattan. En couleurs sombres. (USA)
699 Pochette pour les enregistrements d'un big band chantant des textes religieux. (USA)
700 Pochette du disque d'un groupe de jazz. Illustration en tons sombres. (USA)
701 Pochette du disque *Rush Hour* (heure de pointe) du big band de David Chesky. Illustration en bleu, jaune, lilas et vert vifs. (USA)

241

Record Covers
Schallplattenhüllen
Pochettes de disques

ARTIST / KÜNSTLER / ARTISTE:

702, 704 Steve Carver
703, 710 Robert Giusti
705 Carol McPherson
706 Robert Grossman
707 Brad Ellis
708 Atsushi Yoshioka
711 Ján Meisner

DESIGNER / GESTALTER / MAQUETTISTE:

702, 704 Tony Lane
703, 710 Lynn Dreese Breslin
705 Carol Friedman
706, 709 John Berg
707 Spencer M. Drate
708 Goro Kunisada

ART DIRECTOR / DIRECTEUR ARTISTIQUE:

702, 704 Tony Lane
703, 710 Lynn Dreese Breslin
705 Carol Friedman
706, 709 John Berg
707 John Gillespie/Spencer M. Drate
708 Goro Kunisada

AGENCY / AGENTUR / AGENCE – STUDIO:

702, 704, 706, 709 CBS Records

PUBLISHER / VERLEGER / EDITEUR:

702, 704, 706, 709 CBS Records
703, 710 Atlantic Recording Corp.
705 Artists House
707 Sire Records Company
708 King Record Co., Ltd.
711 Opus

702 The recordings for this CBS record of a jazz drummer were done with well-known jazz musicians in various places, as shown by the changing landscape of the sleeve's illustration. (USA)
703, 710 Complete record sleeve and illustration for the record *Street of Dreams* by Frank Carillo, on *Atlantic Records*. (USA)
704 Full-colour sleeve for the CBS jazz record *No One Home*. The painting in naive style is entitled *Street Life*. (USA)
705 Sleeve for *Tales of Captain Black*, an *Artists House* record. (USA)
706 Full-colour record sleeve for a CBS recording of Ramsey Lewis and his Big Band. (USA)
707 Sleeve for the record *Love goes on* by Sire Records. (USA)
708 Sleeve for a recording by a Swedish Big Band with music based on Japanese folk music. A *King Record* production. (JPN)
709 Black-and-white sleeve for a jazz-rock band on CBS. (USA)
711 Opened record sleeve for a live recording of part of the Bratislava Jazz Festival. Orange-pink wings on blue. (CSR)

702 Die Aufnahmen für diese Platte eines Jazz-Drummers wurde mit bekannten Jazz-Musikern an verschiedenen Orten gemacht, was durch die wechselnde Landschaft angedeutet wird. (USA)
703, 710 Vollständige Plattenhülle und Illustration für die Platte *Street of Dreams* von Frank Carillo. (USA)
704 Mehrfarbige Hülle für die Jazz-Platte *No One Home*. Das in naivem Stil ausgeführte Gemälde zeigt Strassenszenen. (USA)
705 Hülle für die Platte *Tales of Captain Black*. (USA)
706 Mehrfarbige Schallplattenhülle für Aufnahmen des Pianisten Ramsey Lewis und seiner Big Band. (USA)
707 Hülle für die Schallplatte *Love goes on*. (USA)
708 Hülle für Aufnahmen einer schwedischen Jazz-Band, deren Stücke auf japanischer Volksmusik beruhen. In Grautönen. (JPN)
709 Schwarzweisse Hülle für die Platte einer Jazz-Rock-Band. (USA)
711 Geöffnete Schallplattenhülle für einen Live-Mitschnitt des Jazz-Festivals in Bratislava. Orange-rosa Flügel auf Blau. (CSR)

702 Les pièces pour ce disque d'un batteur accompagné de divers musiciens de jazz renommés, ont été enregistrées dans différents endroits, ce que symbolise le paysage changeant. (USA)
703, 710 Pochette complète et illustration pour le disque *Street of Dreams* (Rue des rêves) de Frank Carillo. (USA)
704 Pochette polychrome d'un enregistrement de jazz intitulé *No One Home*. Peinture en style naïf de scènes de la rue. (USA)
705 Pour un disque intitulé «Contes du Capitaine Black». (USA)
706 Pochette polychrome pour les enregistrements du pianiste Ramsey Lewis et de son big band. (USA)
707 Pochette pour le disque «L'amour continu». (USA)
708 Pochette pour les enregistrements d'un groupe de jazz suédois, dont les pièces sont basées sur la musique populaire japonaise. (JPN)
709 Pochette noir-blanc pour le disque d'un groupe de jazz. (USA)
711 Recto et verso d'une pochette pour un enregistrement direct d'un festival de jazz à Bratislava. Ailes en orange sur fond bleu. (CSR)

702

703

704

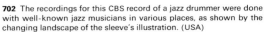

705

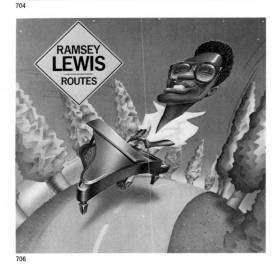

706

707

708

709

710

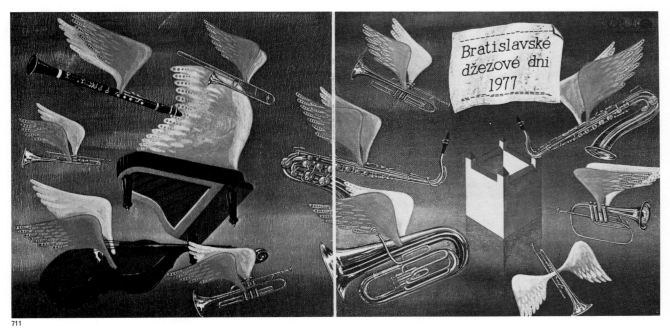

711

712

713

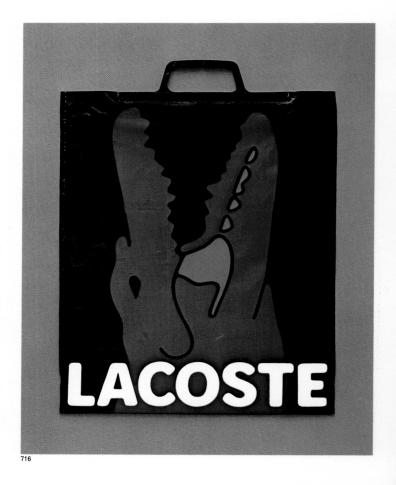

716

ARTIST / KÜNSTLER / ARTISTE:

712 Robert Marshall

DESIGNER / GESTALTER / MAQUETTISTE:

712 Robert Marshall
713 Terry Lesniewicz/Al Navarre
714 Marty Neumeier/Byron Glaser
715 John Nowland/Lynne Seppelt-Deakin
716 Irmgard Ebert
717, 718 Takenobu Igarashi

712 Advertising package of the *Hercules Packaging Group,* containing samples of corrugated cardboard. (AUS)
713 Examples from a series of self-promotional packages of the Owens-Corning Fiberglas Corp. (USA)
714 *Western Medical* packaging for a net-like bandage sold to hospitals for use on burn patients. (USA)
715 This *Eziheat* package contains a complete Barbecue fire pack. (USA)
716 Plastic carrier-bag distributed to sports shops by *Lacoste,* the manufacturer of sports clothing. The green crocodile is the *Lacoste* trademark. (GER)
717, 718 Black-and-white carrier-bags by *Zen Environmental Design,* with lettering on four sides. (JPN)

712 Diese Werbepackung einer Verpackungsfirma enthält Muster aus Wellkarton. (AUS)
713 Beispiele aus einer Reihe von Eigenwerbungspackungen eines Unternehmens, das hauptsächlich Schallisolations-Elemente aus Fiberglas herstellt. (USA)
714 Verpackungen für eine netzartige Bandage, die in Spitälern für Verbrennungspatienten gebraucht wird. (USA)
715 Verpackung für Brennmaterial, das ungeöffnet in den Grill gelegt und angezündet werden kann. (USA)
716 Vom Sportbekleidungs-Hersteller *Lacoste* an Sport-Geschäfte abgegebene Plastiktragtasche. Das grüne Krokodil ist das Markenzeichen von *Lacoste.* (GER)
717, 718 Tragtaschen (schwarzweiss) von *Zen Environmental Design,* mit Schriftzug über vier Seiten. (JPN)

712 Boîtes autopromotionnelles d'un fabricant d'emballages contenant des échantillons de carton ondulé. (AUS)
713 Exemples d'une gamme d'emballages autopromotionnels d'une entreprise fabriquant essentiellement des éléments d'insonorisation en fibre de verre. (USA)
714 Emballage pour un pansement à filet fin utilisé dans les hôpitaux pour couvrir les brûlures. (USA)
715 Ce sac, contenant des combustibles pour le grillage, peut être allumé tel quel. (USA)
716 Sac en plastique distribué aux magasins d'articles de sport par le fabricant de vêtements de sport *Lacoste.* Le crocodil vert est la marque de fabrique. (GER)
717, 718 Sacs en papier (noir-blanc) de *Zen Environmental Design* avec logo sur les quatre côtés. (JPN)

ART DIRECTOR / DIRECTEUR ARTISTIQUE:

712 Barrie Tucker
713 Terry Lesniewicz/Al Navarre
714 Marty Neumeier
715 John Nowland
716 Irmgard Ebert

AGENCY / AGENTUR / AGENCE – STUDIO:

712 Tucker & Kidd
713 Lesniewicz/Navarre
714 Neumeier Design Team
715 John Nowland Graphic Design
716 Alain Fion
717, 718 Takenobu Igarashi Design

714

715

Packaging/Packungen/Emballages

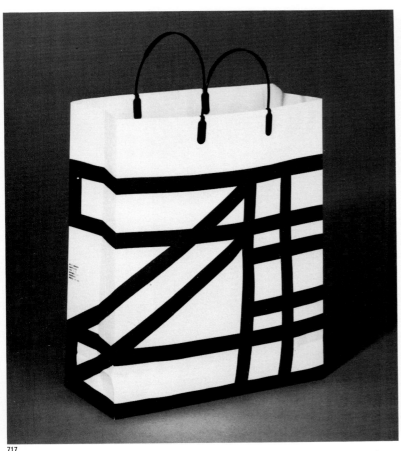

717

718

719

720

ARTIST / KÜNSTLER / ARTISTE:

719 Bob Maile
720 Lars Hokanson
723, 724 Shigeru Akizuki

DESIGNER / GESTALTER / MAQUETTISTE:

719 Julie Riefler/Hannah Leung
720 K. Schultheis
723, 724 Shigeru Akizuki

ART DIRECTOR / DIRECTEUR ARTISTIQUE:

719 Keith Bright
720 Michael Peters
723, 724 Shigeru Akizuki

AGENCY / AGENTUR / AGENCE – STUDIO:

719 Bright & Associates
720 Michael Peters & Partners
721, 722 Gottschalk & Ash Ltd.

719 Bottle design and box for six bottles of *Medaillon* special beer. Blue medallion on white. (USA)
720 Tankard for a new moderately priced *Whitbread* lager. A German name was coined for it *(Heldenbräu* means "heroes brew") and a synthetic heraldic bird invented to suggest tradition. Orange-brown on blue. (GBR)
721, 722 Bottle design for a dry white wine and a light red wine. (CAN)
723 Paper bag and wrapping paper of the Reika Company, a jewellery firm. (JPN)
724 Gift packs for traditional Japanese confectionery made by the Chitose Confectionery Co. (JPN)

719 Flaschengestaltung und Tragkarton für sechs Flaschen eines Spezialbiers. Blaues Medaillon auf Weiss. (USA)
720 Humpen für ein neues *Whitbread*-Lagerbier mit deutschem Namen und Wappentier, um den Eindruck von alter Tradition zu vermitteln. Adler in Orange-braun auf Blau. (GBR)
721, 722 Flaschengestaltung für einen trockenen Weisswein und einen leichten Rotwein. (CAN)
723 Papiertüte und Einwickelpapier eines Juweliergeschäfts. (JPN)
724 Geschenkschachteln für traditonelles japanisches Gebäck. (JPN)

719 Bouteille et carton portable pour six bouteilles d'une bière spéciale. Médaillon bleu sur blanc. (USA)
720 Choppe à bière pour une blonde à prix modique. Le nom choisi est allemand, *Heldenbräu* signifiant «bière des héros». L'oiseau héraldique, exécuté en brun orangé sur bleu, doit évoquer la tradition. (GBR)
721, 722 Conception de deux bouteilles pour un vin blanc sec et un rouge léger. (CAN)
723 Sac en papier et papier d'emballage d'une bijouterie. (JPN)
724 Boîtes-cadeaux pour un assortiment de gâteaux japonais. (JPN)

723

721

722

724

725

726

ARTIST / KÜNSTLER / ARTISTE:

727 Seymour Chwast
728 Steve Graham
730 Mark Jones/Sarah Waldron

DESIGNER / GESTALTER / MAQUETTISTE:

725 John McConnell/David Stuart
726 F. Maumary
727 Seymour Chwast
728 Barrie Tucker
729, 731 Helmut Schmid
730 Primo Angeli

ART DIRECTOR / DIRECTEUR ARTISTIQUE:

727 Seymour Chwast
728 Barrie Tucker
729, 731 Helmut Schmid
730 Primo Angeli

AGENCY / AGENTUR / AGENCE – STUDIO:

725 Pentagram
727 Push Pin Studios, Inc.
728 Tucker & Kidd
729, 731 Nippon International Agency
730 Primo Angeli Graphics

727

728

729

Packaging
Packungen
Emballages

725 Bottle and label design for three types of *Watney's* beer. They are part of a packaging series with cans, bottles and packs. (GBR)
726 Six-pack of a table drink based on lactic acid for the French market. Red and white, flowers in red and blue. (FRA)
727 Can for a *Pushpinoff* mixture of fruit sweets and nuts, distributed by Push Pin Productions, Inc. (USA)
728 Invitation in the form of marmalade tins to the opening of a shopping centre. The centre, called *The Jam Factory*, is in a 125 year-old marmalade factory. Advertisements for this occasion in Figs. 67–69. (AUS)
729 This package contains an instant drink in powder form which has electrolytes for replenishing body fluids, manufactured by *Otsuka Pharmaceuticals*. The waves symbolize positive and negative effects of ions. (JPN)
730 The sausage manufacturer *Molinari* and the *Primo Angeli* advertising studio sent their clients an Italian salami as Season's greetings. (USA)
731 Two packages for products manufactured by *Otsuka Pharmaceuticals*. (JPN)

725 Flaschen- und Etikettgestaltung für drei Biersorten von *Watney's*. Sie sind Teil einer Packungsreihe mit Büchsen, Flaschen und Tragkartons. (GBR)
726 Für Frankreich bestimmte Sechser-Packung eines Tafelgetränks auf Milchsäurebasis. Rot und Weiss, Blumen in Rot und Blau. (FRA)
727 Dose für eine *Pushpinoff* Fruchtbonbons- und Nuss-Mischung, die von der Push Pin Productions, Inc. vertrieben wird. (USA)
728 Mit dieser Marmeladenbüchse wurde zur Eröffnung eines Einkaufszentrums eingeladen, das sich in einer 125 Jahre alten Marmeladenfabrik befindet. Siehe auch Anzeigen zu diesem Ereignis, Abb. 67–69. (AUS)
729 Diese Packung enthält ein Sofortgetränk in Pulverform, das die Elektrolyten im Körper nach körperlicher Anstrengung ersetzt. Die Wellen symbolisieren den positiven und negativen Effekt der Ionen. (JPN)
730 Der Wurstfabrikant *Molinari* und das Werbestudio *Primo Angeli* schickten ihren Kunden zu Weihnachten einen italienischen Salami. (USA)
731 Zwei Packungen für ein Beta-Stimulans und einen Beta-Blocker. (JPN)

725 Bouteilles et étiquettes pour trois bières: nouvelle conception appliquée pour la gamme entière des produits, y compris boîtes et cartons portables. (GBR)
726 Carton portable, destiné exclusivement au marché français, pour six bouteilles de *Rivella*, boisson sans alcool à base lactique. (FRA)
727 Boîte pour des bonbons et des noix mélangées de *Pushpinoff*, distribuée par *Push Pin Productions*. (USA)
728 Boîtes de confiture distribuées à titre d'invitation pour l'ouverture d'un supermarché qui se trouve dans une fabrique de confiture construite il y a 125 ans. Voir aussi les annonces en figs. 67–69. (USA)
729 Cette boîte contient une boisson soluble en poudre qui remplace les électrolytes dans le corps après des efforts physiques. Les lignes ondulées symbolisent l'effet positif et négatif des ions. (JPN)
730 Pour une joyeuse fête de Noël, le fabricant de saucissons *Molinari* et l'agence *Primo Angeli* ont envoyé un salami italien à leurs clients. (USA)
731 Boîtes pour un stimulant et un blocker béta. (JPN)

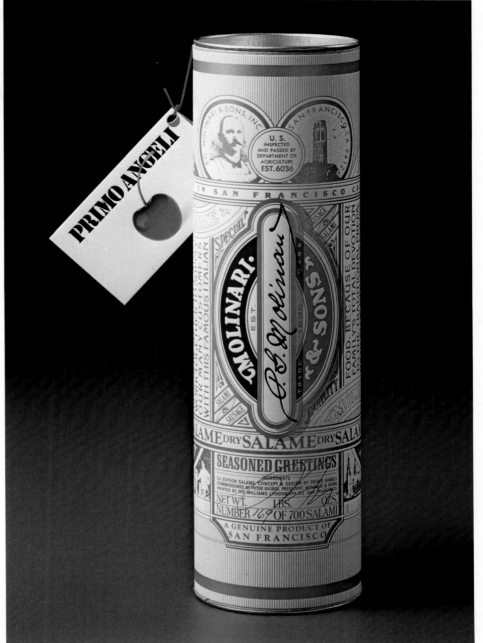

730

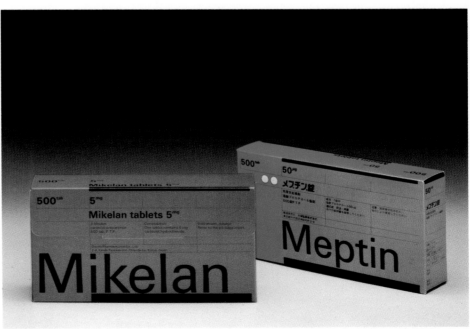

731

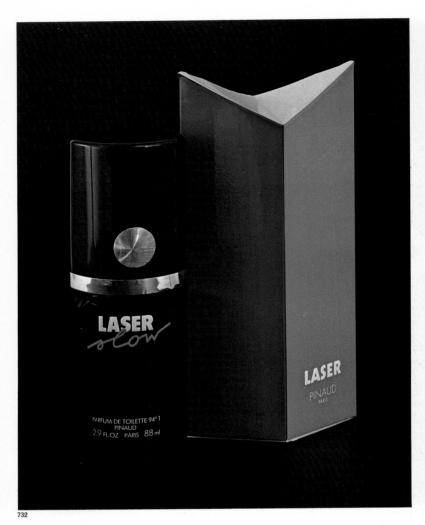

732

733

735

736

734

DESIGNER / GESTALTER / MAQUETTISTE:

734 Philipp Largiadèr
735 Patrick Soo Hoo
736 James J. Marsala
737 Gordon Tani

ART DIRECTOR / DIRECTEUR ARTISTIQUE:

732, 733 Joel Desgrippes
734 Jacques Hauser
735 Patrick Soo Hoo
736 James J. Marsala
737 Douglas Boyd/Scott A. Mednick

AGENCY / AGENTUR / AGENCE – STUDIO:

732, 733 Desgrippes, Beauchant, Gobé
735 Patrick Soo Hoo Designers, Inc.
737 Douglas Boyd Design & Marketing

ARTIST / KÜNSTLER / ARTISTE:

734 Philipp Largiadèr
736 Robert Liebold
737 Rick Wolin-Semple (Photo)

732 Rhombus package and sprayer for the *Laser* perfume by *Pinaud*. (FRA)
733 Bottle, label and packaging design for an Eau de Toilette. The bottle has the form of an old perfume flacon. Packaging in fine corrugated cardboard. (FRA)
734 Promotional pack with various packages of *Kneipp* herbal baths and a brochure for *Kneipp* treatments. The illustrations show Dr. Kneipp and various baths. (SWI)
735 Packaging for Confidence Golf Co. golf-balls. Red on black. (USA)
736 Folding box for *Kotex* tampons manufactured by *Kimberly-Clark*. (USA)
737 An *Associated Film Distributors'* press kit with promotional material. (USA)

732 Packung (Rhombus) und Zerstäuber für das Parfum *Laser* von *Pinaud*. (FRA)
733 Flacon-, Etikett- und Packungsgestaltung für ein Eau de Toilette, das nach einer frisch gemähten Sommerwiese duftet. Das Flacon mit Glasverschluss erinnert an alte Parfumfläschchen. Packung aus feinem Wellkarton. (FRA)
734 Diese als Bade- und Heil-Anstalt aufgemachte Werbepackung enthält verschiedene Packungen mit *Kneipp*-Heilpflanzen-Bädern und eine Broschüre für *Kneipp*-Kuren. Die Illustrationen zeigen Dr. Kneipp und verschiedene Bäder. (SWI)
735 Packung für Golfbälle. Rotes Karomuster auf Schwarz. (USA)
736 Faltschachtel für *Kotex*-Tampons von *Kimberly-Clark*. (USA)
737 Pressemappe im wörtlichsten Sinn mit Informationen über einen Kinofilm. (USA)

732 Emballage (losange) et atomiseur pour le parfum *Laser* de *Pinaud*. (FRA)
733 Flacon, étiquette et emballage pour l'eau de toilette *New Mown Hey* de *Pinaud*, au parfum d'herbe fraîchement fauchée. Le flacon avec bouchon en verre ressemble aux anciens flacons de parfum. Emballage en carton ondulé. (FRA)
734 Emballage promotionnel sous forme d'un ancien établissement de cure contenant des échantillons de bains salubres aux plantes médicinales et une brochure pour les cures du Dr Kneipp. Elément de promotion de *Hoffmann-La Roche*. (SWI)
735 Emballage pour des balles de golf. Rouge sur fond noir. (USA)
736 Boîte pliante pour les tampons *Kotex*. (USA)
737 Documentation de presse contenant des informations sur un film. (USA)

737

Paper / Papier: Papierfabrik Biberist–Biber GS SK3, blade coated,
pure white 120 gm² and Biber Offset SK3, pure white, machine-
finished, 140 gm² / Biber GS SK3, hochweiss, satiniert, 120 gm²
und Biber-Offset SK3, hochweiss, maschinenglatt, 140 gm²

Printed by / gedruckt von: Sigg Söhne AG, Winterthur
(Colour and black-and-white pages / Farbseiten und Schwarzweisseiten,
dust jacket / Schutzumschlag)

Typesetting / Lichtsatz: Sauerländer AG, Aarau (Univers,
MONOTYPE-Lasercomp)

Cover / Einband: Buchbinderei Eibert AG, Eschenbach SG

Glossy lamination / Glanzfoliierung: Durolit AG, Pfäffikon SZ

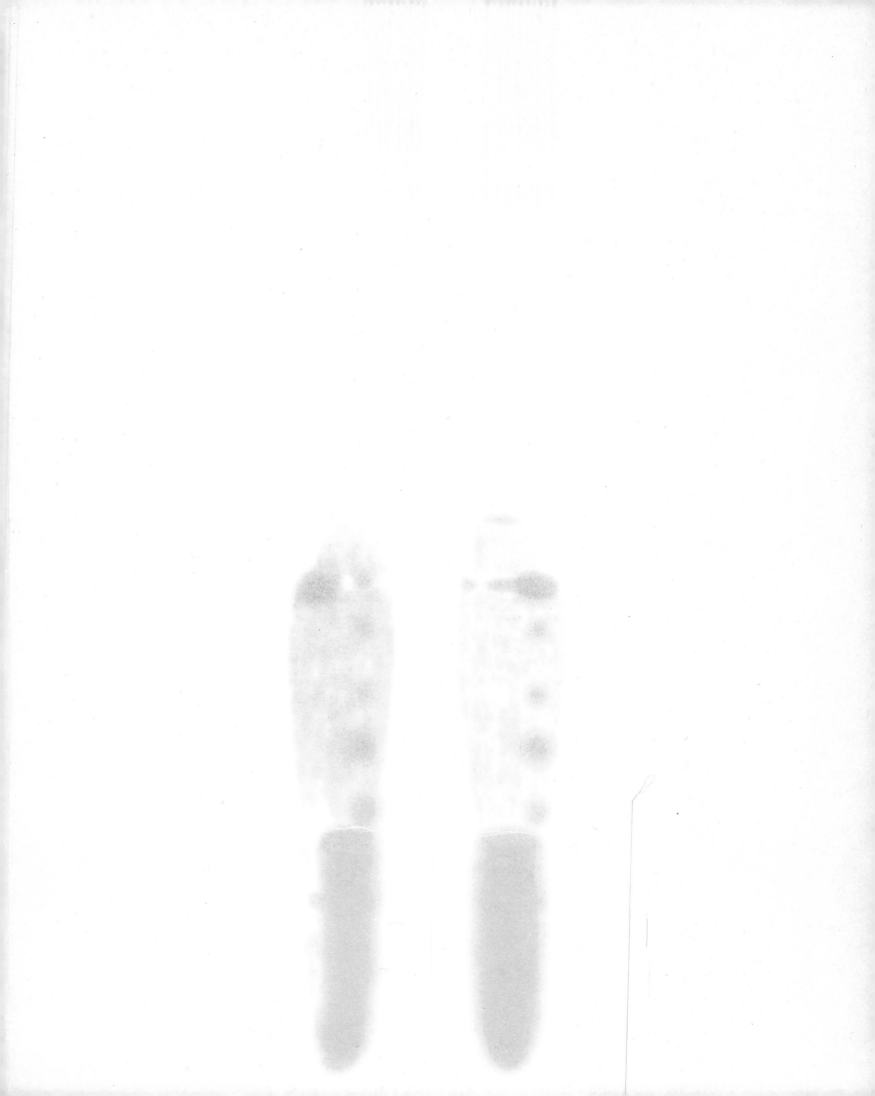